SU
KREITZMAN

Cambridge

Slim Cuisine Diet

EBURY PRESS
LONDON

DEDICATION

For my Slim Cuisine Study Subjects

FIRST PUBLISHED BY EBURY PRESS
an imprint of The Random Century Group
Random Century House, 20 Vauxhall Bridge Road, London SW1V 2SA.

Illustrator STAN BEIRNE
Editors ESTHER JAGGER & BARBARA CROXFORD
Designer PETER BRIDGEWATER

British Library Cataloguing in Publication Data
Kreitzman, Sue
Slim cuisine diet.
1. Physical fitness. Slimming. Diet
I. Title
613.25

ISBN 0-85223-893-2 (hardback)
0-09174-996-4 (paperback)

Typeset in Bodoni Book by TEK ART LIMITED, Croydon, Surrey
Printed and bound in Great Britain by
MACKAYS OF CHATHAM, PLC, Kent

ACKNOWLEDGEMENTS

Many, many thanks to Dr. Alan N. Howard and the Howard Foundation for their support of my research, and to Dr. Stephen Kreitzman (Dr. Husband) who directed my research: their dedication to science, and compassion and empathy for individuals plagued by the pain of obesity, is a constant inspiration.

A special thank you to my assistant, Sandie Perry, and my secretary, Rosemarie Espley, who loyally volunteered to be my very first Slim Cuisine study subjects. Their enthusiasm and dedication make my working life a pleasure. Heartfelt thanks as well to Mary Hardy and Brenda Huebler who have helped in countless invaluable ways.

Several people read the manuscript in early drafts and contributed valuable comments and criticisms. I particularly wish to thank Annie Coxon, Mary Clyne and Margaret Pederson for their comments and insights. Vicki Kimm also read and commented on an early stage of the work, and helped taste test many of the recipes. Both her friendship and her downright visceral love of food and cookery warm the cockles of my heart.

I'm extremely grateful to Gail Rebuck, who – as an editor – is inspiring to say the least. And what delight it has been to have had the opportunity to team up once more with Stan Beirne. Stan is a joy to work with, and his drawings are always totally engaging: my staff and I always await each new faxed sketch with delighted anticipation.

Affectionate thanks as well to my agent, David Grossman, whose warmth and enthusiastic good nature are much appreciated; to Dr. Jill Walls, Val Beeson, Katherine Ray and Mary Dean at the Cambridge Science Park who cheerfully helped with weights, measures and metabolic studies during the Slim Cuisine Studies, and to Dr. Roger Howard who has always been supportive of the Slim Cuisine concepts of weight maintenance and gastronomy.

Finally, an enormous bearhug to my son, Shawm, who – even though he's left home to continue his studies in London – has continued to tickle my funny bone, calm my jitters, enrich my understanding of the universe (particularly the more perplexing bits) and – in general – improve the quality of my life.

CONTENTS

PREFACE

If you have a blind, dogged, pig-headed desire to get as thin as possible as fast as possible, any way possible, and that's all, go away. This plan is not for you. If, on the other hand, you'd love to lose some weight, but you'd love even more to develop a healthy, comfortable relationship with food; a new gastronomic lifestyle that leaves you well-fed at all times, happy with your food choices, and able to sustain your particular weight loss for the *rest of your life*, then stick around; I'm delighted to welcome you to my new book. If you are willing to spend a bit of time and effort on the retraining of your food cravings and food habits, and the examination of the environmental factors that caused your problem in the first place, then I have some happy news for you. *Large portions* are in your future. Crisps, milk shakes, ice cream and steak; pasta, potatoes, Chinese food and curries: a world of good food is wide open to you. Attempting to lose weight through suffering and denial leads to destructive bingeing, out-of-control weight gain and a permanent psychological unease. Ironically, giving up the battle and submerging yourself in the mainstream of high-fat food leads to the same thing. Why subject yourself to such hurtful, unhealthy and futile practices? This four-week plan will enable you to take off the excess weight, retrain the bad habits, and avoid the fattening traps of our fattening society. In the process, you will find that you have become an extraordinary cook. Enjoy the journey – it's going to change your life.

SUE KREITZMAN, CAMBRIDGESHIRE, 1991

BEFORE YOU BEGIN

The Diet, and a day-by-day discussion to help you navigate each step, begins on page 33. A handy guide, *The Plan*, begins on page 16. But first read the introductory material all the way through. Then, before you begin each level of the diet read all the way through the section dealing with that level. Think about what I am saying before you start *each level*. In your haste to embark on your weight loss, don't just read a page here and another one there. Read the whole section. Think! Know what you are doing before you do it.

INTRODUCTION

OUR FATTENING SOCIETY

What always astonishes me is not that there are so many fat people in our society, but that there are so many who are *not* fat. Given the state of the food industry, the science of cookery, and the dogma and prejudices of gastronomy, everyone should be suffering from extreme obesity. We live in a fat-based society. In restaurants, snack shops and groceries, in cookery books, schools and manuals, fats (or oils) are prominent and vital. Indeed, fat is the basis of all cookery. It doesn't matter if it is cordon bleu or catering college, peasant grub or aristocratic cuisine, fat of one sort or another (often great gobs of it) is essential to the basic techniques.

Eat excess fat and you will carry excess fat on your body. Fat, *no matter what its form* – oil, butter, margarine, dripping, lard and so on – contains 9 Calories per gram (120 Calories per 15 ml/1 tbsp), more than twice that of carbohydrate and protein. And those fat Calories go straight to your fat stores in a much more efficient way than carbohydrate or protein Calories. You must have heard that old saying 'A moment on the lips, a lifetime on the hips.' In a very real sense you might as well apply the margarine, whipped cream, chocolate and so on directly on to your behind and have done with it.

As a result of this dietary fat bounty, and the biochemistry of fat metabolism, many of us suffer grievously. We exist in a food-affluent society, living lives of reduced physical activity and consuming outrageous amounts of fat in our diet. An increase in body weight is almost inevitable, but we shun it as unnatural and frightening; indeed, we are obsessed by it. A large portion of the population diets obsessively, or spends a lifetime on the mentally and physically debilitating 'yo-yo'. Some people try to opt out of the obsession and stop worrying. For many such people, this means wallowing in their own fat and assuring themselves – and others like them – that they are happy as they are. But no matter how hard a fat person tries to live with excess body fat, the pain of being overweight is very real – a pain caused by profound medical, cosmetic and sociological factors.

> *Frankly, I think most fat people are more self-conscious than they need to be. Most people don't stare at us for long periods of time – it's just that we think they do and that hurts inside. Nobody thin could possibly understand. It affects you mentally.*
>
> MR D. B., IN AN INTERVIEW

Various people seem almost to be predestined to be fat for many reasons: fat cells developed in childhood; a lifestyle that uses food as a solace and a stress defuser; a sedentary life coupled with a gourmet philosophy about food; a genetic endomorphic body structure; or other environmental, genetic, psychological or medical variables. Given the minefield of dietary fat these people must negotiate every day of their lives, becoming overweight is inevitable. If they are physically 'healthy' fat people – no cardiac problems, high blood pressure, high cholesterol, diabetes and so on – can they lead emotionally healthy lives despite their fat? Taking into account the stigma and prejudice that centres on their fat, it is extremely unlikely. Anti-fat hysteria is rampant in today's society.

> *There are people in the world who get turned off with fat people. They don't even like them around – it makes them nervous. They're thinking, 'This is a person with no self-discipline, this is a person who cares little about herself, this is a person with no ambition.' All the clichés they've got in their heads. 'Otherwise she would weigh ninety pounds, have on a sleeveless dress or wear a bikini.'*
>
> MRS J.C., SCHOOL BOARD PRESIDENT, IN AN INTERVIEW

Most fat people are all too conscious of their status as spiritual criminals, as unaesthetic blobs on the thin scene, as objects of ridicule and contempt, and as disease-ridden, hopeless cases. A fat person walking down the street eating a chocolate bar is a sinner – in the eyes of most beholders, he or she is committing a sin against his or her own body, and a sin against society by keeping himself or herself in such disgusting fat shape. What's more, by eating the chocolate in public, the fat person is showing the world that he or she is a slob – and just doesn't care. A slim person walking down the same street eating a similar bar of chocolate is just a guy eating a chocolate bar. In fact, if that slim person is a young woman, she may also – by the very act of publicly scoffing the chocolate – appear to be adorable, delightful and downright sexy.

> *When I travel I have to get two seats on the airplane. I had to start taking showers because I got stuck in the bathtub. I got stuck one time in a seat at a concert and couldn't get in or out. They had to take the arm off the chair to get me out. I got caught one time in a revolving door – they had to take that door down and slide me out of it like a sardine.*
>
> MRS J.C., SCHOOL BOARD PRESIDENT, IN AN INTERVIEW

A fat individual in this conforming and overcrowded world seems to invade the living space of the thin person, particularly in such places as lifts, theatres and public transport, and thus may be seen to be a threat. Our puritanical ethic does not allow us to view fat people who have been – obviously, to the puritan – over-indulging, giving in, and in general having a fine, sensual, gastronomic time, without severe disapproval and contempt. There is often a touch of envy, too: 'They're eating and enjoying themselves the way I wish I could but don't dare to – how gross and infantile they must be.'

For most congenitally fat people, the reaction to this social pressure is constant, drastic dieting, the unending cycle of binge/starvation, the repetitive ups and downs of weight gains and losses. All of this puts the body and mind in a perilous situation. Add to that the stress of being stigmatized – of being programmed, so to speak, for ugliness and failure in society – and the result may be individuals who, if they weren't emotionally disturbed and physically unwell before, are on their way to being so now: just punishment, according to puritanical thinkers, for the sin of fatness.

> *I would like to believe that the problem of being overweight is something for which I am not responsible at all. That would be really nice. But I'm not able to convince myself that I am such a glutton in proportion to other people that all of my weight is simply the result of gluttony. There's some place in between that makes my body different from the bodies of other people, and yet, since no one's been able to define that very clearly, I have to assume the responsibility for putting more Calories into my body than it needs in order to survive. I wish it were not that way.*
>
> DR M. F., IN AN INTERVIEW

To me, the solution to the whole problem of being overweight seems easy and obvious. As a 'controlled' fat person, who has engineered her own control, I feel impelled to tell the entire overweight population how to take similar control. Simply eliminate all unnecessary fat from your diet. If fat makes you fat, shun it like the plague. Everyone needs a certain (very small!) amount of fat in their diet, but a good variety of fish, poultry, lean meat, vegetables, fruit and whole grains provides plenty. Why lard yourself up with oils, dripping, butter, cream, margarine, the lot? Eat these fats, and you are feeding your fat in a very real sense. The only way to exercise this control is to take matters into your own hands. Starve your fat, but feed *yourself* lavishly. If you depend on fast foods, packet and prepared foods, frozen and chilled foods, restaurants and conventional cookery methods, you might as well resign yourself to being overweight. The only way to take control is to *do* so, to become the person responsible for your own care and well-being.

The purpose of this book is to teach you how to do just that. If you follow the plan step by step, you will find that it really is easy. It is also pleasurable, exciting and exhilarating. This book is an insurgent's manual, a plan of guerrilla action to enable you to undermine the system that is dedicated to the care and feeding of your overweight. Opt out of the fat game. Put in some intelligent time and effort, devote yourself *to* yourself, and you will be rewarded with a lifetime of healthy slimness and gastronomic satisfaction. Desperation has led fat people to frightening and demeaning treatments: the stapling of their stomachs, the hoovering away of their fat deposits, the wiring of their jaws, the removal of large pieces of their intestines, the binding of their midriffs with cords, the permanent fear of food.

The very fashionable and very thin Mrs H. was the envy of all the ladies . . . . How she kept up her svelte, non-Germanic figure was no secret because she herself would tell you it was done by a tapeworm in her innards. I remember Mrs H. telling my astonished parents that she had come to the conclusion that a tapeworm alone would keep her trim without having to sacrifice all the rich goodies and cakes she loved. So, having procured a very young and small tapeworm from I don't know where, she swallowed it with a drink of water and became thin in a short time.

UPS AND DOWNS, A MEMOIR BY NIKA HAZELTON

Here is the antidote to this appalling state of affairs. Embark on this project, and enter a new, lifelong love affair with food that *will not lead* to a lifetime of miserable fatness.

HOW I OPTED OUT OF THE OBESITY GAME

Once I was a fat woman, getting fatter all the time. In the ten years after 1972, when I left my job as a primary schoolteacher and turned my hobby (food and cookery) into a full-fledged profession, my weight soared from 60.3 kg (9½ stone) to 100 kg (15½ stone). The weight gain was hard enough to deal with, but the constant *escalation* was even worse. I never stabilized – my weight would simply reach a new height, and then press onward and upward. Before that time, when I was a schoolteacher who dabbled passionately in cookery in my spare time, I was a classic 'yo-yo'. My weight would creep up until self-disgust at my appearance exceeded my passion for food, and it was time to embark on yet another drastic and punishing diet. When I was eating, I wished I was dieting, and vice versa. After a bout of dieting and the resultant hard-won weight loss, my weight would slowly but surely inch up again until it *exceeded* my last top weight. Eventually self-disgust would set in once more, and the whole vicious cycle began again.

I stood there, massive in my loose, warm nightdress. What was wrong with me? It was then the reason dawned on me: I was immensely too fat. I was overweight, I thought, to the point that anyone employing me must be kinky . . . . From that night I decided to eat and drink half. Only half of everything I normally ate, in any circumstances . . . . Just to consume half, or perhaps even a quarter, until I reached a reasonable weight and size. And I started next morning eating less, drinking less.

A FAR CRY FROM KENSINGTON, A NOVEL BY MURIEL SPARK

But in the early seventies things changed. My son was an infant, I was on maternity leave from my teaching job, and my weight was at a particularly good point. Through a series of lucky breaks the opportunity to write my first cookery book came along, foodie opportunity after opportunity came my way, and I never returned to primary schoolteaching. Food editor, bistro chef, cookery school director, restaurant reviewer, food columnist, university lecturer on food in society and food in literature, presenter of a late-night food fantasy call-in radio programme – you name it in the Food Biz, I did it. During that very intense ten-year period I was fuelled by passion, and I grew – quite literally – with my work. I hated being on the fat track again, and I hated the inexorable steady ballooning even more, but I *loved* my work, and that turned out to be the stronger emotion. Any time I tried – half-heartedly – to pull back, my overwhelming interest in the fabulously seductive food, the incredibly juicy and *fun* assignments, won over any residual longings to be slim. If ever a chef or an editor felt that I was entertaining the thought – however vague – of attempting to diet, that chef or editor would gaze deeply and sincerely into my eyes and assure me: 'Sue, darling, surely *you're* not supposed to go on a diet. We can't imagine you any other way.'

During this period of my life I kept hearing rumours about that fabulous creature, the thin restaurant reviewer. This slim and sophisticated legend had a philosophy: you don't have to finish everything on your plate. Eat half (or even less) of everything put in front of you, was her motto. My relationship with food never allowed me to follow her advice, and thus to join her legendary svelte ranks. My philosophy was this: if the food is truly awful, or if it is (as often happened) drearily mediocre, eat only enough to enable the resulting review to be devastatingly accurate and honest. Leave the rest on the plate, ignoring any maternal echoes from the past about starving children in China. (This was not a rational decision. I was simply unable – in the line of duty or for any other reason – to eat such food.) If, on the other hand, the food was outstanding, delicious, seductive and glorious, Eat It *all*! Clean your plate, sigh ecstatically, then look around for more. My restaurant reviews were the talk of the town, avidly read for their honesty and the poetic, gastro-erotic vision of their food descriptions; my recipes were cooked in countless homes; my late-night radio call-in programme always had jammed lines, with people queuing up to discuss their never-before verbalized food fantasies on the air; and my girth was approaching that of a small vehicle.

But suddenly in 1982 my dedication began to wear thin, and my excess weight began to wear heavy on my bones and conscience. At the very time of my discontent Professor Steve Kreitzman (I call him Dr Husband), then director of the Centre for Nutrition at a large American university, began a scientific study to test the safety and efficacy of a new diet concept, the VLCD (very low-calorie diet) – in this particular case, the Cambridge Diet. For me, his study came at exactly the right moment: 100 kg (15½ stone) was just too much. Even worse, my wardrobe constantly had to be replenished, and almost as soon as I purchased clothes they became too small. I was tired of my lumbering, waddling gait, my several chins, my flabby and enormous behind. Anyone who has ever been fat knows what I mean: that air of being upholstered, rather than dressed, that feeling of being condemned to dowdiness because the Lady or Gentleman Elephant department has such a limited choice of colour and style. Self-dissatisfaction led me to do a very brave thing, in the light of my career involvement and my all-too-flourishing passion: I volunteered to be a study subject on Dr Husband's VLCD trial. A VLCD regime means that one consumes a nutrition-rich, calorie-shy liquid formula, three times a day. *Nothing else*, except enough water to float a small tanker.

Of course, I had to retire – temporarily – from restaurant reviewing. No one, however talented, can write an impassioned and accurate review of a meal based only on the way it looks and smells. Wine tasting was out of the question as well. But I continued to lecture, teach and write my food columns. It doesn't pay to turn one's back on a successful career, and one certainly does not abandon a full-fledged passion. Food (one of my best friends) was not gone forever; we had simply put our intimate relationship on hold for a while. My vicarious pleasure was extraordinary. I watched – with great enjoyment – my students consume intricate and enormous meals: Thai, Korean, Indian, French, All American, Mexican . . . . And I continued lovingly to develop and test for my column new recipes, which I would evaluate by nose and eye before ferrying to friends, neighbours and colleagues for tasting. All in all, the time on 'sole source' (several four-week periods) was intense and enlightening. I became more creative than ever before in my life. Although not really *hungry*, I fantasized about food constantly, even dreamed about it. Oh, the things I did to various foodstuffs in my imagination! I learned a lot about myself, and my relationship to food. And, of course, the best part was the weight loss. It was as if I were dabbling in personal archaeology: the willowy shape and tiny waist of my young womanhood were still there, just waiting to be uncovered. I emerged from the study a new woman. Losing 35 kg (5½ stone) impelled me to have my hair cut, my colours co-ordinated, my make-up revamped.

I was left with two glorious rewards. First, I won the prestigious National American/Canadian Food Writers' 'Vesta' award for stories written and recipes developed during my adherence to the VLCD study. In other words, my abstention and resulting rampant fantasizing paid off. In fact, not long afterwards my agent secured a nifty contract for a book about garlic, based on truly visionary flights of garlic-imbued fancy experienced during 'sole source'. And secondly, of course, I was intoxicatingly, brilliantly, elegantly *slim*!!

But let's stop and think for a moment. What happens next? There I was: slimmed down, more successful than ever, over the moon with excitement at my wonderful new appearance, my glowing health, my still vigorous career. Do I ride off into the sunset to the sound of soaring strings and rejoicing woodwinds, to begin my well-earned stint of Happily Ever After? Do I declare: 'I'm a slim person now, all my problems are over, it's time to resume life as it was before the diet'?

Anyone who has ever struggled with obesity and the 'yo-yo' is way ahead of me. The answer is 'Hell, no!' So-called 'Target Weight' is just the beginning. One thing that 'sole source' on a VLCD teaches you is that you really can survive a period of time without those things you hold so dear: chocolates, cream cakes, double cream, ice cream, soft drinks, crisps, alcohol, butter sauces, fish and chips, hamburgers . . . . You may fantasize wildly about these things, and long fiercely for the day you can engulf them once more, but in the meantime you exist beautifully without them. Indeed, their temporary lack causes your weight to decrease, your skin to clear up and any blood pressure problems to normalize.

So what happens, on that joyous day of achieving target weight? The seething pit of fat-imbued junk food, 'fun food', convenience food, haute cuisine *et al* is still there, just waiting for you to finish your regime. Do you clap your hands with glee and dive right back in? Many people do, even though all the food and drink once scoffed down so greedily now tastes rather strange. Whole milk seems unpleasantly thick; crisps, and fish and chips, taste impossibly greasy. Béarnaise and Hollandaise sauces coat the tongue like unguent ointments. Most puddings and candy appear cloyingly rich and sweet. What most folks do is doggedly chomp, munch and slurp their way through day after day of the same old problem food, until they *retrain* themselves into the destructive eating patterns that made them fat in the first place. And *voilà*! Presto! Surprise! Before long they *are* fat again.

I was determined not to fall into this vicious trap. Restaurant reviewing suddenly held no glamour whatsoever. Conventional cookery methods, fat and oil-based as they are, had not only become unpalatable, but I finally realized that they were dangerous – both to my spiffy new figure, and to my health. The whole concept of Slim Cuisine is a direct result of that newborn perception of the outrageously fatty, oily nature of the food universe. I vowed to escape the recidivism (regain of lost weight) that is the fate of 95 per cent of successful dieters, and I vowed to do it in a way that would allow me to continue to enjoy a sensual and emotionally nourishing relationship with food; one that would not involve a dreary lifetime of counting Calories and weighing portions. Dieticians' advice and state-of-the-art low-fat cookbooks seemed awful to me; either they didn't cut down nearly enough on fat (substituting polyunsaturates and monosaturates for saturated fat does nothing whatever for *weight control*, whatever debatable benefit it may have for your heart and arteries) or – if they were truly low-fat – they were terminally *boring*. Mediocre food was still – after all – quite impossible to bear. All my passion, expertise and experience went into developing a new, revolutionary (literally so) cuisine. Can you imagine the challenge? There I was, the butter and oil queen of North America, the woman who had majored in Hollandaise sauce and vinaigrette (heavy on the extra-virgin olive oil), about to embark on a no-fat crusade. Having faced the fact that the old fat-based conventions of cookery were obsolete, I had to start from the very beginning, ditching what I knew about the classic fat-based processes and developing new techniques and methods.

It wasn't easy. Since I had learned cookery the classic way – involving quantities of the usual oil, butter and so on – unlearning proved a great trial. Restaurant reviewing, which I resumed (reluctantly) when my VLCD regime ended, was a disaster. Four or five (or more) elaborate restaurant meals a week were threatening to bring the old fat me back into full flower in no time at all. And I still thought – in blind, stupid foolishness – that anniversaries, birthdays, celebrations of any kind were occasions to throw dietary caution to the winds. So – even though I meant well, and had learned an enormous amount – I found myself approaching the 'yo-yo' again.

> *Constantine begins the evening's lecture. He has two of them, which he alternates as he watches his weight; starvation on even days, gluttony on odd.*
>
> *THE KITCHEN MAN*, A NOVEL BY IRA WARD

Drastic measures were needed. I gave up restaurant reviewing altogether, finished off my obligations to my publisher and determined never to write another 'conventional' cookery book again. Holidays and celebrations remained a problem until I realized that I wasn't really enjoying the celebratory (high-fat) food, and I hated the inevitable weight gain that resulted from even temporary indulgence in such food. Why not just stop eating such destructive fodder completely? I developed a strategy to rid myself of the new weight gain (this plan is the direct result of that strategy), and established the totally low-fat regime that is now my gastronomic lifestyle. I still celebrate birthdays, anniversaries, successes and so on with food – how dull life would be without gastronomic celebration – but I do it my way, with lavish meals of Slim Cuisine. Very low-fat cookery has become a way of life – slipping into the old ways is totally unthinkable. Why should I slip? High-fat food has become unpalatable, Slim Cuisine is delicious, and my weight is stable.

The purpose of this book is to help *you* achieve this happy state of affairs. It goes beyond the ground broken by my first three Slim Cuisine books. They are cookbooks, dedicated to the new techniques and recipes of my very low-fat crusade. This book is meant to teach you total control. To *lose* weight, should you need to; to *keep* the weight off forever; and – most important of all – to retrain your taste perceptions and cravings, so that fat addiction is a thing of the past.

Don't ever count Calories again; get off the 'yo-yo', and enjoy your food with all of your heart and soul. Welcome to the revolution!

ABOUT THE SLIM CUISINE DIET

THE PREMISE

The premise of this weight loss plan is simple: if added fat is ruthlessly eliminated from one's diet, weight *loss* becomes mindlessly and painlessly simple, and weight *maintenance* is a snap. By *added* fat I mean all cooking fats and oils (even so-called 'low-fat' spreads), all dairy products that are not made from skimmed milk, and all high-fat foodstuffs (see lists on pages 22–23). Although fat is forbidden, salt is not, but must only be used very sparingly. Sugar is forbidden in the first few weeks.

Despite these drastic exclusions, this plan is upbeat, sensual and 'foodie' in the extreme; in fact it is an incredible reward, a luxurious food splurge, to follow my regime. When fat is removed, lots of Calories automatically follow. As a result, not only do large servings and between-meal snacking become possible, but they become necessary – even on the weight loss regime – because good nutrition is important to the basic plan. And the techniques of Slim Cuisine make no-fat cookery – usually dry, boring and terrifyingly undelicious – a vivid, exciting, deeply flavoured experience. The reward – the luxurious food splurge – is reality, not mere hyperbole.

This guide is a lifetime plan for good health, and slimness. It eliminates the need for tiresome Calorie counting, and its hedonistic, sensuous and permissive approach to food is soul-satisfying in the extreme. The splendidly satisfying dishes produced by the Slim Cuisine techniques will become staple family food. This is not a programme to be endured until one can return to 'real' food. Slim Cuisine will become your new gastronomic reality.

THE PURPOSE

The purpose of the plan is threefold:

1 To lose weight in a safe, no-suffering way.

2 To keep the weight off for the rest of your life – again safely and painlessly.

3 To retrain your palate and happily change your bad habits, so that the precepts of Slim Cuisine become joyful second nature.

THE PLAN

The weight loss regime is divided into four weeks: each week brings new additions and special treats. Here are some of the high points.

The *One-day Blitz*. A single day of raw vegetables and salads, (from a specified list) and skimmed milk products (quark, yogurt, skimmed milk, buttermilk, fromage frais, cottage cheese and curd cheese.) There is no limit on the amount of salads, vegetables and dairy products. Wine vinegar, seasonings, mustard and other specified condiments are allowed to dress the vegetables and season the dips. At no time should you be hungry; if hunger strikes, eat more of the allowed foods.

The *Therapeutic Binge* vegetarian week. All the vegetables (cooked and raw) and all the skimmed milk dairy products desired, but nothing else: no grains (until the fourth day); no bread or pasta; no fruit; no pulses, meat, poultry, fish and so on. The list of allowed vegetables is large, and the skimmed milk dairy products allowed are as listed in the One-day Blitz. Recipes are a very important part of this week; the 'free' vegetables and dairy products are used in all sorts of sumptuously delicious recipes, so that taste boredom and hunger will never set in. These recipes, especially the Therapeutic Binge ones, will eventually become well-loved staples in the long-term maintenance plan. All of them will utilize Slim Cuisine cookery techniques. Two large potatoes a day are also allowed.

The *addition of fruit*. This may be the most dramatic moment in your gastronomic life. After six days of eating no sweet foods, the first taste of a perfect piece of exquisitely chosen fruit hits your tastebuds with the force of the 4th of July, the 14th of July and the 5th of November *put together*. That perfect pear or apple or strawberry will burst with flavour and ravish your palate the way no cream cake or chocolate bar ever has.

Then, as the days go by, you can add bread, fish, poultry, pasta, grains and finally lean meats in prescribed quantities. The basic list of vegetables – first described in the One-day Blitz and expanded in the Vegetarian Week – remain the same, and remain *free*, that is they are allowed in unlimited quantities.

When your target weight is reached, fish, lean meat and poultry are allowed in larger quantities, and you can eat more fruit, more pasta and grains, pulses, and occasional small amounts of medium-fat cheeses (in recipes). If at any time you slip – revert to junk food, succumb to an over-the-top family holiday dinner, are seduced by a weekend in France or a trip to Italy, or fall into any of the fat-lined pitfalls that can ensnare all ex-fatties, then you go *immediately* back to the One-day Blitz. Then, unless your reversal is very severe and you have gained a significant amount of weight, you may return to Maintenance.

WEEK 1: THE VEGETARIAN WEEK

DAY 1: ONE-DAY BLITZ

Unlimited raw vegetables and skimmed milk products (for details see page 34).

DAY 2: THERAPEUTIC BINGE

Unlimited raw and cooked vegetables, skimmed milk dairy products, 450 g (1 lb) potatoes (for details see page 40).

DAY 3

Same as Day 2.

DAY 4

Add breakfast (cereal or crackers); for details see page 50.

DAYS 5 AND 6

Same as Day 4.

DAY 7

Add one piece of fruit in the evening (for details see page 51).

WEEK 2: SWEET REWARDS

DAY 8

Begin eating two pieces of fruit a day (for details see page 54).

DAY 9

Begin eating two pieces of bread a day (for details see page 54).

DAYS 10 AND 11

Same as Day 9.

DAY 12

Add milk shakes, fruit creams and Slim Cuisine 'whipped' cream (for details see page 57).

DAYS 13 AND 14

Same as Day 12.

WEEK 3: THE OMNIVORE

DAY 15

Add one more serving of fruit, bringing your daily fruit total to three, plus one boneless, skinless chicken breast *or* one fish fillet *or* one can 185 g (6½ oz) drained tuna in brine or water per day (for details see page 58).

DAYS 16, 17, 18, 19 AND 20

Same as Day 15.

DAY 21

Substitute if you wish 300 ml (½ pint) cooked grains (couscous, pasta, polenta, buckwheat groats or bulghur) for one slice of bread, or your breakfast cereal or crackers (for details see page 60).

WEEK 4: CHEESECAKE AND STEAK

DAY 22

If you wish, add one more chicken breast or fish fillet per day, or you may have instead canned salmon, sardines, mackerel or pilchards (no added oil!) or any shellfish. At this point, you may have a few vegetarian days (no fish or chicken) each week if you wish; in fact it is strongly recommended that you do so. And do make sure you are eating a good variety and quantity of vegetables, as you should every day (for details see page 62). And today, you may begin eating *cheesecake* (for details see page 62)!

DAYS 23, 24 AND 25

Same as Day 22.

DAY 26

Add 150 g (5 oz) green peas and/or 150 g (5 oz) sweetcorn each day, if you wish (for details see page 64).

DAY 27

Same as Day 26.

DAY 28

If you wish, substitute an occasional serving of pork (tenderloin) or beef (goose skirt steak or point-end brisket), or very lean mince, for one serving of fish or chicken. A *serving* is 110–150 g (4–5 oz) raw weight (for details see page 65).

Stay on this level until you hit target weight. If you hit a 'plateau' – that maddening period of time that dieters often experience, when weight refuses to budge, then you may, if you want to, go back a level or two, until the downward process begins again. In fact any level (except the One-day Blitz) that pleases you – a level on which you are comfortable, losing easily with no suffering and no inconvenience – can be yours for as long as you like. Take your time, and stay on that level until you feel ready to move on. If you stay on any level (before the final one) until you reach target weight, do not immediately go to Maintenance. Move up, day by day, to Day 28 – then switch to Maintenance.

The Diet, with day-by-day advice and discussion, begins on page 33.

ACHIEVING YOUR GOALS

This diet plan has many goals. First, of course, the goal is to help you *lose weight*. But – even more important – this plan is tailored to help you *keep the weight off*, once you have reached your target. And here is the *most* important gift that this diet can give you: a state of complete and uncompromised happiness with your daily food choices. The regime is designed to retrain you, your habits and your food perceptions so that fatty, greasy, sugary and salty foods become – eventually – unnecessary and unpalatable.

THE ART OF BINGEING: THE THERAPEUTIC BINGE

If your weight problem is partly caused by your tendency to binge, I think you should retain the right to binge. I want to switch you, however, from destructive bingeing to therapeutic bingeing. A binge can be delightfully comforting when life is less than perfect. And when life *is* going very well, a binge can be a fabulous reward. And food is not only a wonderful comfort in itself – it is a hedge against more sinister comforts such as drugs, tobacco, alcohol and various forms of anti-social behaviour. But, as you know, food will make you fat and ill if your bingeing sessions centre on high-fat junk. This diet plan will enable you to break the fat-sugar-salt addiction of a lifetime, and retrain your tastebuds so that you crave low-fat healthy foods – the sort you can binge on to your heart's content. Then you will be mentally and spiritually soothed, as well as exquisitely nourished from a physical point of view.

This is the Therapeutic Binge symbol. All recipes so marked in any of my cookery books are suitable for eating at any time, in any amount, on any stage of this plan, from Day 2 on into lifetime maintenance. Always have Therapeutic Binges available in your fridge and freezer. It means planning ahead, but it will be the most important thing you do for your weight control and gastronomic satisfaction. Depend on these foods for your physical and mental health.

HOW MUCH SHOULD YOU WEIGH?

I asked my husband, Dr Stephen Kreitzman (a PhD in Nutritional Biochemistry and Metabolism, and a researcher in the field of obesity at Cambridge University), to answer this question. Steve, who once weighed 158.7 kg (25 stone) and now weighs 69.9 kg (11 stone), has devoted his not inconsiderable talent and expertise to the study of the problems, causes and treatment of obesity. It is very tempting to decide that the arguments for becoming slim are spurious, and based on arbitrary and meaningless sociological and even sexist factors. After all, fashions and tastes change: sometimes the ideal feminine beauty is voluptuous, fleshy, bosomy and overblown, sometimes she is reed-thin, flat-chested and scrawny. Rubens's beauties practically billowed off the canvas; the flappers of the twenties tried to bind their disorderly breasts out of existence; the pin-ups of the fifties flaunted their extravagant hourglass curves and filled their sweaters beyond capacity; and the teenagers of the Twiggy era starved themselves to skeletal extremes. Why should we blindly follow fashion? Why should we worry at all? Why not give in to our destiny, whether it's a curvy destiny or a skinny one?

> *. . . we should remember that beauty and its corollary, sexual appeal, are not timeless ideals but fluid, shifting concepts. Today the rosy, bulging goddesses who Rubens and his contemporaries considered so desirable would hasten to a fat farm; the pale, frail jeunes filles admired in the early 19th century would rush to a doctor or a health club.*
>
> ALISON LURIE IN *LEAR'S MAGAZINE*

IDEAL WEIGHT BY DR STEPHEN KREITZMAN

The image that people have of their ideal weight, realistic or not, can be extremely important to their psychological health. Vanity is not always frivolous, as the social consequences of being more (or less) than 'normal' standards can often be quite severe. Vanity, however, is only one criterion for target weight and not necessarily the most valid one. Approximately three people out of every ten in the UK have a body weight that is considered to be a risk to health.

Insurance companies love to collect premiums, but are reluctant to pay out. Several years ago insurance company statisticians in the United States conducted a massive study to try to identify those people who would be most likely to require pay-out on their life insurance policies. This was not an academic exercise: they were trying to save themselves billions of dollars. What they found therefore goes far beyond vanity, and should be taken extremely seriously.

They found that a measure of body fatness, the 'Body Mass Index' (BMI), was very markedly related to the risk of death and so of their having to pay up on their policies. When BMI goes up beyond 25, the gamble that the company would be taking to insure your life increases rapidly. The ideal range from their point of view is between 20 and 25.

To find your BMI you need to know your height and weight, and then look at the chart opposite. Desirable weight is below BMI 25 for medical reasons and within the range 20 to 25 for reasons of self-esteem and personal body image. So your target weight should be in the range 20 to 25 according to personal preference. Obesity (BMI 30 to 35), super obesity (BMI 35 to 40), morbid obesity (BMI 40 to 45) and super morbid obesity (BMI 45 plus) all represent a dramatically accelerating increase in medical risk.

HEIGHT

WEIGHT (STONE)	4′ 9″	4′ 10″	4′ 11″	5′	5′ 1″	5′ 2″	5′ 3″	5′ 4″	5′ 5″	5′ 6″	5′ 7″	5′ 8″	5′ 9″	5′ 10″	5′ 11″	6′	6′ 1″	6′ 2″	6′ 3″	6′ 4″	6′ 5″	KILOGRAMS
METRES	1 45	1 47	1 50	1 52	1 55	1 57	1 60	1 63	1 65	1 68	1 70	1 73	1 75	1 78	1 80	1 83	1 85	1 88	1 90	1 93	1 96	
6½	20																					41.3
6¾	20	20																				42.9
7	21	20	20																			44.5
7¼	22	21	21	20																		46.0
7½	23	22	21	21	20																	47.6
7¾	23	23	22	21	21	20																49.2
8	24	23	23	22	21	20	20															50.8
8¼	25	24	23	23	22	21	20	20														52.4
8½	26	25	24	23	22	22	21	20	20													54.0
8¾	27	26	25	24	23	22	22	21	20	20												55.6
9	27	26	25	25	24	23	22	22	21	20	20											57.2
9¼	28	27	26	25	24	24	23	22	22	21	20	20										58.7
9½	29	28	27	26	25	24	24	23	22	21	21	20	20									60.3
9¾	30	29	28	27	26	25	24	23	23	22	21	21	20	20								61.9
10	30	29	28	27	26	26	25	24	23	23	22	21	21	20	20							63.5
10¼	31	30	29	28	27	26	25	25	24	23	22	22	21	21	20							65.1
10½	32	31	30	29	28	27	26	25	24	24	23	22	22	21	21	20						66.7
10¾	33	31	30	29	28	28	27	26	25	24	24	23	22	22	21	20	20					68.3
11	33	32	31	30	29	28	27	26	26	25	24	23	23	22	21	21	20	20				69.9
11¼	34	33	32	31	30	29	28	27	26	25	25	24	23	23	22	21	21	20	20			71.4
11½	35	34	33	31	30	29	29	28	27	26	25	24	24	23	22	22	21	21	20	20		73.0
11¾		34	33	32	31	30	29	28	27	27	26	25	24	24	23	22	22	21	21	20	20	74.6
12		35	34	33	32	31	30	29	28	27	26	26	25	24	23	23	22	22	21	20	20	76.2
12¼			35	33	32	31	30	29	29	28	27	26	25	25	24	23	23	22	21	21	20	77.8
12½			35	34	33	32	31	30	29	28	27	27	26	25	24	24	23	22	22	21	21	79.4
12¾				35	34	33	32	31	30	29	28	27	26	26	25	24	24	23	22	22	21	81.0
13					34	33	32	31	30	29	29	28	27	26	25	25	24	23	23	22	22	82.6
13¼					35	34	33	32	31	30	29	28	27	27	26	25	24	24	23	23	22	84.1
13½						35	33	32	31	31	30	29	28	27	26	26	25	24	24	23	22	85.7
13¾						35	34	33	32	31	30	29	28	28	27	26	25	25	24	23	23	87.3
14							35	34	33	32	31	30	29	28	27	27	26	25	24	24	23	88.9
14¼							35	34	33	32	31	30	29	29	28	27	26	26	25	24	24	90.5
14½								35	34	33	32	31	30	29	28	28	27	26	25	25	24	92.1
14¾								35	34	33	32	31	30	30	29	28	27	27	26	25	24	93.7
15									35	34	33	32	31	30	29	28	28	27	26	26	25	95.3
15¼										34	33	32	32	31	30	29	28	27	27	26	25	96.8
15½										35	34	33	32	31	30	29	29	28	27	26	26	98.4
15¾											35	34	33	32	31	30	29	28	28	27	26	100.0
16											35	34	33	32	31	30	30	29	28	27	27	101.6
16¼												35	34	33	32	31	30	29	28	28	27	103.2
16½												35	34	33	32	31	30	30	29	28	27	104.8
16¾													35	34	33	32	31	30	29	29	28	106.4
17													35	34	33	32	31	31	30	29	28	108.0
17¼														35	34	33	32	31	30	29	29	109.5
17½														35	34	33	32	31	31	30	29	111.1
17¾															35	34	33	32	31	30	29	112.7
18															35	34	33	32	31	31	30	114.3
18¼																35	34	33	32	31	30	115.9
18½																35	34	33	32	32	31	117.5
18¾																	35	34	33	32	31	119.1
19																	35	34	33	32	32	120.7
19¼																		35	34	33	32	122.2
19½																		35	34	33	32	123.8
19¾																			35	34	33	125.4
20																			35	34	33	127.0
20¼																			35	35	34	128.6
20½																				35	34	130.2
20¾																				35	34	131.8
21																					35	133.4
21¼																					35	134.9

What your BMI means
20 – 25 normal weight range
25 – 30 overweight
30 –35 obese
35 – 40 super obese

To find your BMI
Read across the chart to find your height, then down to your approximate weight. The point where the two cross gives your BMI

Body composition is an important subject of obesity research these days. Accurate and efficient methods of measuring body composition have been developed recently, so weight and physical appearance are not the only things considered in current obesity treatment. The important factor is the actual percentage of body fat. Very recent research suggests that the percentage of *dietary* fat consumed determines in large measure the amount of *body* fat. Thus an individual whose diet consists of 40 per cent fat over the long run will eventually have a body composition of approximately 40 per cent fat.

> *Suck it in! I sucked. Nothing moved. Small breasts fuller but sagging on the sides. Torso wide, stomach and hips huge. I looked like a snowwoman, built in tiers. Man, get a load a dem thighs! Gen-u-ine, industrial strength, pony express-sized saddlebags. Kneecaps a couple of indented dimples in the middle of my legs. Thick calves. Thick ankles. Fat feet. Chubby toes. Th-th-th-that's all, folks. C'mon, there's got to be something salvageable. 'You have great naturally curly hair,' I said. 'Breathtakingly beautiful eyes.' I batted puffy lids. 'You have strong finger- and toenails and wonderfully delicate earlobes.' I pressed my nose against my reflection. You're bright, creative and can type. It ain't much, kid, but it's a beginning.'*
>
> *THE DIETER*, A NOVEL BY SUSAN SUSSMAN

You can adjust your amount of body fat by calibrating the amount of dietary fat you consume. Slim Cuisine provides enough fat (approximately 20 per cent of your diet is fat by the time you get to maintenance) to cushion your organs and to keep you warm, good-looking and well nourished. Less would be unhealthy and make you look skeletal, more would encourage overweight. Percentage of body fat is regulated by the average percentage of fat we consume *over the long run*, so this regime *must* be a long-term one. This plan results in a fast initial loss – very good for morale and motivation. This is followed by a slow, steady and inexorable loss of fat, and an eventual stabilization of the loss, which will last a lifetime under the aegis of Slim Cuisine.

STARVE YOUR FAT

Your body fat thrives on the dietary fat you feed it day after day. If you want to eliminate the fat deposits from your body, why continue mindlessly and obligingly nourishing them? Instead, ruthlessly eliminate the following items from your diet:

THE OBVIOUS FATS

Butter •*All* oils • Solid shortenings • Margarine • Low-fat spreads • Vegetable shortenings • Dripping • Lard • Suet • Poultry fat • Poultry skin • Bacon fat •Full-fat and semi-skimmed milk products including full-fat and semi-skimmed hard cheeses, soft cheeses, yogurts, fromage frais, cottage cheese, cream, soured cream, clotted cream, etc. • Mayonnaise and salad dressings • Fatty meats

THE LESS OBVIOUS FATS

Cut these out as well:

All nuts (except chestnuts, which are *not* high in fat) • Egg yolks (the whites are fine) • Avocados • Coconut • Olives

THE HIDDEN FATS

Eliminate, as well, all prepared foods, from frozen foods to baked goods to snacks and convenience food, and everything in between, that contain *added fat*. For the most part the food industry is not interested in your desperate battle of the bulge. Even many so-called 'Calorie-controlled' and 'low-fat' products contain far too many fat Calories to suit an individual who is waging a serious war against his or her fat deposits. You must learn to read labels closely, even if it means carrying a magnifying glass when you shop, and decide for yourself whether a particular 'diet' or 'low-fat' product is suitable. Less than 1 per cent fat is what you want to aim for in dairy products, no *added* fat in other products.

DEMON FAT

Why *no* oil or butter or marge at all? Why not just a few drops here to sauté your onions, and a scraping there to butter your toast? First of all, even a little bit of fat or oil is Calorie-intense. But even more important is this: fat and oil are too insidious to use in such a manner. When you set out to break an alcohol addiction, you do not quaff a little bit each day. And were you to try to kick a heroin habit, you would not plan to shoot up just a bit occasionally. The only way to deal with an addiction is to *stop*. Oil, butter, marge, cream, 'low-fat' spread – the lot – are too compelling to play such games with. A scraping here, a dribble there; soon you will be back in the coils of Demon Fat once more, and fatter (and more despairing) than ever.

RECIPE OF THE WEEK FRIED SUGAR BALLS

1½ cups granulated sugar/¼ cup powdered sugar/1½ cups lard/3 sticks margarine

Heat lard in skillet. Melt margarine, mix in granulated sugar and form balls, about 1 inch thick. Drop sugar balls into hot lard. Remove when golden brown. Serve hot on styrofoam plates, sprinkled generously with powdered sugar. This is a favorite of kids and grandparents alike. Even people who say they don't like lard like this dish.

BLOOMINGTON [INDIANA] HERALD TIMES, QUOTED IN THE *NEW YORKER*

'POLYWHATS'ER NAMES'

A GUIDE THROUGH THE SUPERMARKET MINEFIELD

If you watch TV commercials, and read magazines and newspapers, you'll have heard plenty about 'good' fats and 'bad' fats; cholesterol; 'low-fat' spreads; saturated fats; unsaturated fats; 'polywhats'er names'; and so on – an unending, mind-numbing assault of confusing (and often misleading) information. Let me try to simplify the whole knotty problem of fats for you.

1 *All* fats – whether they are saturated animal fats including poultry fat, lard, dripping, suet and butter fats; polyunsaturated or monounsaturated oils; margarines (many are highly saturated, although some are richer in mono-and polyunsaturates); the fats or oils in nuts, avocados and coconuts – *all of them* contain 9 Calories per gram (approximately 120 Calories per 15 ml/1 tbsp). These Calories are metabolized into body fat in an extremely quick and efficient fashion.

2 'Low-fat' spreads may contain less fat than butter or margarine because they have been diluted with something (water or air or buttermilk, for instance), but they still contain substantial amounts of health-threatening and calorie-dense *fat*. I've never understood the need for 'low-fat spreads'. You can't cook with them – they are too watery. Their sole purpose seems to be to grease up your bread or toast. Give me a break! Use skimmed milk quark, or skimmed milk fromage frais, or a mashed ripe banana (after Day 7). For what possible reason would you want to add fat to your diet simply to ruin your toast and your beautiful bread? The mind boggles.

3 The whole saturated/unsaturated (mono and poly) story is incredibly confusing to many people. Just what does it mean anyway? All edible fats are mixtures of saturated and unsaturated compounds. Animal fats, including dairy fats (butter, cream and whole milk products), lard, poultry dripping, suet and so on, contain a high *percentage* of *saturated* fat. The word 'saturated' refers to the actual chemical make-up of the fat molecules. Interestingly enough, three vegetable oils (palm oil, palm kernel oil and coconut oil) are even higher in saturates than butter. So if a product is labelled 'made with vegetable shortening only', or 'contains vegetable fat', it does not automatically follow that the product is high in unsaturates.

Other vegetable oils are higher in monounsaturates and polyunsaturates, although they will also contain *some* saturates. Again, the terms monounsaturates and polyunsaturates refer to the chemical bonding within the fat molecules. Since a fat with a higher proportion of unsaturation is often a liquid at room temperature, some solid margarines and solid vegetable shortening are manufactured by putting highly unsaturated vegetable oil through a hydrogenation process to firm it up, so that it will be 'spreadable'. This hydrogenation process actually causes the oil to become saturated; in fact, saturated in a way that is even *more* suspected of causing health problems than naturally saturated fats.

So what? is the question I hear ringing through the air, loud and clear. What can it all mean? Well, as you already know, all fat is equally fattening, whatever the make-up of its chemical bonds. An impressive history of solid scientific research reveals a connection between highly saturated fats and disease, especially (but by no means only) heart and artery disease. But the unsaturated fats have also been implicated in disease (several kinds of cancer, for instance). So cutting back only on highly saturated fats makes no sense at all, either for weight control or for health. But eliminating *all* added fats and high-fat foods makes perfect sense. Don't let aggressive and intelligence-insulting advertising manipulate you into making dangerous (and fattening) dietary choices.

4 It is true that the human body needs a certain amount of dietary fat to function. But guess what? There is plenty in a bountiful diet of fish, lean meat and poultry, vegetables and grains: just what you'll be eating on this plan. And the masses of vegetables, whole grains, poultry, fish, fruit and lean meat (and skimmed milk powder) will give you a full complement of fat-soluble vitamins as well.

5 Now what about cholesterol? Cholesterol is a fatty substance that is manufactured in the body, and is important to the body's functioning. It is the cholesterol levels in the blood that concern medical researchers. On the scientific level, controversy rages. Does dietary cholesterol affect levels of blood cholesterol? Does it contribute to heart disease? And what about 'good' cholesterol and 'bad' cholesterol? Does olive oil (and other highly monounsaturated oils) *really* raise levels of 'good' cholesterol – as has been claimed with great fanfare lately?

Although many books recently published in both the UK and the USA purport to give concrete answers to these highly perplexing questions, the truth is that there are no easy answers. The whole cholesterol story, on both the medical and scientific levels, is fraught with debate and conflicting theories. But again, for practical purposes you have 'no worries', as our Australian friends say. If you ruthlessly cut added fats and high-fat foods from your diet, you will have done much towards reducing your total blood cholesterol levels and restoring the proper balance between so-called 'good' (HDL) and 'bad' (LDL) cholesterol. It is now generally believed that it is the *total fat intake* that may have the effect of raising blood cholesterol levels, not just frequent consumption of high-cholesterol foodstuffs. So try to ignore current exhortations to eat lashings of olive oil or canola oil or other highly monounsaturated oils to benefit your cholesterol levels. They are all pure fat.

> *It is odd that it is now much easier to buy good olive oil in this country than it is to buy good butter. Is this because olive oil has become the butter of the health-conscious? Or is it simply the liquid engineering of our taste buds by a number of canny olive oil importers?*
>
> SIMONE SEKERS, KITCHEN COLUMN, *SUNDAY TELEGRAPH*

6 Perhaps you have read about fish oil recently. Epidemiological studies on the Greenland Eskimos seem to show that it is beneficial to the heart. The incidence of heart disease among these people is low, and they eat a diet high in fat fish.

After Day 15 of the plan do eat fish, both fatty and lean, several times a week. Fish fat may well be beneficial, and fish is rich in fat-soluble vitamins as well. Do not, however, supplement your diet with fish oil capsules, or liquid fish oil out of a bottle. Such large concentrated doses of pure fish oil are not necessary: there is never any need to ingest *pure oil*. The fish alone is enough. Interestingly enough, squid and shellfish – although not particularly fatty – contain a high proportion of omega-3 fatty acids (the compounds in fish fat that are believed to be beneficial to the heart). It is wise to make both shellfish and other fish a regular part of your diet. Keep this in mind: even the fattest fish is relatively low in Calories, and fish fat (as is the fat in whole grains) is *just* the kind of fat your body needs. Remember, Slim Cuisine is not a totally fat-free diet. Such a diet would be dangerous and almost impossible to achieve. It's a diet of no *added* fat.

GROUP DYNAMICS

Dieting with a group is so much easier than dieting alone, especially if that group is filled with sympathetic friends who share similar problems. Why not gather together a group of like-minded people to form a Slim Cuisine diet club? The first day One-day Blitz is so much less of a challenge, and so much fun, when the experience is a shared one. For the first three or four days, plan for your club to meet each afternoon or evening. Keep charts for every member: at the beginning of each meeting weigh and measure, and enter the figures on the charts. Then begin the deeply satisfying part of the meeting: True Confessions. Each member must have a turn to talk. Use this time to explore the reasons for each member's overweight. Do you eat to punish yourself or to punish others? Or do you eat because you have an endless hunger that you seem unable to assuage? Perhaps you eat simply because the food is *there*, with no thought for its taste or goodness (or lack of it) – a sort of human hoover, sucking up everything in sight, even if it is other people's leftovers. The first day is the most revealing.

> *By this time I was eating steadily, doggedly, stubbornly, anything I could get. The war between myself and my mother was on in earnest; the disputed territory was my body. I didn't quite know this though I sensed it in a hazy way; but I reacted to the diet booklets she left on my pillow, to the bribes of dresses she would give me if I would reduce to fit them – formal gowns with layers of tulle and wired busts, perky little frocks, skirts with slim waists and frothy crinolines – to her cutting remarks about my size, to her pleas about my health (I would die of a heart attack, I would get high blood pressure), to the specialists she sent me to and the pills they prescribed, to all of these things, with another Mars Bar or a double helping of French fries. I swelled visibly, relentlessly, before her very eyes, I rose like dough, my body advanced inch by inch towards her across the dining room table, in this at least I was undefeated. I was five feet four and still growing, and I weighed a hundred and eighty-two pounds.*
>
> *LADY ORACLE*, A NOVEL BY MARGARET ATWOOD

At the time when you would usually reach for milky coffee and three doughnuts, for a bar of chocolate and a bag of crisps, for a fast food burger and fries, for a packet of biscuits, for a beer and a double handful of peanuts, what did you think, how did you feel as the time came and passed, and you munched raw vegetables instead? This regime is meant to break your food addictions. Talk each day's experiences through with your friends in the group. Everyone should get enough time to whinge, to self-analyse, to probe, discuss, exult and exhaust the day's anecdotes. After everyone has had their say, serve lavish refreshments based on the day's food choices.

On the second day, after weights and measures and True Confessions, serve a buffet supper. It should be what Americans call a Covered Dish Supper: everyone brings a dish, and sets it on the table. Such parties result in a gorgeous array of food; each member of the group gets to eat a bit of everything. For each Slim Cuisine Diet Research Study I've run I have always served such a lavish buffet on the second night, although my assistant, Sandie, and I – not the study subjects – do the cooking. It is an encouraging, intoxicating and quite unbelievable experience to be able to feast to total satisfaction on an array of perfectly splendid, colourful food, and to know that this is your *diet*; all these dishes are allowed, and some of them are Therapeutic Binges! When the second day meeting is over everyone will go home very full, very happy and full of hope that this is a diet they can live with.

Here is a suggested menu for the second night buffet. Ask each member of the group to choose one dish. The host or hostess should provide plenty of coffee, tea and mineral water to accompany it.

'Fried' Onions • Roast Potatoes • Sautéed Mushrooms • Potato Crisps • Colourful Potato and Vegetable Casserole • Gratin of Mediterranean Vegetables • Vegetable Chilli • Mashed Potatoes with Gravy • Peperonata • Vegetable 'Lasagne' • Simple Vegetable Soup • Ratatouille • Creamy Parsnip Soup • Vegetable Curry (at least one version, perhaps several) • Curried Cauliflower

After the third day, meetings need to take place once a week only, but the members should act as a support group for one another between meetings. It's vital to have someone to depend on when you are depressed, when circumstances seem to be forcing you off your regime, when you hit a plateau in your weight loss and when you feel discouraged. I think you will find that friends made in a support group like this remain friends forever. Just remember – in such a group you expect (and you should receive) love, support, understanding, emotional indulgence, pampering and several shoulders to cry on. But you must *give* these things, as well, or the group experience will not work at all.

FEEDING THE MASSES

If you are responsible for cooking for your family, your housemates or your friends, it's quite absurd to cook one way (high-fat, creamy, buttery, health-threatening) for them, and another way (very low-fat, healthy, disease-fighting) for yourself. And it's *really* stupid to have stashes of destructive 'goodies' (sweets, biscuits, doughnuts, shop-bought crisps and so on) for them that you are not allowed to touch. Cooking daily, and all the related shopping and planning, are difficult and time-consuming enough when everyone is eating the same menu. If you have to double that work by implementing a separate shopping and cooking strategy for you and for them, you will kill yourself with exhaustion. And as far as the 'goodies' are concerned, it is hard enough ignoring their siren song when you are out and about – how much more difficult to ignore them in your own home. Don't do such destructive things to yourself. And – just as important – don't do such destructive things to *them*. Even if your family, friends and housemates are the kind who can seemingly eat anything they like without putting on weight, do they really *need* butter, cream, high-fat meats and sugary, fatty sweets? Do they *have* to have deep-fried chips regularly? Why is it proper for you to cherish your heart, arteries and general physical well-being, but not theirs?

I'll tell you a great truth about Slim Cuisine. The techniques are such that it does not taste like 'slimming food'. If you have already experienced Slim Cuisine through my cookery books, then you already know: this is real food – food that delivers deep flavour and profound satisfaction. Should you try to cook Slim Cuisine for yourself and Fat Cuisine for the rest, you will find that they eye your ice cream, your milk shakes, your curries, your crisps and chips, your 'fried' chicken and fish with serious larceny in their eyes. The ones who do not need to lose weight can eat easily prepared extras: simple lean chops, medium-fat cheeses, more bread, pulses (including baked beans if they like them), plenty of pasta and grains and so on. (When you reach Maintenance, you can eat those things too.)

Children (who should not be put on a drastically low-fat diet) can eat in addition semi-skimmed milk and semi-skimmed milk products, and plenty of fish, poultry, lean meat and dried fruit. They need plenty of Calories for growth and development, and they need some fat too – but they *never* need rubbish: biscuits, sweets, pastries, commercial crisps, deep-fried chips, deep-fried fish, fatty fast food hamburgers and so on. Why predestine them for later suffering, why muddy their taste perceptions, and why encourage them to develop bad habits? This is a revolution for everyone.

FOR WOMEN ONLY

The best time to start your diet is just after your monthly period is over. If you start before, you'll suffer needlessly. Many women, in the week or ten days before the onset of their period, are overtaken by a food frenzy: it's as if we could devour the world (especially the chocolate-flavoured bits) and still feel unsatisfied. That monthly bottomless appetite and mindless craving for all the wrong things may sabotage your good intentions. And should you manage to overcome the cravings, the appetite and the irritability, and stick to the plan despite the exhortations of your raucous hormones, you may find that your weight does not fall as it should – indeed it may increase somewhat because of water retention. The first week of the diet does have a diuretic effect, so if you are prone to pre-menstrual water retention it might not be as severe as usual, but it will still probably slow down your progress.

So wait until your period is over. The plan is a twenty-eight-day one. When you reach craving time again, you may be surprised: what you crave this time won't be the same as what you craved the last time around, pre-diet. But be good to yourself during this mercilessly reappearing time of the month. This time around feed your cavernous hunger with mashed potatoes and Therapeutic Binges. Feed your throbbing sweet tooth with milk shakes, cheesecake and Slim Cuisine ice cream. Crunch your way through a bowl of Slim Cuisine crisps. I think your chocolate craving may not appear this time around, but if it does, and it threatens to propel you to the corner shop for a bagful of garbage (chocolate biscuits, chocolate bars and so on) *Stop*! Don't do it. Turn to page 131 and admire the recipe there. Yes, on Day 12 and afterwards you may have a chocolate shake. Drink it slowly. Roll it around on your tongue. Revel in it. This is chocolate as it should be. And for maintenance (and for the next lot of monthly heebie-jeebies) this should be your chocolate experience, when you need it.

EXERCISE

This is *not* a book about exercise, but no plan concentrating on health, fitness and weight can ignore this subject. It is by no means a foregone conclusion that regular strenuous exercise hastens weight loss; experimental results are ambiguous on this point. But regular exercise of some sort *is* important to general fitness, cardiac health and mental well-being, and there is no doubt that your Calorie expenditure increases while exercising. If you are not a sports-minded person, and have the coordination and grace of an inebriated clodhopper, there are still plenty of painless ways to add some activity to your life.

1 Walk! For some individuals the car seems to be an actual physical extension of their body. Remove your backside from the car seat and put your legs in motion: get yourself a pair of decent walking shoes (if you don't want to spend a bundle, get trainers, or – for women – a good pair of rubber-soled nurse's shoes), and hit the pavement. The best thing about walking (especially city walking) is that it's so interesting: so many people, so many shop windows, so many city dramas and escapades to whet your curiosity. But don't meander or stroll. Stride along as though you mean it.

2 Climb the stairs. Why let lifts and escalators do all the work? Stair climbing (both up and down) gives your body a good workout, especially if you're carrying packages as well. There is an unbelievably expensive exercise machine that is having an enormous vogue right now in the USA called the Stairmaster. This is puzzling. Who needs a pricey machine? There they are for free – in the tube, in department stores, in blocks of flats. Hit those stairs!

3 Swim. There is not a muscle in your body that will not benefit from a swimming workout. And frolicking in water is one of the best things that you can do for your mental health as well; most humans find water play infinitely soothing. If you are embarrassed to swim in public because you hate the way that you look in a swimsuit, go swimming with your support group instead of braving the water alone with a bunch of thin strangers.

DAILY ROUTINE

1 Keep a diary. Label each day: Day 1, Day 2, Day 3 and so on, so that you always know where you are in the progression of the diet plan. Carry the diary with you each day. Write down what you eat, what time you ate it, and how you felt about it. Did you love it or hate it? Did it satisfy you or did it make you hungry enough to eat the furniture? Did you wish it was something else? Write it all down. When you crave something (chocolate, crisps, whatever) write it down and describe your feelings. If you think you can't survive another day without a cream cake, write it down. If you think you can't eat another vegetable, write it down. If you are filled with hope and excitement because you think you *can* do it, write it down. Use your diary to talk to yourself, argue with yourself, comfort yourself. Be graphic, be detailed, be specific, even be abusive if you wish. If writing doesn't come easily to you, get yourself a small tape recorder and a bunch of blank tapes and talk to yourself through the little machine.

You are embarking on a four-week plan, designed to help you break your addiction to fats and your destructive food habits. Use the tape machine (or the diary) to establish a dialogue with yourself. Argue with yourself, cajole, despair and encourage. Talk about your food choices, record your difficulties and successes. Keep the dialogue going right through to maintenance. Only you can take charge of your life: talking to yourself about it will help immeasurably.

2 Don't skip meals. Make sure that you eat at least three meals a day. You may snack between meals if you wish. *But do not eat or drink anything not on the list*!

There was an old man on the Rhine
Who was asked at what hour he'd dine.
He replied, 'At eleven,
Four, six, three, and seven.
Not to mention a quarter to nine.'

FRANCES PARKINSON KEYES

3 Take your measurements every morning, and record them in your diary. Inches lost are a graphic indication of vanishing fat.

4 Try to weigh yourself once a week only – in the morning before you have had your coffee or tea and breakfast. Record the results of both 3 and 4.

IMPORTANT POINTS TO REMEMBER AS YOU FOLLOW THE PLAN

1 Eat! Food is not the enemy, even of fat people. The act of eating will keep your metabolic rate ticking away nicely. And food nourishes, comforts, enhances social occasions and provides intense pleasure. By simply following directions, day by day, you will be able to enjoy these glorious aspects of food without overloading your heart, your arteries, your muscles and your fat stores.

2 Snacking between meals is allowed.

But it was Aristotle who identified anger as one of the Six Basic Human Emotions, along with Lust, Greed, Envy, Fear of Attorneys and the Need to Snack.

DAVE BARRY, IN A COLUMN FOR THE KNIGHT-RIDDER NEWSPAPERS SYNDICATE

3 Don't count Calories – it reduces the art of eating to a drudgery.

4 It is important to eat a large variety of foods. Sometimes overweight people become so obsessed with dieting and weight loss that they forget the main purpose of food: to nourish. Obsessive dieting and cutting back can easily lead to malnutrition, and/or destructive bingeing. Don't let this happen to you – eat a varied diet to ensure that it will not.

5 Don't be obsessed with the scales. This plan will result in a steady and natural loss which will be evident in the way your clothes fit and in the wonderfully improved image you see in the mirror. After the first two or three days weigh yourself once a week or so, not daily. Do measure yourself every day. Inches often seem to come off faster than pounds – although, on this diet, the pounds come off pretty fast, too.

6 Eating for comfort is not a bad thing. There are biochemical reasons for the comfort power of certain foods: potatoes, pasta, bread and chocolate, for instance. As you work your way through this plan, you will learn how to use such foods so they comfort but do not fatten.

> *She was brought up among holocaust survivors – twelve families given shelter by her grandparents . . . . 'When I was only three, I would sing and dance after dinner, my sole purpose being to stop them talking about the butchery they had suffered. The fear I lived with was suffocating. The only time I felt safe was when I was with my grandmother . . . eating.'*
>
> INTERVIEW WITH TV STAR ROSEANNE BARR, IN *THE SUNDAY EXPRESS MAGAZINE*

7 There is plenty of advice sprinkled throughout this book on surviving the restaurant experience, and surviving travel. Pay attention to such advice. Why use travel and restaurant meals as excuses for reverting to destructive eating habits?

8 Fat Calories are very different from carbohydrate and protein Calories. There are more than twice as many Calories per gram of fat as there are per gram of protein and carbohydrate. And the fat Calories are metabolized differently from the way that protein and carbohydrate Calories are: the fat Calories go straight to the body's fat stores with deadly efficiency. It is because of these biochemical facts that ruthlessly cutting out dietary fat causes such dramatic results. Follow the instructions carefully. There are good, solid scientific and psychological reasons for every single step.

THE SLIM CUISINE DIET

~

Read each section carefully before you begin. For day-to-day convenience, while you are following the plan, refer to The Plan on pages 16–18

WEEK 1

THE VEGETARIAN WEEK

DAY 1: ONE-DAY BLITZ

The first day of your lifetime plan is a very dramatic one. The one-day raw vegetable blitz is the important first step in putting the brakes on bad eating habits. Psychologically, this day is a one-day fast, a symbolic 'cold turkey' day, a farewell to cream cakes, fast food burgers, chocolate bars, grease-laden fish and chips, Hollandaise sauce, and all the rest of the fattening, health-destroying rubbish that fills our lives. It is a spartan day, but an exhilarating one as well, because it represents a commitment, a brave new beginning.

At no time during this day should hunger, weakness or dizziness occur. There is *no limit* to the amount of food you eat, as long as the choice falls within the specified guidelines. In other words it is a *feasting* fast! Plenty of recipe suggestions are included for salads, salad dressings and dips (see pages 76–82). You will begin to realize, on this vitally important single day, that there are many possibilities for good taste sensations and creativity using the so-called 'diet' foods.

DAY 1 'FREE' (EAT ALL YOU WANT) RAW VEGETABLE LIST

Asparagus • bean sprouts • beetroot • broccoli (calabrese) • cabbage (white and red) • carrots • cauliflower • celery • chicory • courgettes • cress • cucumber • endive • fennel • garlic • herbs (fresh) • leeks • lettuce (all kinds) • mange-tout • mooli • mushrooms • onions (all kinds) • peppers (green, yellow, red) • radishes • runner beans • spinach • sweetcorn cobs (tiny) • tomatoes (cherry tomatoes are delicious) • turnips • watercress

> *I could make do with that as long as I ate at home, since I'm passionately fond of raw vegetables and could satisfy myself leaning on the counter gnawing on raw carrots, raw potatoes, and raw broccoli and, for dessert, raw tomato slices placed sandwich-style between two wedges of raw cabbage. Going out to dinner was the problem. Hostesses, to put a good face on the meal, felt obliged to cook the vegetables, except that having heard that overcooked vegetables will kill you, they didn't really cook them. They'd steam them for just a few seconds, not long enough to cook them, but just long enough to take all the taste out of them. Then you had to eat them without salt.*
>
> 'EAT WHAT YOU ARE'. AN ESSAY BY RUSSELL BAKER

DAY 1 SKIMMED MILK PRODUCTS

Skimmed milk • skimmed milk powder • skimmed milk plain quark • skimmed milk plain fromage frais • skimmed milk plain yogurt • buttermilk, cultured from skimmed milk • skimmed milk cottage and curd cheese

IMPORTANT!

Read the labels! Make sure all dairy products are made from skimmed milk and contain *less than* 1 per cent fat. This diet will not work if you use dairy products that are not made from skimmed milk. Semi-skimmed will not do! And products made from skimmed milk with *vegetable fat added* will certainly not do either.

CONDIMENTS, SEASONINGS AND THREE COOKED VEGETABLES ALLOWED ON DAY 1 TO MAKE DRESSINGS AND DIPS

Made mustard (read the label – the mustard should contain no *oil, fat, sugar, flour or cornflour. Dijon mustard is perfect)* • *lemon and lime juice* • *wine vinegars* • *dried herbs and spices* • *capers (in a jar)* • *canned pimientos (red peppers) in brine* • *Baked Beetroot (see recipe on page 74)* • *Baked Garlic (see recipe on page 74)*

SLIM CUISINE TECHNIQUES FOR BLITZ DAY (PAGE 74)

Baked Beetroot • *Baked Garlic*

SUGGESTED RECIPES FOR BLITZ DAY (PAGES 74-82)

Creamy Cucumber Dip • *Minted Cucumbers* • *Marinated Peppers* • *Tomato Herb Salad* • *Filipino Tomato Salad* • *Spinach-Mushroom Salad* • *Dips, Spreads and Dressings*

BEFORE THE BLITZ

The day before you begin, read the lists of fats on pages 22–23. All of those are your sworn enemies. Stalk through your kitchen and pantry with the eye of an eagle and the nose of a bloodhound. Be ruthless. Dump the biscuits, crisps and candy. Divest your shelves of the olive oil, the marge, the 'low-fat' spread, the butter, the mixed nuts, the cream, the whole and semi-skimmed milk. Eliminate the cheeses, the mayonnaise, the lard, the ice cream. Make a ritual of it: *anything* not on the plan must be *gone*. Throw it away, give it away, or use it in some non-food manner but *don't leave it in your kitchen to sabotage your good work at a later date.* You are not wasting it. *Wasting* is throwing it down your gullet to ruin your health and your shape. Be brave and steadfast; have a total clean-out.

HAPPY BLITZ DAY

Be good to yourself during your One-day Blitz. Plan ahead. Think through what you are going to eat for breakfast, lunch and dinner, and plan to have plenty of food available for snacks as well. Make the food look beautiful. When you are hungry during Blitz Day, I don't want you reduced to standing in front of the open fridge, staring pathetically and helplessly at a bag of old carrots and a bunch of wilting celery. Make your Blitz Day a celebration. This is – in a very real sense – 'the first day of the rest of your life'. It should be a glorious occasion.

The night before, prepare masses of crudités. Crudités are raw vegetables, cut into bite-sized pieces. Choose a colourful variety from the Day 1 list. If you like to fiddle about you might carve the radishes into roses and form the spring onions into brushes, but vegetables are so beautiful just trimmed and cut simply that it is not necessary. On Blitz Day morning arrange them beautifully on platters, with an eye to colour and shape. Have your dips ready too, and put them into clear glass bowls, if you have them, to show off their colour, texture and creaminess. Have spare tubs of less than 1 per cent fat fromage frais, yogurt, curd cheese and quark on hand too, for snacking. Wash and carefully dry a variety of salad greens: spinach, endive, radicchio, cos lettuce, crisphead and so on. Store them in plastic bags in the fridge. Make up several different Slim Cuisine dressings and refrigerate them in jars. Have plenty of fresh herbs ready for snipping into your salads.

If you are away during the day, bring Blitz food with you. And remember, a quick trip to the supermarket on Blitz Day will yield a good choice of skimmed milk products and – in some supermarkets – a choice of prepared, ready-to-eat vegetables from washed spinach, to carrot and celery sticks, to cherry tomatoes, to broccoli and cauliflower florets.

I can't repeat this often enough: *think ahead!* Don't let yourself get caught on Blitz Day without suitable food. Don't sabotage yourself. Don't make it easy to say, righteously, 'Well, I was starving, I was about to hallucinate and faint, *of course* I had to eat a Mars bar (or a doughnut, or a bag of crisps).' Rubbish! Nonsense! You are the master of your own destiny. *Be prepared!*

If you love raw vegetables, and eat them frequently, Blitz Day will be a great pleasure. If you are not in the habit of munching on raw veggies, however, you may be prone to wind and mild stomach cramps on Blitz Day. To circumvent this problem avoid raw cauliflower, broccoli, cabbage, radishes and unpeeled peppers.

SUGGESTED MENUS FOR THE ONE-DAY BLITZ

Here you go. The habits of a lifetime are about to be broken – shattered, you might say. The first day is dramatic; breakfast, especially so. What, no toast, eggs, cereal, fruit juice? Where's the butter, the jam, the sausages? Forget them! For today only, you are in a gastronomic netherworld. All the usual rules of 'meal-shapes' are temporarily revoked. If you *hate* the oddness, remember: it's just for one day – *you can do it*! The results will be more than worth it. Take any frustrations out on your diary or tape recorder.

But you may be quite surprised. One of my study subjects had her Blitz breakfast – carrot, celery and mushrooms with fromage frais – and wrote in her diary: 'Not as bad as I expected – very filling and good.' Another wrote: 'Had my first salad breakfast ever, which consisted of lettuce, tomato, spring onion, small baby corn, carrot and beetroot with fromage frais.' Another decided not to eat at conventional times during her One-day Blitz, but instead to 'graze' all day. 'Haven't had a proper meal, just kept on nibbling vegetables and dips all day. Although I have been on the go all day, I have felt very relaxed.' Another study member, who also decided to 'graze' during all of Blitz Day, wrote: 'No problems, I'm relaxed and quite full. I haven't been hungry all day.' You may find that grazing (eating what you want from the lists whenever you want it) may be the best, the most fun and the most comfortable way to go. Just be sure that you read through the advice on page 35 so that your fridge is filled with a full and tempting complement of Blitz food.

If you would rather eat 'meals' on Blitz Day, a selection of suggested menus follows to help you plan your day's eating. Each suggestion comes from actual meals recorded by me and by my study members during our Blitz Days. Choose what pleases you. And remember to snack between meals on anything that you fancy from the Blitz Day list.

SUGGESTED BREAKFASTS

1 Crudités (mixed raw vegetables) with fromage frais or Chive Spread.

2 Sliced tomatoes with Minted Cucumbers.

3 Cottage cheese or quark whirled in the processor with ground cinnamon and a pinch of nutmeg, served with raw vegetables.

4 Halved cherry tomatoes, quartered button mushrooms and chopped fresh herbs, mixed into fromage frais.

SUGGESTED LUNCHES

1 Spinach-Mushroom Salad, Herbed Tomato Salad.

2 Beetroot Purée with Cos lettuce leaves, chicory leaves and peeled peppers.

3 Salsa Cruda, vegetable crudités, salad of mixed greens with Creamy Herb Dressing.

SUGGESTED EVENING MEALS

1 A huge salad of mixed vegetables and mixed greens (as many as you can find). A selection of dips and dressings.

2 A bed of mixed greens. Arrange shredded beetroot, shredded mooli, shredded white turnip, bean sprouts, julienned courgettes and grated cabbage on the greens. Serve with Creamy Salad Dressing.

3 Filipino Tomato Salad. Creamy Cucumber Dip with peeled strips of red, yellow and green peppers, and peeled baby carrots.

4 A big bowl of fromage frais mixed with fresh herbs and chopped vegetables: carrots, spring onions, radishes and cucumbers. Sprinkle the top with paprika. Surround with watercress.

5 Chicory leaves, button mushroom caps and 'boats' of peeled red, green and yellow peppers – some filled with quark mixed with Baked Garlic purée, some filled with Beetroot Purée, some filled with Red Pepper-Chive Spread. Or fill bowls with the spreads and dips, place them on a huge platter, and surround them with the mushrooms, leaves and pepper pieces.

Mix and match these menu suggestions any way you wish, eat as *much* as you wish, or else graze all day. Don't let yourself get hungry!

OFFICIAL WORDS OF WISDOM AND ENCOURAGEMENT

The first day is a little bit unusual. All right, it's very unusual. Carrot and celery sticks with dip is not our ordinary, everyday breakfast. And raw vegetables *all day long* is not the way we want to spend our lives.

But it is for *one day only*. Be brave and stick it out. The raw vegetable day is an important part of the plan to retrain your palate and to break some of the bad food habits of a lifetime. I want you to be able eventually to eat *all you want* of delicious food, enjoy every bite, and at the same time be slim and well nourished. The all-day-raw-vegetable-blitz is the first step.

If by the afternoon you are bored with salads and raw veggies, soldier on. Just think, tomorrow you can eat *mashed potatoes*! Tomorrow you can eat soup. Tomorrow you can eat all sorts of wonderful *cooked things*, and there will be no limit to the amount. So hang on. It's only one day. Besides, all these salads and raw vegetables and dips *are delicious*. Are you hungry? Eat more. *Don't* starve yourself! Just stick to the lists.

RECIPE NOTE: All the suggested recipes listed in the technique and recipe sections are just that – suggestions. You may make and use any recipe you like, as long as you do not stray one iota from the ingredient list. Use my recipes as written, if you wish, or use them as inspirations for your own creations.

DRINKS ALLOWED

Water – tap or bottled; fizzy mineral water is fine. Coffee – regular or decaffeinated – and tea – regular or herb teas that contain no sugar or fruit pieces. If you wish to sweeten it, use artificial sweetener only. If you want to whiten it, use skimmed milk only. Lemon in tea is okay.

If you are away from home all day, carry a little plastic bag of milk powder –it is just about impossible to obtain skimmed milk for your coffee if you don't bring it yourself. If the little pots of long-life milk offered seem to be skimmed, read the fine print: vegetable oil may be added. And if powdered non-dairy coffee whitener is available, beware! Have you ever read the label on that awful stuff? Carry your own skimmed milk powder; it's the only way. If you hate adding powder to your coffee, reconstitute it with some tap water first. It really is important to pay attention even to such a tiny detail as the milk for your coffee or tea. Even the small amount of whole or part-skimmed or vegetable fat-added milk that you might put into a daily cup of coffee or two will interfere with the retraining of your palate.

NOTE: If you want to, you may add fresh lemon or lime juice to your mineral water. And you may drink iced tea or iced coffee. Or, if you want to make your own soft drink, try half cold coffee or cold tea, and half sparkling mineral water with a splash of fresh lemon or lime. Sweeten with NutraSweet if you wish.

No fruit juices, no tomato juice, no fizzy drinks (other than mineral water), no squashes and no soft drinks. And no alcoholic beverages whatsoever. Soft drinks and fizzy drinks will interfere with the intense retraining your palate will be undergoing during this regime; fruit juices give you the sugar and concentrated calories of fruit with little of the fibre and lip-smacking chewing/eating satisfaction of whole fruit. And alcohol is full of empty (no nutrients) Calories that sabotage your willpower and good intentions.

Very important: drink at *least* eight full glasses of water a day. This is *vital*! It will help your weight loss, and enable your body to expel the waste products of that weight loss efficiently. You will feel better if you drink your water quota each day (you will also feel the need to know where the nearest loo is at all times!)

I know it's a nuisance. I know some of you will have no patience for glugging down eight full glasses of the stuff a day. But the water is very important to your general well-being and health. It doesn't *have* to be a chore. Get yourself a beautiful glass, one that suits your personality and fits into your hand as if it were made for that hand alone. I have two that I use, according to my mood: a gracefully ballooning brandy snifter, and an old-fashioned American Soda Fountain glass imprinted with the head of the Statue of Liberty, and the words 'Liberty 1886 – 1986.' At my desk, at the cooker, at the chopping board – wherever I am, one of those glasses is at hand, filled with sparkling, cold and refreshing water.

I'm trying very hard to make this water business sound pleasant, delicious, even glamorous. When I moved from America to England almost six years ago, and went for the first time to see the doctor at my local surgery, he looked me over and queried, 'How are your waterworks?' I goggled at him in complete incomprehension. Much of what English people said to me in those days was almost totally unfathomable; it *sounded* like the same language I had spoken for all my life, but it wasn't. So when he said, 'How are your waterworks?' I thought, 'Hmm . . . is it a quaint old English custom that when two people meet for the first time they politely enquire on the state of each other's household plumbing?' Given the state of the plumbing in my old village house, I thought it entirely possible. Then the penny dropped, and I realized that he meant *my* waterworks, my very own personal ones. Yes, waterworks *are* important, and keeping things flowing nicely is vital when you are losing weight. Follow my advice, choose a glass that impeccably matches your personality and keep that glass filled with pure and sparkling H_2O.

DIET SOFT DRINKS

It's true that most diet soft drinks contain no Calories, or one Calorie, but even so they are forbidden on the Slim Cuisine regime. Some diet soft drinks contain sodium, which might cause you to retain water and so experience a temporary plateau or even weight gain, but – even more important – I feel very strongly that the artificial flavours and harsh, bludgeoning tastes of many soft drinks, diet and otherwise, degrade the palate, and make it impossible to purify and retrain it. That's why I advise *no* diet soft drinks of any kind, either during the weight loss regime or during maintenance.

DAY 2: POTATOES & THE THERAPEUTIC BINGE

The raw vegetable day is over. The time has come for *real food.* For the next few days you are going to remain a vegetarian – no meat, no fish, no poultry. Not yet. And, for the time being, no bread or cereals either. These will be added soon, but not quite yet. But today you may eat soup. You may feast on potatoes.

POTATOES

Starting today, you may eat potatoes. Although when they first arrived from the New World they were considered poisonous, decadent and destructive to the soil, we now know that potatoes are a near-perfect package of nutrients. And not so long ago, they were considered fattening. Nonsense. Your daily potato ration is very important: for its filling power, its nutritional density, its versatility and its serenity-inducing properties. And potatoes taste so good.

DAY 2 POTATO LIST

Two large (approximately 225 g/8 oz each) baking potatoes • or sixteen small (approximately 25 g/1 oz each) new potatoes • or an equivalent amount of all-purpose potatoes (450 g/1 lb) • or one large or two small sachets instant mashed potato (see page 95 for information on palatable sachet potatoes)

If you feel you can't manage the whole potato ration on any day you don't *have* to eat it all, but do *not*, on any day, eat *no* potatoes at all. Eat at least half the ration each day. On the other hand, do not *exceed* the potato ration on any day.

You may divide or mix and match this potato bounty any way you wish. For instance, you may eat a small sachet of mashed potatoes at lunch and a large jacket potato at suppertime. Or you may have eight roasted new potatoes (see page 94) at lunch, and Slim Cuisine Chips made from one large baking potato (see page 92) at suppertime. If you *love* mashed potatoes, as many do, you may have a small sachet at lunch and a small sachet at supper – or you can even save up your potato ration and have a potato pig-out: one *large* sachet at suppertime.

Of course, you will not be eating these wonderful potatoes all by themselves – life is much more exciting than that. Fill jacket potatoes with any one of the dips from your first day, or with Beetroot Purée, Mushroom Ragoût, Tomato Sauce, Salsa, Browned Onions or anything else from the list of recipes that tickles your fancy. Add a good dollop or two of fromage frais or of Creamy Herb Sauce (page 81). Mashed potatoes are wonderful mixed with enough fromage frais or buttermilk to make them creamy. Or try mixing them with skimmed milk into which you have whisked 15–30 ml (1–2 tbsp) skimmed milk powder. Add salt and pepper to taste. Eat them with Tomato Ragoût, Tomato Sauce, Vegetable Curry or Sautéed Mushrooms. Use new potatoes in potato salad or roast them. Or make chips or crisps with baking potatoes (see pages 92 and 94 for the recipes).

THE THERAPEUTIC BINGE

The vegetables on your vegetable lists are 'free' – that is, you may eat all you want, whenever you want. Potatoes are rationed, but 'free' vegetables are not. All recipes are Therapeutic Binges. They utilize your 'free' vegetables, and thus may be indulged in without limit. Enjoy! This food will help you become slim, will make your skin glow, your hair come to life and your well-being soar. And it all tastes so good! I'll repeat it, because it really is important: although your daily potatoes are rationed, your 'free' vegetables are not. Eat *all you want*, raw or cooked. Just follow the Slim Cuisine rules. Use *no added fat.* No margarine, low-fat spread, butter, oil, dripping, yak fat, blubber or anything else fat-wise.

EAT YOUR VEGETABLES

At the heart of this plan is an overflowing bounty of vegetables. The technique and recipe sections will teach you how to cook masses of vegetables without fat or oil, so that they taste quite unbelievably rich and 'non-dietetic'. You should be eating *plenty*; make huge and frequent servings of your favourite recipes. Because of the high water and fibre content of vegetables they make you feel full and satisfied, and you will certainly *not* suffer from constipation. The vegetable Therapeutic Binges not only keep your stomach full, your metabolic rate up and your weight loss steady, but they are profoundly important to your general health and well-being.

Vegetables high in beta carotene (the precursor of vitamin A) are believed to be significant protectors against the development of cancers affecting the skin and lining tissues, for instance lung and breast cancers; bladder and digestive tract cancers; and prostate and cervical cancers. Vegetables high in beta carotene include asparagus, beetroot, broccoli, carrots, red and yellow peppers, dark green leafy vegetables (such as spinach, chard and watercress), tomatoes and sweetcorn.

Another class of vegetables believed to be cancer-protective are the brassicas or cabbage family, including Brussels sprouts, all cabbages, broccoli, kale and (if you are lucky enough to find them) kohlrabi. Large and frequent servings of such vegetables may help reduce the risk of cancers of the stomach and large intestine.

Many studies also seem to indicate that a high percentage of fat in the diet may be linked to increased incidence of certain cancers (breast, uterus, colon and prostate); not just the saturated fats, but monounsaturates and polyunsaturates as well. So adopting a gastronomic lifestyle that uses large amounts of vegetables and no added fat may be life-affirming as well as slimming.

METABOLIC RATE

Most diets temporarily lower one's metabolic rate. No matter how much we long to lose weight, our bodies are not always willing to co-operate. A period of Calorie deprivation, however modest, usually convinces the body that it might be experiencing a famine, and it slows down the metabolic rate as a helpful method of conserving available Calories. As a result, we function on fewer Calories and weight loss slows down. This diminished metabolic rate is only temporary. When the dieting stops, the metabolic rate is restored to normal, consistent with the lost weight – for some people, in a week or so, for others somewhat longer. But here is the good news: this diet may *not* lower your metabolic rate.

The actual act of eating, carbohydrate and protein foods especially, raises the metabolic rate: that is one of the reasons that Therapeutic Binges, skimmed milk dairy products and so on are not only fun and enjoyable but are necessary to the success of this plan. This regime keeps your metabolic rate ticking away nicely. There will be no decrease in Calorie utilization. So don't assume that the less you eat, the faster you'll lose. Just the opposite can be true. But you must stick to your lists or the whole plan will fail. Remember, added fats are forbidden. Without them, the Calorie density of your food is drastically reduced. Large amounts of Slim Cuisine will keep you nourished and happy and will keep your metabolic rate from dropping. Your body will not scream 'Famine!', because there *is* no famine.

DAY 2 'FREE' (EAT ALL YOU WANT) VEGETABLE LIST

You may continue to eat all the vegetables from the Day 1 list, raw *or* cooked. Add to that list:

Artichokes (fresh or canned, globe or Jerusalem) • *aubergines* • *Brussels sprouts* • *celeriac* • *greens (all kinds: chard, beet greens, etc)* • *kohlrabi* • *marrow* • *parsnips* • *spaghetti marrow* • *swedes* • *tomatoes (canned)* • *tomato purée*

DAY 2 SKIMMED MILK PRODUCTS

Same as Day 1. Make sure you *read the label.* Buy products that are *less than* 1 per cent fat. No fat at all is best.

DAY 2 ADDITIONAL CONDIMENTS

Dry red wine, white wine, sherry or white vermouth may be used as a cooking ingredient. You *may not* drink it. Alcohol contains seven 'empty' (no nutrients) Calories per gram, which – like fat Calories – go to your fat stores more efficiently than do carbohydrate and protein Calories. In other words, alcohol Calories make you fatter faster. Also, alcohol Calories play havoc with your willpower, so that you find yourself willing to stray from grace diet-wise. But when you cook with wine you evaporate the alcohol and eliminate the problem. It is quite all right to use it as suggested in the various recipes. Just follow the directions in the specific recipe.

Soy sauce or Teriyaki sauce (both are available in most supermarkets) can be used for sautéing mushrooms (see technique on page 86).

SLIM CUISINE TECHNIQUES FOR DAY 2 (PAGES 83–96)

HOW TO SAUTÉ AND PAN FRY: Sautéed Onions • *Sautéed Mushrooms* • *Stir-'Fried' Peppers*

HOW TO GRILL VEGETABLES: Grilled Aubergine • *Grilled Courgettes* • *Grilled Peppers*

HOW TO BAKE VEGETABLES: Baked Root Vegetables • *Baked Aubergine* • *Baked Onion* • *Baked Potatoes* • *'Fried' Potatoes* • *Potato Crisps* • *Roast Potatoes* • *Mashed Potatoes*

HOW TO BRAISE VEGETABLES: Braised Vegetables

WINE

Dry vermouth and sherry are fortified wines: once opened, they will keep for a while. But dry red and white wine will not keep once opened. If you use 120 ml (4 fl oz) of wine (or even just a splash) in a recipe and want to prevent the rest from spoiling until you need it again, try one of these methods:

1 Believe it or not, you can freeze wine in small quantities (use small plastic tubs, or even ice cube trays or bags) and thaw what you need for a recipe. When thawed, red wine throws a sediment, so strain it through a nylon tea strainer into the pot. There will be *no* loss of quality.

2 When you have used part of a bottle, decant the wine into a smaller vessel and close tightly. Air is the enemy of wine: if the wine fills the bottle or jar so that there is no air, it will not spoil.

3 You can buy a convenient vacuum gadget in many houseware departments that reseals partially empty wine bottles by pumping air out of the bottle. They cost only a few pounds, and are very easy to use.

SUGGESTED RECIPES FOR DAY 2 (PAGES 96–126)
Curried Gratin of Puréed Baked Vegetables • Aubergine 'Caviare' • Peperonata • Braised Onion • Simple Vegetable Soup • Soup of Potato and Caramelized Onions • Soup of Creamy Greens • Herbed Onion-Tomato Soup • Creamy Parsnip Soup • Ratatouille • Gratin of Mediterranean Vegetables • Vegetable 'Lasagne' • Vegetable Filled Cabbage Rolls • New Mexican Salad • Potato Tzatziki Salad • Braised Aubergine, Chinese Style • Potato-Cauliflower Curry • Vegetable Curry I • Vegetable Curry II • Vegetable Bhajee with Corn Cobs • Vegetable Chilli with Potatoes • Lesco-Potato Stew • Potato-Fennel Gratin • Tomato Ragoût • Curried Cauliflower • Curried Cabbage
SAUCES: *Tomato Sauce • Roasted Tomato Ketchup • Chunky Tomato and Pepper Relish • Tomato-Carrot Sauce • Gravy • Pepper Sauce*

MEAL PLANNING ADVICE FOR WEEK 1

Make your meals interesting. Begin with a bowl of soup. Serve some steamed vegetables or a vegetable casserole, prepare a salad, and have your potatoes in the casserole, in the soup, or baked, mashed, oven-'fried', roasted – any way you wish. Plunder the recipe section for inspiration. And see pages 48–50 for menus.

BREAKFAST NOTE

For two days you will be eating lavish vegetarian meals with plenty of skimmed milk dairy products, but you will have no 'normal' breakfast foods. Here are three suggestions for breakfast for Days 1 and 2. They may be eccentric, but they are a delicious way to start the day all the same.

1 Raw vegetables with dip. Not only does this make a wonderful snack, it makes a great breakfast as well: colourful, full of texture and good-tasting.
2 Soup. This is a warm and reassuring way to start any day. A big, steaming, savoury bowl of morning soup prepares one to meet any challenge the world may offer. Tomato Ragoût (see recipe on page 117) is particularly good, as is Soup of Creamy Greens (page 100), and both are very easy to make. Make a huge batch the night before. Then brief heating is all that is needed in the morning.
3 A big bowl of Slim Cuisine Potato Crisps (page 94). It will put you in a good mood for the entire day.

DAY 3

Your routine for today is exactly the same as yesterday:
1 Two large baking potatoes, or sixteen new potatoes, or an equivalent amount of all-purpose potatoes, or two small or one large sachet of mashed potatoes. You may mix and match, or divide your potato ration any way you wish.
2 Unlimited vegetables, raw or cooked, from your vegetable lists.
3 Unlimited *skimmed milk* dairy products from your lists.
4 Eight (250 ml/8 fl oz) glasses of water a day, and unlimited coffee and tea. Sweeten coffee and tea with artificial sweetener, if you wish.
5 *This is important*: eat a good variety of vegetables during the day. Find the time to cook yourself some wonderful things. Read the recipes and use them.
6 When you feel the need to snack, do so – on raw vegetables and dips, on soup, on quark or fromage frais, on steamed vegetables with Slim Cuisine sauces, or anything else that takes your fancy from the lists of approved foods, or from the Therapeutic Binges. *Remember*: if it is not on your list, don't eat it! If it *is* on the list, indulge freely.

BALSAMIC VINEGAR

Nectar, that's what it is! Balsamic vinegar is like no other vinegar you've ever tasted. It's sweet, thick and heady, and makes an incomparable dressing for salads, steamed vegetables and potatoes. I'm delighted to see that many supermarkets are now stocking the compelling stuff. Remember, you will *not* be buying butter, oil, marge, sweets, crisps and other such destructive foodstuffs. Invest some of the money *not* spent on those items on a bottle of balsamic vinegar and a small pocket flask. Fill the pocket flask with vinegar and carry it with you at all times, using it to dress up healthy restaurant or canteen meals.

EATING OUT DURING THE VEGETARIAN WEEK

How nice if we could convince restaurateurs to introduce Slim Cuisine choices, prepared using the no-fat Slim Cuisine techniques, on to their menus. How I wish

I could walk into a restaurant and order Vegetable Curry (page 112), Vegetable Chilli (page 115), Gratin of Mediterranean Vegetables (page 115), salads with Slim Cuisine dressings, herb fillings (page 104) for baked potatoes, and the like. Until that happens, order naked (no-dressing) salads, unfilled baked potatoes and plates of cooked vegetables. When ordering your vegetable plate, ask for a huge serving of *all* the vegetables the kitchen can assemble, beautifully arrayed on a large plate. *Always* say: 'No fat, no oil, no butter or margarine, no cream, and nothing fried please.' Bring your flask of balsamic vinegar to dress your salad and season your vegetable plate, or ask for lemon or lime wedges and the pepper mill. And it doesn't hurt to pop a tub of fromage frais in your briefcase or tote bag on your way to lunch. Apply it generously but discreetly to your jacket potato.

DEALING WITH RESTAURANT STAFF DURING YOUR SLIM CUISINE REGIME

Don't be intimidated by waiters and waitresses. You *must* be the master of your own destiny. When you ask for things specially prepared without fat, oil, margarine and so on, you may be greeted with contemptuous glances, exclamations of disbelief, or even – as has happened to me many times – hoots of derisive laughter.

It does not matter!! *You* are the one who knows what you are doing; *you* are the one who is taking matters into your own hands, and caring for your health and appearance. And *you* are the one who will accumulate unwanted flab on your butt if you succumb to the blandishments or contempt of a snobbish and uncaring waitperson. Stand up for yourself, send things back if the kitchen has produced butter-drenched vegetables or oil-glistening salads. Smile, be polite and stay calm, but be firm, purposeful and unwavering.

EXCUSES

One relatively sure way of getting what you want is to call ahead. Phone and ask if a restaurant will cater to a diner who cannot tolerate fat, oil, butter, margarine and whole milk dairy products. And don't be afraid to imply that you have a medical problem with these forbidden foods. No restaurateur wants a diner to drop dead at the table because of the food. After all, you do have an 'allergy' to fat; it makes you break out in ugly lumps. And if you have a condition that is exacerbated by obesity and/or high fat intake – high blood pressure, cardiac problems, back trouble, a wonky gall bladder – then no exaggeration is involved at all.

I knew a retired chef-pâtissier in Provence, very fat and married to a wife his size. They had a fox terrier to match. The three ran a small restaurant near Aix, and from the hors d'oeuvre through the dessert every course was based on or accompanied by a variation of his conditioned accomplishment: plain hard and plain flaky pastry, brioche pastry, cream puff and puff pastry, in shells-squares-timbales-pies-tarts-molds, fleurons, sticks, hot and cold pâtés. He made pastries of butter, suet, lard, oil. He was a maniac, not able to sleep much, potentially dangerous unless he was kneading and rolling and baking. He would stand at the door of the small dining room and watch as we ate, at first with delectation and then more slowly, until he could produce his predictable surprise, a dessert never on the menu, which a man with gun at his temple could not but savor. We stopped going there.

WITH BOLD KNIFE AND FORK, A MEMOIR BY M. F. K. FISHER

DINNER PARTIES

It's best to refuse dinner party invitations during the Vegetarian Week. Imposing your temporary restrictions on an unsuspecting host or hostess seems a little unfair. But later in the regime, and during lifetime Maintenance, there's no reason not to accept invitations. You will have to – very discreetly and courteously, of course – explain your dietary requirements to your host or hostess when you accept the invitation. Don't be embarrassed to say that you cannot eat fat, oil and whole milk dairy products. After all, if you were an Orthodox Jew, you would not eat pork or other non-kosher food at a dinner party. If you were a vegetarian, you would have no qualms about expressing that fact to your potential host. And if you had any other medical problem that required avoidance of certain foodstuffs – diabetes, a heart condition, high blood pressure, food allergies and so on – you would say so.

If you are going to a wedding, a formal dinner at a hotel, or any other sort of set meal or buffet where you suspect that there will be acres of food, most of it unsuitable, do what your mother probably told you never to do: spoil your appetite. In other words, eat something wonderful before you leave: bread spread with one of the Slim Cuisine spreads, soup, a vegetable casserole. And have plenty of food ready in the fridge for when you return, as well. Then, when you are confronted with the frightening array of food you shouldn't eat, and really don't want to eat, you will not be so ravenous, and so sorry for yourself, and so deprived-feeling, that you fall face forward on to the buffet table and start noshing mindlessly. You will have the strength to eat what is suitable and ignore the rest.

> *In the excitement of trying on dresses, she had forgotten Mammy's ironclad rule, that before going to any party, the O'Hara girls must be crammed so full of food they would be unable to eat any refreshments at the party.*
>
> *GONE WITH THE WIND*, A NOVEL BY MARGARET MITCHELL

As far as giving a dinner party yourself, even during the first week of the regime, nothing could be easier. There are *many* gorgeous recipes that could come together to form an exceptional dinner party menu, and none of the guests would feel that they had been 'dieted' to distraction. See the menu sections for specific ideas.

A FEW WORDS ABOUT THE MENUS

Writing daily and weekly menus is hard. Such lists make me laugh. No one really eats like that. How do they really eat? (By *they* I mean people like *us*, like you and me.) We open the fridge and stare in dreamily. We grab something and eat it right then and there. Then a little more. If it is really good (like cold spaghetti, or a big hunk of leftover cheesecake, or a couple of meatballs shedding gouts of solidified sauce), we polish it off. 'Eating standing up in front of the fridge doesn't count,' we tell ourselves. 'And it's cold. Nothing eaten cold, without a fork, standing up, can possibly have any Calories that count.' And then we eat a little

FULL OF FOOD

You will be eating quite a bit of food on this diet. At the end of the day you may feel quite full – in fact, your belt or waistband will probably feel rather snug. This is normal: it simply means that you have eaten well. Don't let that full feeling make you suffer pangs of guilt, and don't let it convince you that you are getting fat rather than losing weight. You deserve to eat (and to enjoy it!) just as much as the thin ones do. The nature of this plan is that you will eat well, and feel full at the end of each day, but *you will still lose weight.* In the morning you'll find that your waistband will actually be a little looser than it was the morning before.

Enjoy yourself! Stop feeling guilty! Eat well!

more. Later, while clearing the lunch or supper dishes, we polish off much of what's left on everyone else's plate. When the leftovers that have escaped our voracious maw are tucked safely away, something lurking in the corner of the fridge catches our eye, and we eat it too (the lurking food, not the eye). At the end of the day we have put away an enormous amount of dibs and dabs: 'non-meal' food, snacks, nibbles – half the time we are not even aware that we are doing it. All these nibbles and snacks add up; they are as important a part of your daily intake as your actual meals. That's why a cold-blooded menu listing of three meals a day seems almost futile. And what about days spent running madly about on household errands, at work and so on?

Still, despite these problems I'm giving you menu lists and suggestions for each level. When you do plan to have a real, sit-down, home meal, these lists will help you shape those meals and give you an idea of what a good day's eating can be. Since on this plan you can eat whenever you want, as much as you want (as long as you stick to your lists), use the menus as guides only. It is all right to graze all day, instead of eating three conventional meals. Vegetable Curry eaten cold with your fingers out of the refrigerator plastic storage container will do you just as much powerful psychological and nutritional good as when it is spooned, hot and steaming, off a good china plate in the dining room. Use the menus to guide you through your particular day, and adapt them to your own tastes and circumstances. You will also notice that many of them can be adapted to restaurant or canteen eating, for those who work and must eat their midday meal out. You can usually order some variation on jacket potatoes/salad/steamed vegetables, etc., without too much trouble.

SUGGESTED MENUS FOR DAYS 2 AND 3

Well, breakfast is still going to be unusual (just for these two days), but not quite as unusual as yesterday. Again, I have taken all suggestions from actual meals recorded in my food diary, and those of my assistants and study subjects. Do remember to snack between meals from your 'unlimited' lists. Don't let yourself get hungry, whatever you do.

SUGGESTED BREAKFASTS

1 Tomato Ragoût

2 Mashed Potatoes and Creamy Parsnip Soup (my assistant's favourite Vegetarian Week breakfast)

3 Slim Cuisine Potato Crisps

SUGGESTED LUNCHES

1 Soup of Creamy Greens • Herbed Tomato Salad

2 Soup of Potato and Caramelized Onions • Crudités with Beetroot Purée • Filipino Tomato Salad

3 Baked potato with fromage frais • Steamed vegetables (as many different kinds as you can manage) with balsamic vinegar or lemon wedges • Big salad of mixed greens, small sweetcorn cobs and cherry tomatoes, with Slim Cuisine dressing of your choice, or balsamic vinegar.

4 Herbed Onion-Tomato Soup • Potato-Tzatziki Salad

SUGGESTED EVENING MEALS

1 Group Buffet (see page 28)

2 Mashed Potatoes and Gravy • Sautéed Onions • Sautéed Mushrooms

3 Curried Gratin of Puréed Baked Vegetables • Tomato Sauce or Tomato Ragoût • Sautéed Mushrooms

4 Vegetable Chilli • Creamy Herb Sauce • Marinated Peppers

5 Simple Vegetable Soup • New Mexican Salad

6 Creamy Parsnip Soup • Vegetable Curry • Creamy Herb Sauce • Curried Cabbage

DAYS 4, 5 AND 6

BREAKFAST

Good morning! Today is the day you eat a breakfast that is not peculiar. Eat your breakfast first thing in the morning *or* mid-morning, according to your schedule and your preference.

Choose one item from the following list:

Shredded Wheat: twelve small (45 g/1¾ oz) • *Shredded Wheat: two large (45 g/1¾ oz)* • *Grape-Nuts: one serving (30 g/1¼ oz)* • *Jordan's Puffed Cereal: one serving (25 g/1 oz)* • *Quaker Puffed Wheat: one serving (25 g/1 oz)* • *Kallo Puffed Rice Cereal: one serving (25 g/1 oz)* • *Ryvita: four pieces* • *Crackerbread: three* • *Finn Crisp Original Rye Crispbread: three* • *Finn Crisp Rye Crispbread: five* • *Rakusen's matzos: two large*

The rye crispbreads, crackerbread and so on may be spread with skimmed milk quark, curd cheese, cottage cheese, yogurt or fromage frais. (*Read the label*: it should be less than 1 per cent fat only.) Add some chopped parsley, chives or other herbs, if you like. Or spread your crackers with one of the Slim Cuisine dips or spreads. The cereal may be mixed with skimmed milk or eaten plain if you like it crunchy. Add a little low-calorie sweetener, if desired. If you can't finish *all* your breakfast, don't worry, but don't save it for later. This list is for the morning only.

For the rest of the day, carry on exactly like Day 3.

THINGS TO REMEMBER

1 You may use dry red or white wine, dry sherry or dry white vermouth for cooking. Make sure that in the cooking you have simmered it enough so that the alcohol (empty Calories) evaporates away.

2 Indulge yourself and eat well. Cook wonderful things for yourself, and make sure you are eating a good variety. If you cook for others as well, they will most likely find your Slim Cuisine recipes delicious and compelling. Make sure there is enough for you! You *must* be the master or mistress of your own destiny. (Or, as my son once said, of your own density.) If you work, take plenty of soup or ragoût and vegetable casseroles with you in vacuum jugs. Don't go hungry!

3 Drink plenty of water.

4 Frozen vegetables are fine to use if they are on the list and if the vegetables have no sugar or fat added.

DAY 7

Same as Days 4, 5 and 6, with this stunning addition:

FRUIT!

Choose your fruit and bring it out in the evening to eat after supper. Buy the juiciest-looking, ripest, most fragrant, most beautiful specimen you can find. Choose one item from the following list:

1 medium bunch grapes • 1 orange • 3 apricots • 2 tangerines • 1 apple • 3 plums • 1 nectarine • 1 box strawberries or any berries • ½ small pineapple • 1 grapefruit • 5 lychees • 1 mango • 1 papaya • 570 ml (1 pint) cherries • 1 pear • 1 banana • 1 peach • 1 sharon fruit (persimmon) • ½ medium melon • 1 kiwi fruit

Make a ceremony of the addition of fruit to your diet. Cut it into pieces and put them on a beautiful plate. Eat them slowly, with your fingers. Don't let anyone disturb you. This is real food: this fruity, complex, sweet/tart, juice-spurting, mouth-filling and nourishing experience is what eating is all about.

Spongy gâteaux oozing ersatz cream; soggy biscuits coated with inferior, vegetable fat-injected chocolate; gummy jellies flavoured with acrid, artificial fruit essences . . . what punishment to have to eat such rubbish! Fortunately, you will never have to touch tongue to such appallingly wretched preparations again.

TRAVEL

I travel quite a bit, what with classes, demonstrations, lectures, TV appearances, book promotions and so on. There is nothing cosier, after a long journey and a late arrival, than curling up in bed with a lavish room service meal. Most hotel kitchens rise beautifully to the occasion when I phone down and ask for a sumptuous array of *all* the steamed fresh vegetables the chef can muster (*no* oil, *no* butter, *no* marge, etc, etc.), a large undressed salad, an unfilled baked potato and a selection of fresh fruit. First, I have to override the room service operator's bewilderment. 'We *have* no vegetables,' she often says.

'Do you have parsnips?' I ask. (I always mention parsnips first. Somehow the mention of those particular roots seems to calm hotel operators.) 'Do you have carrots, cauliflower, sprouts, spring onions, celery, mushrooms or runner beans?'

'Hold on,' she says. Faint muttering in the background. 'Oh, yeah – they say they've got some of *those*.'

'Well, then,' I say, 'just remember – *no* oil, *no* butter, *no* marge, etc, etc.' (I can say it in my sleep by now.)

Inevitably the rolling table arrives, simply overflowing with gorgeous freshly cooked veg. Sometimes (oh, joy) there are steamed new potatoes in addition to a baked potato. Sometimes there are tiny sweetcorn cobs, sticks of crisp-tender parsnip, snowy cauliflower florets, bright green branches of broccoli. I always ask for plenty of lemon wedges to squeeze over the bounty, and I flourish my balsamic vinegar flask over the salad. The fruit is almost always ripe and lovely, and there may be enough for me to take a few pieces along the next morning as I begin my labours.

Some of the most spectacular low-fat travel meals I've ever encountered have been on business trips in Switzerland and Denmark. When planning a trip in a foreign country I always write ahead, through someone who can present my request in the proper language, and – after the initial inevitable bewilderment ('How in the world can I cook *anything* without fat or oil?' think the affronted chefs) – the results can be dazzling, delicious and inspiring. So don't let travel undermine your regime. A little care and forethought will work wonders.

SUGGESTED MENUS FOR DAYS 4–7

If you have enjoyed your odd breakfasts (soup, raw vegetables, mashed potatoes and so on), by all means continue them, but if you're longing for a more conventional breakfast, today's your day. From now on, you may begin the day with cereal (see list on page 50).

For midday and evening meals see the menu suggestions for Day 2, plus the suggestions below. Don't forget – on Day 7, in the evening – to eat a ceremonial piece of fruit. And keep snacking throughout the day on vegetables – raw and cooked, however you like them.

SUGGESTED LUNCHES

1 Baked potato • Tomato Sauce – fromage frais • Salad of mixed greens and vegetables with a Slim Cuisine dressing, or balsamic vinegar

2 Baked potato stuffed with Beetroot Purée • Peperonata

3 Baked potato stuffed with Aubergine 'Caviare' • Baby sweetcorn cobs, cherry tomatoes, button mushrooms with Chive Dip

4 Steamed vegetables with Roasted Tomato Ketchup, or Chunky Tomato-Pepper Relish • Spinach Salad with Beetroot Purée

SUGGESTED EVENING MEALS

1 Potato-Fennel Gratin • Ratatouille

2 Soup of Creamy Greens • A selection of grilled vegetables: aubergine, peppers, courgettes

3 Vegetable 'Lasagne' • Sautéed Mushrooms

4 Roast Potatoes with Gravy • Braised Onions • Stir-'Fried' Peppers

5 Lesco-Potato Stew • Fromage frais with fresh dill

6 Potato Crisps with Rémoulade Dip • Gratin of Mediterranean Vegetables

7 Chips • Tomato Sauce or Roasted Tomato Sauce, and fromage frais • Braised Cauliflower

WEEK 2

SWEET REWARDS

DAY 8

Eat two servings of fruit a day, beginning today (see fruit list on page 51). Don't save up your fruit to eat all at once. Eat one serving with breakfast and one for dessert after dinner, or eat one for a mid-morning snack and one for an evening snack. Divide them any way you wish – just don't eat it all at once.

You may eat your fruit plain, or in Slim Cuisine ice cream. If you decide to make ice cream (*of course* you will decide to make ice cream!) make plenty, because all the family will want it too. Slim Cuisine ice cream is an instant recipe, and one of the richest-tasting, most delicious of puddings. What a way to get slim!

SLIM CUISINE TECHNIQUES FOR DAY 8 (PAGES 127–128)

Ice Cream • Grilled Banana • Banana Cream Mousse

SUGGESTED MENUS FOR DAY 8

See menus for Days 2–7, plus suggestions below. You may add fruit to your breakfast cereal, and another serving of fruit, Slim Cuisine ice cream or Banana Mousse either after lunch, after dinner, or for a snack.

1 Vegetable Filled Cabbage Rolls • Sautéed Mushrooms • Herbed Tomato Salad

2 Vegetable 'Lasagne' • Spinach and Cos Lettuce Salad with baby sweetcorn cobs, sliced button mushrooms and mustard dressing

3 Mashed Potatoes beaten with Baked Onion purée and Baked Garlic purée • Pepper Sauce • Grilled Courgettes

4 Braised Aubergine, Chinese Style • Sautéed Mushrooms (include shiitake mushrooms if you can find them) • Filipino Tomato Salad

5 Baked potato with Tomato-Carrot Sauce • Braised Fennel and Courgettes

DAYS 9–11

You may eat two slices of bread (approximately 25 g/1 oz each) a day, beginning today, or their equivalent: one bagel, one roll or one large pita. Make sure the bread you choose contains *no added fat*. Think of the possibilities: pita pockets stuffed to overflowing with salad; banana sandwiches made with crisp baguettes; toasted bagels spread with quark; Beetroot Purée and shredded raw spinach leaves on rye . . . let your imagination run wild! The bread can be white, brown, or black – as long as it contains no added fat. Quiz the baker, scrutinize the labels and remain steadfast: you want bread with *no added fat*. Some bakers may try to tell you that bread without fat does not exist, cannot be achieved, will taste like a brick, and what kind of idiot are you for wanting it anyway? Ignore such comments – they are ignorant – and keep searching. Plenty of excellent fat-free breads exist.

WHOLEMEAL BREAD

You want a loaf of bread that contains no *added* fat. So when you buy, read the *ingredients* on the label first, and make sure no oil or fat of any kind is listed.

Whole grain, however, contains fat, so even though no *added* fat may have been used in the baking of the bread, the *nutritional analysis*, if it appears on the label, will include a few grams of fat. Don't worry – that's as it should be. The naturally occurring fat in the whole grain is beneficial, and helps provide your body with the essential fatty acids that it needs. As long as there is no fat listed in the *ingredients*, all is well.

The same rule of label-reading applies for cereals, crackers or any other whole grain products.

RESTAURANT TREAT

If you wish, this week you may order a pizza. Go to a high-quality pizzeria or Italian restaurant and ask for a pizza (*not* a deep dish pizza) with any or all the vegetables you desire (obviously you will *not* ask for sausage, salami, ham or anything else that is fatty), then say: '*No* oil, *no* salt and *no* cheese, please. If they make a mistake and send you one with oil or cheese, send it back; you don't have to eat it or pay for it. They should rectify the mistake.

This pizza will be your bread quota for the day (in fact, it will go a bit above your quota) – but what a wonderful way to eat your bread! You may do this once a week if you wish.

SUGGESTED MENUS FOR DAYS 9–11

For breakfast, try cereal with skimmed milk and fruit; or crackers (see lists on pages 50–51) spread with quark or fromage frais (plus mashed banana, crushed berries, mashed pears and so on if you wish). From now on you may have a sandwich for your lunch, evening meal or a snack if you like.

SANDWICH MEAL SUGGESTIONS

1 Pita Pizza. Spread Slim Cuisine Tomato Sauce or Pepper Sauce on a pita. If you split the pita into two, you can make two thin crust pizzas, or you can save the second half for a different meal. Top the sauce-spread pita with a sprinkling of fresh herbs and any Slim Cuisine vegetable you fancy: sautéed onions or mushrooms, grilled peppers, aubergine, courgettes, braised fennel . . .

2 Banana Sandwich. This is a very popular sandwich – perfect when you are on the go, and want to grab a sandwich while you are out. Have you ever asked at a sandwich bar for a sandwich with no butter or mayonnaise? The person behind the counter looks at you as if you were threatening to start a riot. Spare yourself. Instead of the sandwich bar, head for the grocery. Buy the crispest small baguette you can find. Buy a ripe banana. Peel the banana. Take out your Swiss Army knife (you should always carry one) and split the banana lengthwise. Split the baguette, but not all the way through. It should open like a hinged book. Insert the banana halves into the baguette. Bite into baguette. Crunchy outside – creamy and banana-y inside. Shards of crumbs on shirt front. Bite again. Mmm . . . .

3 Freshly Baked Filled Baguettes. Have you seen those wonderful ready-to-bake French baguettes in the chill cabinets of some supermarkets? They come four to a cylinder – simply pop open the cylinder, roll up the pieces of dough and put them – on a non-stick tray – into a hot oven. Twelve minutes later, hot bread! One baguette is your bread quota for the day. Eat one, and feed the rest to family and friends, or – once baked – freeze them. Thaw and reheat on another day. To make a hot, filled baguette, before rolling the dough spread it with something. Baked Garlic Purée is great – so are Tomato Sauce, Ratatouille, Sautéed Mushrooms, Sautéed Onions, good mustard, Vegetable Curry . . . you get the idea.

4 Split a bagel like this (it's the only proper way). Perforate it all around its perimeter with a fork, then pull the bagel apart on the dotted line. This method yields two bagel halves that each have a *rough* surface. If you cut the bagel with a knife, you get a smooth-surfaced bagel. A smooth-surfaced bagel is an insipid bagel – don't even consider it. Spread the bagel halves with Chive Spread (page 80), and top with slices of the ripest, juiciest tomato you can find. Grind on a little black pepper.

5 Take a piece of black German rye bread (you can buy it, wrapped in cellophane, in many supermarkets). Spread with Beetroot Purée. Top with shredded raw spinach leaves.

6 Halve pita bread crosswise, yielding two pockets. Fill the pockets with great stuff: salad, curry, chilli, grilled vegetables, braised vegetables, Creamy Cucumber Dip, Herbed Tomatoes, Peperonata, Aubergine 'Caviare' . . . .

7 How about a chip buttie? Fill a bap with Slim Cuisine 'Fried' Potatoes, then smear the top half of the bap with Slim Cuisine Mayonnaise and the bottom half with Roasted Tomato Ketchup. This is the chip buttie elevated to ambrosia.

8 Here's a taste of Provence (minus the olive oil). Split a crusty small baguette, fill it with sliced ripe, juicy tomatoes, or halved ripe cherry tomatoes, add some very thinly slivered onion or sliced spring onion, some crushed garlic, some shredded basil and chopped parsley, and a sprinkling of balsamic vinegar. Wrap and weight (with a plate topped by a heavy tin) for a few minutes, so that the juices permeate the bread.

DAYS 12–14

Starting today, you may add milk shakes and fruit mousses to your diet, along with Slim Cuisine 'Whipped Cream' for your fruit or ice cream.

TECHNIQUES FOR DAYS 12–14 (PAGES 129–133)

Milk Shakes • Slim Cuisine 'Whipped Cream'

SUGGESTED MENUS FOR DAYS 12–14

Follow the previous days' menu suggestions for breakfasts, sandwiches (if you wish) and vegetarian meals. But now you can add ice cream and milk shakes – they make great snacks – and you can put 'whipped cream' on your fruit.

WEEK 3

THE OMNIVORE

DAYS 15–20

For the next six days, here is your plan:

1 Add one more serving of fruit, bringing your total up to *three* servings a day – in ice cream, milk shakes or other recipes if you wish.

2 Eat one fish fillet (any size) or one skinless, boneless chicken breast a day, or you may have 175 g (6 oz) turkey breast, chicken breast, smoked turkey breast or smoked chicken breast from the supermarket deli counter, or you may have one 200 g (7½ oz) can of tuna in water or brine, drained. (If the tuna is in brine, rinse it after draining to rid it of excess salt.) If you prepare a roast chicken, eat one breast (no skin); the family can eat the rest.

If you use the pan juices, make sure they have been skimmed of *all* fat. To skim the fat, pour the pan juices into a glass jar or jug and place in the freezer for about fifteen minutes so that the fat can rise to the top. (The roast chicken can stay on a platter, tented loosely with foil. It will benefit from the rest after cooking.) Then skim the fat off and discard it, and reheat the pan juices. You may eat your chicken, fish or turkey either at midday or at the evening meal. You can use *plain* breadcrumbs or matzo meal to make 'fried' chicken or 'fried' fish (see the recipe on page 138).

3 Unlimited vegetables from your vegetable lists. Eat plenty – they are important. Cook them creatively. Make them delicious.

4 Skimmed milk products – as much as you need for recipes and so on. See list on page 34.

5 Two large baking potatoes, or sixteen small new potatoes, or an equivalent amount of all-purpose potatoes, or one large or two small sachets of instant mashed potatoes.

6 Two slices of bread, one pita, or one roll, or one bagel.

7 Condiments and seasonings as needed (see list on page 35) including wine for cooking, and breadcrumbs or matzo meal for your chicken and fish.

8 Continue eating your breakfast as on page 50.

SUGGESTED RECIPES FOR DAYS 15–20 (PAGES 134–149)

Fish Soup • Italian Fish Soup • Fish in a Bag • Tuna Pâté • Grilled Chicken Breasts • Oven-Fried Chicken Breasts with Matzo Meal • Grilled Chicken Breasts with Breadcrumbs • Baked Crispy Chicken Breasts • Grilled Chicken Breasts • Chicken Breasts – Pan Sauté Method • Stir-'Fried' Chicken • Salil's Chicken Curry • Eddie Mui's Steamed Chicken • Rosie's Family Heirloom Curry • Tandoori Chicken • Lemon Roasted Chicken • Luxurious Potato-Turkey Salad • Fruit Fondue

FROZEN DIET DINNERS

If you hope to control your weight by consuming commercial frozen diet dinners on busy evenings, beware: they may contain fat. What's more, the fat may amount to as much as 30 per cent of the Calories of the whole (not very large) dish. Such frozen meals may also contain a high amount of salt. If you are curious about these meals, read the label and then – if you are serious about your weight control, your taste perceptions and your health – put them back in the freezer cabinet and walk away.

If you are a very busy person, and have no time to make your own frozen Slim Cuisine dinners, you may consider paying someone else to do it for you instead of paying at the supermarket. And if you are a homemaker who does not work at an outside job, and wants to earn some extra money, you might consider making Slim Cuisine diet meals for other dieters to buy for freezer stocking. Any recipe marked with a ❄ is suitable for freezing.

SUGGESTED MENUS FOR DAYS 15–20

Breakfasts remain the same. Continue having sandwiches for lunch, if you wish, but you now may occasionally have fish, turkey or chicken in those sandwiches. (Try your forked-open, quark-spread bagel topped with a slice or two of smoked salmon). If you are eating a meal out, you have much more flexibility now. A jacket potato, a plate of steamed vegetables and a big salad still make a convenient and 'safe' restaurant meal (the tub of fromage frais and flask of balsamic vinegar that you bring with you give the meal some pizazz), but you now can have grilled, poached, steamed or smoked fish as well. As always, you must communicate your needs to the restaurant staff: *no* oil, *no* butter, *no* marge . . . .

In the evening, if you have had fish or chicken for lunch, have a vegetarian meal (see previous menu listings). If not, base your evening meal around the fin or the feather (suggestions follow). Have your plain fruit, fruit fondue, ice cream, milk shakes, fruit mousses and so on as snacks, as sweet meals or as dessert.

1 Grilled chicken breasts on a bed of Peperonata, steamed broccoli and cauliflower, lemon wedges.

2 Creamy Parsnip Soup • Salil's Chicken Curry • Curried Cabbage • Creamy Herb Sauce

3 Italian Fish Soup • Mixed green salad with balsamic vinegar • Garlic Bread (lightly toasted baguette slice spread with Baked Garlic purée)

4 Soup of Creamy Greens • Fish and Vegetables steamed in a bag

5 Black bread spread with Aubergine 'Caviare' • Luxurious Potato-Turkey Salad • Tomato Herb Salad

6 Pan Sautéed Chicken Breasts with Mushroom-Tarragon Sauce • Fennel-Potato Gratin • Ratatouille

7 Lemon Roasted Chicken • Roast Potatoes • A selection of steamed or braised vegetables

8 Simple Vegetable Soup • Stir-'Fried' Chicken • Filipino Tomato Salad

9 Baked Crispy Chicken Breasts with Chunky Tomato-Pepper Relish • Mashed Potatoes (with Baked Garlic purée if desired) • Braised Onions

10 Rosie's Family Heirloom Curry (great if you have leftover chicken) • Creamy Herb Sauce • Baked Potato Halves

DAY 21

NEW GRAINS

Beginning today, you may add a bit of flexibility to your daily food regime. The following grains may be added to your list of permitted foods: substitute your choice from this list for one slice of bread *or* your breakfast cereal and crackers. You may eat your serving of new grains at any meal.

300 ml (½ pint) cooked rice (white or brown – basmati, American long grain or Italian Arborio. Pudding rice is OK too). Approximately 75 g (3 oz) raw rice = 300 ml (½ pint) cooked.

OR 300 ml (½ pint) cooked bulghur (cracked wheat). Approximately 75 g (3 oz) raw bulghur = 300 ml (½ pint) cooked.

OR 300 ml (½ pint) cooked pasta (white or brown). Approximately 75 g (3 oz) raw pasta = 300 ml (½ pint) cooked.

OR 300 ml (½ pint) cooked buckwheat groats (kasha). Approximately 75 g (3 oz) raw kasha = 300 ml (½ pint) cooked.

OR 300 ml (½ pint) cooked couscous. Approximately 75 g (3 oz) raw couscous = 300 ml (½ pint) cooked.

OR 300 ml (½ pint) cooked polenta (maize meal). Approximately 50 g (2 oz) raw polenta = 300 ml (½ pint) cooked.

IMPORTANT!

Keep eating lots of vegetables! • Drink lots of water! • Don't be hungry, don't be sad, enjoy your food! • Eat a good variety from your lists.

SUGGESTED RECIPES FOR THE EXTRA GRAINS (PAGES 151–155)

Wheat Pilaf • Bulghur-Tuna Salad • Tomato-Tuna Sauce • Polenta Pizza

SUGGESTED MENUS USING THE EXTRA GRAINS

I'm going to give you some sample *days* at this point, because you will have to learn – from today until target weight – to balance your grain allowances. You may have one serving of extra grain (polenta, pasta, bulghur, kasha, rice or couscous) in place of your breakfast cereal or crackers, or in place of one piece of bread. Let me point out that you don't have to eat *all* of what is allowed each day. It is there for you if you need it, but you don't *have* to. But do eat *lots of vegetables* every day.

1 *BREAKFAST*

Cereal with skimmed milk and fruit

LUNCH

Baked Potato with Tomato Sauce • Grilled Vegetables

MIDDAY SNACK

Salad-filled Roll

EVENING MEAL

Stir-'Fried' Chicken and vegetables • Grated vegetable salad with Slim Cuisine dressing or balsamic vinegar • Slim Cuisine Ice Cream

EVENING SNACK

Milk Shake

2 *BREAKFAST*

Fruit Milk Shake

LUNCH

Smoked Turkey Sandwich with Rémoulade Spread • Herbed Tomato Salad

MIDDAY SNACK

Raw Vegetables with Dip

EVENING MEAL

Soup of Creamy Greens • Polenta Pizza • Ice Cream

EVENING SNACK

Fruit

3 *BREAKFAST*

One slice of toast spread with a mashed banana or crushed berries, and quark

LUNCH

Grilled fish and grilled vegetables • Salad of spinach leaves, and dark greens, balsamic vinegar or Slim Cuisine dressing • Fruit

MIDDAY SNACK

One slice toast spread with Beetroot Purée

EVENING MEAL

Soup of Potato and Caramelized Onions • Pasta with Tomato Ragoût • Slim Cuisine Ice Cream

EVENING SNACK

Vanilla or Mocha Milk Shake

4 *BREAKFAST*

Cereal with skimmed milk and fruit

LUNCH

Baked Potato with Creamy Herb Sauce • Large mixed salad • Stir-'Fried' or steamed vegetable selection

MIDDAY SNACK

Slim Cuisine Milk Shake

EVENING MEAL

Pasta with Tomato-Tuna Sauce • Bread

WEEK 4

CHEESECAKE AND STEAK

DAYS 22–25

You may add these things:

1 If you wish: one more serving per day of chicken breast, turkey breast, fish fillet or tuna. Alternatively you may eat canned salmon, squid or any shellfish: prawns, shrimps, cockles, scallops, lobster, mussels, clams, langoustines, oysters and so on. Or you may eat sardines, pilchards or mackerel canned with tomato sauce. (Read the label – *no* oil!) You don't have to have chicken or fish every single day, if you don't want to. By all means have a vegetarian day every once in a while. And continue to make sure you eat a large variety of vegetables *every* day.

2 You may also have *cheesecake* starting today. The cheesecake crust is made from Grape-Nuts cereal, so from today on, you may have your cereal ration at whatever time of day you wish to have your cheesecake.

SUGGESTED RECIPES (PAGES 156–159)

Orange Cheesecake • Banana Cream Cheesecake • Strawberry Cheesecake

SUGGESTED MENUS FOR DAYS 22–25

1 *BREAKFAST*

Fruit (choose one: strawberries, melon, sliced oranges, banana) with fruit sauce (raspberry, strawberry or mango)

LUNCH

Tuna Pâté Sandwich • Slim Cuisine Potato Crisps • Mixed green salad with balsamic vinegar or Slim Cuisine dressing

MIDDAY SNACK

Slim Cuisine Ice Cream

EVENING MEAL

Eddie Mui's Steamed Chicken • Steamed rice • Stir-'Fried' mixed vegetables (mange-tout, courgette sticks, asparagus (in season), peeled pepper strips and so on)

EVENING SNACK

Milk Shake

2 *BREAKFAST*

Cheesecake

LUNCH

Spinach-Mushroom Salad with prawns and Rémoulade Sauce, or Slim Cuisine Mayonnaise

MIDDAY SNACK

Slim Cuisine Potato Crisps with dip

EVENING MEAL

Tandoori Chicken • Basmati Rice • Curried Gratin of Puréed Vegetables

EVENING SNACK

1 slice bread with mashed banana or other fruit

3 *Breakfast*

Cereal with fruit and milk

LUNCH

Grilled Chicken Breast in a pita pocket (half a pita) with Roasted Tomato Sauce or Chunky Tomato-Pepper Relish, and a dollop of Slim Cuisine Mayonnaise • Slim Cuisine 'Fried' Potatoes

MIDDAY SNACK

Slim Cuisine Ice Cream

EVENING MEAL

Creamy Parsnip Soup • Cous cous with Vegetable Curry • Creamy Cucumber Dip • Fruit Fondue

EVENING SNACK

Raw vegetables with dip, or Vanilla Milk Shake

4 *BREAKFAST*

Cereal with milk and fruit

LUNCH

Smoked mackerel or smoked salmon on a slice of black bread or wholemeal bread, with Rémoulade Sauce • Cucumber, tomato, beetroot salad on greens with Slim Cuisine dressing

MIDDAY SNACK

Banana Mousse

EVENING MEAL

Baked Crispy Chicken Breasts with Sautéed Mushrooms • Wheat Pilaf • Gravy or Tomato-Carrot Sauce

EVENING SNACK

Ice Cream or Milk Shake

5 *BREAKFAST*

1 piece toast with fruit and quark or fromage frais

LUNCH

Baked Potato with Beetroot Purée • Fruit

MIDDAY SNACK

Cheesecake

EVENING MEAL

Tandoori Chicken • Vegetable Bhajee with Corn Cobs • Basmati Rice • Fruit Fondue

EVENING SNACK

Milk Shake

DAYS 26 AND 27

Add sweetcorn to the list of vegetables you may eat – up to 300 ml (½ pint) a day; also green peas in the same amount. Keep eating *plenty* of vegetables, raw and cooked (especially cooked), and drinking lots of water.

SUGGESTED RECIPES (PAGES 160–161)

Polenta with Tomato-Sweetcorn Sauce • Corn Salad • Herbed Pea Purée

SUGGESTED MENUS FOR DAYS 26 AND 27

1 *BREAKFAST*

Cereal with fruit and milk

LUNCH

Slim Cuisine Crisps with Herbed Pea Purée • Tomato filled with Tuna Pâté

MIDDAY SNACK

Banana Sandwich

EVENING MEAL

Oven-'Fried' Fish • Corn Salad • Slim Cuisine Chips • Ice Cream

EVENING SNACK

Milk Shake or raw vegetables and dip

2 *BREAKFAST*

Cheesecake

LUNCH

Pasta with Tomato-Carrot Sauce • Melon with Raspberry Coulis

MIDDAY SNACK

Pita pocket (½ pita) filled with salad

EVENING MEAL

Rosie's Family Heirloom Curry with garden peas • Curried Cabbage • Ice Cream

EVENING SNACK

Milk Shake or Raw Vegetables with Dips

DAY 28

If you wish, substitute a serving of lean pork or lean beef for fish or chicken a few times a week. If you choose beef, buy goose skirt steak or point end brisket (see page 162); if pork, pork tenderloin. A *serving* is 110–150 g (4–5 oz). Alternatively, you may add 110 g (4 oz) extra-lean mince (beef, pork, veal or lamb). The ideal is to buy a piece of *very* lean, perfectly trimmed meat from the butcher, and have him mince it for you, or else bring the meat home and mince it yourself. You do not have to eat chicken, fish or meat every single day. Remember, one or two total vegetable days a week will not hurt – indeed, they are strongly recommended.

Stay on this level (Day 28) until you reach your target weight. If you are feeling very happy, well fed and comfortable (and losing nicely) on any level that occurs *before* Day 28, you may stay on that level as long as you like. But don't make that day the One-day Blitz; that is – as it says – meant to be experienced for a single day only. Use the One-day Blitz as an emergency brake. If you have fallen from grace and feel out of control, off the track and in the coils of Demon Fat once more, go immediately back to the One-day Blitz. It shouldn't happen, but – alas – it does. Christmas back home with the extended family; weddings, funerals and other emotionally charged group events; holidays – all these things may tip you back into the fat-lined pit.

I hope this plan will enable you eventually to weather such situations, but should you succumb, immediately return to your symbolic fast, the taste-purifying One-day Blitz. Then, if your digression was very severe and you have regained a considerable amount of weight, follow the plan through once more. If your weight gain was negligible, but you just needed to experience the Blitz in order to regain control, return to the level you had achieved before your scuffle with Demon Fat and continue from there.

SUGGESTED RECIPES (PAGES 162–176)

Chinese Stir-'Fried' Goose Skirt Steak • Open Face Steak Sandwiches with Mushrooms • Chinese Beef with Spring Onions • Goose Skirt Steak Braised with Wine and Onions • Old fashioned Pot Roast • Brisket and Onions • Roast Pork • Breaded Medallions of Pork with Onion Sauce • Shami Kebab • Hamburgers • Veal-Mushroom Patties • Bolognese Sauce • Shepherd's Pie

SUGGESTED MENUS FOR DAY 28

You will now – if you wish – be able to add a meat meal now and then. The technique and recipe section will teach you how to buy and cook the leanest cuts of meat. The iron in meat comes in the form that is most easily absorbed by the human body; the zinc as well. *Lean* meat-eating is not a bad thing, especially for pre-menopausal women who need plenty of easily absorbed dietary iron. So follow the menu suggestions for the previous level, but add a meat meal a few times a week.

SUGGESTED MEAT MEALS

1 Chinese Beef with Spring Onions • Steamed Rice • Braised Aubergine, Chinese Style

2 Veal-Mushroom Patties with Tomato-Carrot Sauce • Potato-Fennel Gratin

3 Shami Kebab with Mint-Coriander Sauce • Vegetable Bhajee with Corn Cobs

4 Old Fashioned Pot Roast • Roast Potatoes • Braised Cauliflower, Courgettes, Sautéed Mushrooms

5 Hamburgers on Buns with Roasted Tomato Ketchup, Chunky Tomato-Pepper Sauce • Herbed Tomato Salad • Shredded cabbage, carrots, and beetroot with Slim Cuisine dressing • Slim Cuisine Potato Crisps

6 Grilled Goose Skirt Steak with Grilled Vegetables (courgettes, peppers, aubergines) • Slim Cuisine 'Fried' Potatoes

MAINTENANCE

How do you know when you are ready to jump from Day 28 to Maintenance?

1 You've reached your target weight.

2 You've stabilized; that is, you have stayed at target weight for three days.

Target weight is a great moment in any ex-fat person's life. Say hello to your willowy waist and flat behind, hello to your cheekbones and firm chinline. How nice to know that they really were there, all those years, buried under the flab. And how nice to know they have emerged while you feasted on cheesecake, ice cream, steak, mashed potatoes, chilli, curry et al!

Now what? You *love* being newly slim, but you also love food as much as ever. Well, there's no problem at all, is there? You have by now learned to prepare glorious food of all kinds without resorting to added fat in any form. You have learned to snack through the day, even to binge, without getting into trouble. Both the taste and texture of full milk products, butter, oil and dripping will seem quite unpalatable now. Diving back into the old buttery, oily, creamy habits would be punishment at this point. Not only would your lovely, slim bits disappear in short order, but the food would taste *awful*.

To hold the flab at bay, and to stay off the diet 'yo-yo' for the rest of your life, cook and eat according to the Slim Cuisine rules for ever. 'Rewarding' yourself with a so-called treat now and then will not work at all. An oil-drenched salad here and a whipped cream-slathered cake there, a pat of butter, a glass of soft drink, a fatty steak, a chocolate bar . . . any of those will taste very odd after your intensive four-week palate retraining, but it doesn't take much sampling to throw that retraining out the window. You are a reformed fat-o-holic. Don't leap right back into the arms of Demon Fat.

If you do, you'll find yourself saying again, just as you did in the old days: 'I'll just have a little bit. I'll be *good* again tomorrow.' You're back on the 'yo-yo', you're back to binge/starve, you're back to suffering, and soon you'll be fat again. There is no need to do such things to yourself. Week 4 should remain your basic pattern for the rest of your life, with the following additions.

1 You can change the amounts of various foods you eat. More bread when you want it, more fruit per day, more pasta and so on.

2 You may eat the *dark* meat of the chicken as well as the breast. But you should *never* eat the skin, or the juices before they have been defatted.

3 You may eat the occasional egg (up to three a week) *if* you have no heart, artery, or cholesterol problems, and no history of such problems in your family.

4 You may add pulses when you want them, including baked beans (read the label and buy a brand with no added sugar or fat).

5 You may use Italian Mozzarella and Parmesan cheese (part-skimmed milk cheeses) occasionally in recipes. Read the labels: they should indicate that the cheese is medium-fat. Mozzarella comes packed in a liquid-filled pouch, Parmesan in a block. (Parmesan also comes ready-grated, but often it is of very poor quality; a sort of cheesy dust. Even high-quality Parmesan, when ready-grated, will not do; it goes stale quickly. It's best to buy a piece and grate it as needed, or else grate the entire piece, and store the grated cheese in the freezer to use as needed.) Cut the block Parmesan into small chunks, and whirl it in the blender to grate it. Save the rind to add to simmering stews and sauces. It will add good flavour, but not disperse in the stew or soup, so the added Calories and fat are minimal. If cheese pushes you over the edge – if you find it impossible to have any in the house without eating it all at once – then *forget* the Mozzarella and Parmesan; you will still eat very well without it.

6 You can use sugar in place of low-Calorie sweetener occasionally. Some baked sweets do not work with NutraSweet (see page 73).

7 You may use dried fruits occasionally in recipes. It is not a good idea to use them as snacks, however: they are full of concentrated sugar, and can pile on the sugar Calories in no time at all. But controlled amounts in baking occasionally will dress up your desserts (see page 184).

8 You may eat chestnuts – the only nut that is not woefully high in fat.

Reread the lists of *obvious fats*, *less obvious fats* and *hidden fats* on pages 22–23. To maintain your target weight for the rest of your life, avoid those fats for the rest of your life. It's that simple.

HOW TO DEAL WITH WEIGHT GAIN WHEN YOU HAVE STUCK TO A NO-ADDED FAT REGIME

1 If you have been sticking to the rules and avoiding *all* added fats and high-fat foods, with the exception of cheese, then cut out the cheese.

2 If that doesn't bring your weight down, cut down on bread and grains.

3 If you still fail to bring your weight down, return to Week 3 (Days 15–20) of the plan, and stay there until your weight is where you want it to be. Just remember that fluctuations of a pound or two (a few pounds for women) are normal. Don't panic unless you are experiencing a steady, inexorable weight gain.

HOW TO DEAL WITH WEIGHT GAIN WHEN YOU HAVE GONE OFF THE RAILS

It happens. A family Christmas, a holiday, an emotional crisis involving your family, a lover, the Inland Revenue, your best friend; you are back in the coils of Demon Fat.

It *shouldn't* happen. When you are on holiday you should learn to say 'no fat or oil, I'm allergic,' in French, Italian, Serbo-Croat, whatever is appropriate. And you must train your family to respect your dieting needs during Christmas and every other time of year. During a crisis, binge away on Therapeutic Binges. But still, life is not perfect. People *do* fall off the wagon occasionally. Just don't use it as an excuse to billow out to your old fat and unhappy self again. Hop right on to the One-day Blitz; that's what it is for. Then stay right on Level One, the Vegetarian Week, until the extra weight has all gone. When you're at target weight again, go back to Maintenance.

SUGGESTED RECIPES FOR MAINTENANCE

Vegetable-Cheese Gratin • Vegetable Lasagne • Potato Pizza • Tuna-Tomato-Bean Salad • Re-fried Beans • Bread Pudding with Raspberries • Orange Bread Pudding • Carrot Cheesecake • Fruit Brulée

SNACKS: *Popcorn • Tortilla Chips*

TECHNIQUES AND RECIPES

~

SYMBOLS USED IN THIS SECTION

 A Teddy Bear means: Therapeutic Binge. There is no limit on this recipe; eat all you want whenever you want. T.B.'s keep you nourished and happy, enjoy them often.

 A Snowflake means: suitable for freezing. I strongly recommend that you cook ahead, and keep your freezer very well stocked, especially with Therapeutic Binges. There will be many times when you want to grab something out of the freezer, pop it in the microwave, and chow down in no time at all. Stock up with goodies so that you can do so.

 A Heart means: suitable for the weight loss regime, although not a Therapeutic Binge. Recipes without a ♡ (or without a  are for Maintenance.

A Clock means: quick and easy to put together and cook. Perfect for those days when you come home late, *ravenous*, in need of comfort PDQ, and the freezer is bare. A clock recipe will take approximately ½ hour to produce.

SOME ADVICE ABOUT INGREDIENTS

DAIRY PRODUCTS

We are very lucky in this country to have some excellent very low-fat (less than 1%) dairy products available in many supermarkets. They make this regime a great pleasure.

Quark: A physicist won't believe you (a physicist thinks that a quark is a subatomic particle) but supermarket shoppers know that quark is a smooth, creamy, skimmed milk curd cheese. I love quark on its own, spread on bread, or in all sorts of dips, spreads, and other recipes. If you *don't* like plain quark spread on bread, try whipping it with the electric mixer first, or whirling it in the food processor. The texture then becomes beautifully fluffy. And, of course, when you whirl it in the processor, you can whirl in a handful of chopped fresh herbs as well, or a pinch or two of cinnamon and nutmeg. After Day 7, you may whirl in some ripe fruit. Some supermarkets carry very low-fat (less than 1%) curd cheese – a smooth creamy cheese that can be used exactly as quark.

Yogurt: In 1973, a Harvard medical professor-adventurer startled the world with reports of the existence of apparent super-geriatric paradises in Russia's Caucasus, and in the Himalayas. For a brief time yogurt – a dietary staple of both populations – became *the* healthy food to scoff down in quantity. These super geriatrics, it seemed, lived the simple life, ate quantities of yogurt, and lived to spry old age (well over 100). But in 1979, all was revealed. Hard evidence turned up, indicating gleeful age exaggeration on the part of status seeking elders, and a confusion of naming patterns and record-keeping, that made differentiation between generations almost impossible. Suddenly, in the western world yogurt lost its cachet, and was no longer devoured with the zeal of Ponce de Leon searching for the Fountain of Youth. But in the meantime something quite interesting had happened; both the English and the Americans found that they had developed a taste for the tangy stuff. They discovered that, though it may not help you live forever, it sure is delicious mixed with crushed fruit, chopped fresh herbs, grated cucumbers, crushed garlic, or even eaten straight out of its tub. Buy the very low-fat yogurt (less than 1% fat). You may have to shop around before you find a brand of very low-fat yogurt that pleases you; some are thin, watery and appallingly sour, others are custardy and pleasantly tart. If you love the taste of yogurt, try draining it overnight, in a muslin bag set in a colander over a bowl. In the morning you will be left with a compelling yogurt 'cream' cheese.

Fromage Frais: Great stuff! Buy the 0% (or less than 1%) fat kind only. French brands will indicate on the carton 'Fromage frais, 0% de matière grasse'. Although I like yogurt, I must say that fromage frais puts it in the shade. It is called 'fromage frais' – fresh cheese – but it is not particularly cheeselike. More like a rich sour cream, I'd say; thick, creamy and not really sour at all – just a slight, pleasing tanginess. You will find fromage frais infinitely useful and appealing, both in recipes and eaten plain. It makes a perfect topping for fruits and berries.

Buttermilk: Real buttermilk is the liquid left over from buttermaking –all the fat has gone into the butter, so the only butter actually contained in the buttermilk is in the name. Serious cooks know that buttermilk is splendid in bread and cake baking. The buttermilk available in supermarkets is not the real thing: it is, rather, a cultured skimmed milk product. It has a lovely creamy texture and, like fromage frais, a pleasant tartness. It is *incomparable* for making Slim Cuisine Ice Cream (see page 127). I *wish* supermarkets were more consistent about stocking the beautiful liquid: you'll buy it in the same supermarket every other day for a year, then – suddenly – there is no trace of it on the shelves, and the shelf-stockers insist that they've never heard of it, the store has never stocked it, and it probably doesn't exist in the known universe. All I can say is keep looking, keep asking! Be insistent. If dairy managers know that you *really* want it, and *really* will buy it if they stock it, they will undoubtedly keep it on the shelves. I spoke to someone at Raines Dairy, the dairy that produces the buttermilk found in many supermarkets, and he advised me that buttermilk can be frozen very successfully *if* your freezer is very cold so that the buttermilk can be frozen *fast*. If it freezes slowly (and if your freezer is not cold enough), the buttermilk may be grainy when thawed, due to the formation of ice crystals in the freezing process. But if your freezer freezes it quickly, it will thaw (in the refrigerator or on the thaw cycle of the microwave) beautifully creamy, with no adverse effects. Should it separate slightly, simply whisk it. If no shop close to you stocks buttermilk, it will pay to buy it in bulk, and store it in the freezer. When thawed, use it in the ice cream recipe.

Skimmed Milk: People are cruel, stupid, and criminal sometimes. Recently, I was giving my usual enthusiastic (over-the-top you might say) Slim Cuisine talk, extolling the versatility of skimmed milk and skimmed milk products. An elderly woman came up to me afterwards, quite distraught. A few weeks before, she – thinking about her health, her husband's health, and her expanding waistline – asked her milkman to switch her milk order to skimmed. He looked at her contemptuously: 'You don't want to do that' he urged. 'Skimmed milk is like water. It's horrible!' And he wouldn't change her order. This man should be drummed out of the milkman corps. Don't let anyone do this to you. Stand up for your rights. It's not that skimmed milk is *watery* – it's that full cream milk is so thick, cloying and unrefreshing. If you are making the big change from whole to skimmed, you'll be astonished at how quickly you adjust.

Skimmed Milk Powder: Keep the powder in the cupboard for emergencies (when you've run out of fresh milk) and use it gleefully in recipes: wait until you taste the milk shake (see page 129)! Skimmed milk powder is fortified with vitamins D and A (two of the fat-soluble vitamins), which makes it a particularly valuable Slim Cuisine ingredient.

OTHER INGREDIENTS

Stock: Making your own chicken and vegetable stock from scratch is a rewarding and satisfying kitchen activity. Homemade, defatted stock can be frozen in small containers, and thawed when needed. Or it can be frozen in ice cube trays, and a cube or two can be popped out when you need it for sautéing. *But* it does – I admit it – take time. Fortunately, there are alternatives to slaving over a steamy stock pot. There are some good vegetable bouillon powders available. I particularly like Frigg's Végétale – a vegetable bouillon *drink*. It makes a wonderful sauté medium. Marigold vegetable bouillon powder is also excellent. And I am delighted to say that you can now buy – in the chill cabinet of some supermarkets – an excellent chicken stock and beef stock, ready made, defatted, and as good as the best homemade stock. The same company – Fonds de Cuisine – make a vegetable stock, but it contains butter.

Sun-dried Tomatoes: You can buy dry pack (no oil) sun-dried tomatoes in Italian delicatessens and some specialist food stores (see page 189) for a mail order source). The intensely flavoured, leathery morsels when added to a sauce or soup become tender in the cooking, and give the sauce or soup a miraculous flavour boost.

Sweeteners: NutraSweet (Aspartame) is a very useful very low Calorie sweetener, synthesised from two amino acids (amino acids are the building blocks of protein). You can buy granulated NutraSweet in large jars. It does not have the bitter aftertaste of saccharine, and it is 200 times sweeter than sugar. When heated, some of its sweetness dissipates, so that it cannot be used in cooked desserts, but it is extremely useful in ice creams, dessert sauces, milkshakes, and so on. If you decide to substitute sugar for NutraSweet in any dessert recipe, you will be adding 34 Calories per 15 ml (1 tbsp) sugar used, to the dish. For the weight loss regime, it is best to stay with NutraSweet. During Maintenance, you may choose to use sugar occasionally.

Eggs: Egg yolks are almost pure fat, and very high in cholesterol, but the egg white is virtually fat-free, and a perfect protein. As a result, many Slim Cuisine recipes call for egg whites – no yolks. 'What do I do with all those yolks?' I hear you cry. Well, you *could* give them away, but there are valuable non-food things you can do with egg yolks that you might want to try. During Maintenance if you do not have cardiac or arterial problems, and if you do not have a high blood cholesterol count, you may eat whole eggs occasionally, but it is not a good idea to consume more than three a week.

SOME ADVICE ABOUT EQUIPMENT

Non-reactive pans: A non-reactive pan is one that will not react with acid ingredients (wine, tomatoes and citrus juices, for example) to produce off colours and tastes in the finished dish. Non-reactive materials are stainless steel, enamelled cast iron, non-stick coatings such as Tefal and Silverstone, and flameproof glass and ceramic. For Slim Cuisine cookery, the best non-reactive pans to use are enamelled cast iron and heavyweight non-stick cookware. And a non-stick wok with a lid, and a steamer rack, is one of the most useful pieces of equipment you can own.

Food processor: If you don't have one of these machines, save your pennies and buy one, if at all possible. It will be one of the best investments you can make for your diet, your health, and your gastronomic happiness.

DAY 1
TECHNIQUES AND RECIPES

BAKED BEETROOT

Use baked beetroot to make a dip or sauce for raw vegetables. (Later, when you begin to eat bread and crackers, use the dip as a spread.) Cut the baked beetroot into chunks and place in a food processor with a spoonful or two of fromage frais or yogurt, a splash of lemon juice or good wine vinegar and a little raw garlic or Baked Garlic purée (see page 75), if you wish. Season with salt and pepper. Process to a rough chunky purée for a dip; process to a perfectly smooth purée for a sauce. Add more fromage frais, lemon juice or wine vinegar, and seasonings, as needed. This is not only extremely good tasting – the colour and texture make this, as you can imagine, a visual knock-out!

Trim the green tops away and wrap whole, unpeeled beetroots in heavy-duty foil, shiny side in (put 3–4 beetroots in one packet). Bake at 200°C, 400°F, Gas Mark 6 for 1–2 hours until tender. (Timing depends on age and size.) Use a skewer for testing doneness. The skewer should insert easily but the beetroots should not be mushy. Cool, then trim and slip off the skins.

BAKED BEETROOT – MICROWAVE VERSION

Trim large beetroots and wrap each in microwave cling film. Microwave on FULL for 15 minutes for 1 beetroot or 20 minutes for 2 beetroots. Turn them over and microwave for another 15 minutes (1 beetroot) or 20 minutes (2 beetroots).

You may use ready-cooked beetroot from the supermarket. (The kind that contains no vinegar; the vinegary beetroot tastes too harsh.)

BAKED GARLIC

Don't be frightened as you don't have to eat garlic if you hate it. The diet will work just fine without it. It's just a special culinary bonus for those who love garlic. Baked garlic is one of my favourite Slim Cuisine ingredients. It is not as shocking as it sounds. Garlic, baked whole, takes on an amazing sweetness, and the texture of the cloves (which soften into a kind of purée) becomes something akin to roasted chestnuts. For this technique, wait until you can buy large, firm heads of garlic, with no sprouts or withered cloves. Store it in a ventilated basket or pierced crock in a cool part of the kitchen (never refrigerate). And don't hold on to the garlic for months, waiting until you gather enough courage to do the deed. Baked ancient garlic is revolting, but fresh, firm heads, when baked, are a revelation! Stir the resulting purée into quark, fromage frais or yogurt to make a very special garlic dip or dressing. Later, from Day 2 on, use it to season sauces and enrich casseroles, to mash into potatoes, or – after Day 9 – to spread on bread. If you hate the stuff, just ignore this completely. (But you'll never know what you're missing!)

To Bake Garlic

1 Preheat the oven to 190°C, 375°F, Gas Mark 5.

2 Remove the papery outer covering of the whole garlic heads, but do not separate the cloves or skin them. Place each whole head of garlic on a square of foil, shiny side up. Fold up the foil and crimp so that the head is completely wrapped in a roomy, tightly sealed pouch.

3 Bake for about 1 hour (timing depends upon the size of the garlic bulb).

4 Remove from the oven, unwrap and cool for at least 5 minutes. Gently separate the cloves and squeeze each one over a fine-mesh sieve so that the softened garlic pops into the sieve.

5 With a wooden spatula or spoon, rub the garlic through the sieve into a small container or bowl. If you are in a hurry, forget the sieve. Simply squeeze the garlic into the bowl, then push it into a mound with a rubber spatula. Cover tightly with cling film and refrigerate until needed.

BAKED GARLIC – MICROWAVE VERSION

1 Remove the papery outer covering from 2–3 large, firm heads of garlic, but do not skin them. Separate the cloves. Scatter them in one layer in an 20 cm (8 inch) square, 2.5–5 cm (1–2 inch) deep glass baking dish. Pour in water to a depth of a little more than 1.25 cm (½ inch). Cover tightly with microwave cling film.

2 Microwave on HIGH for 10 minutes. Carefully pierce the cling film in several places to release steam (stand back) and leave to stand for 10 minutes.

3 With tongs, peel away a corner of the cling film on the side away from you, to allow any residual steam to escape. Be very careful: the steam is hot, and you don't want to get burned. With the tongs, remove the cling film.

4 When the garlic is cool enough to handle, remove the skins – they will slip off easily. Drain the garlic and place in a bowl. Mash with a fork or a wooden pestle. If liked, push through a sieve to make a very fine purée.

CREAMY CUCUMBER DIP

MAKES 1.7 LITRES (3 PINTS)

~

Seeding and slicing cucumbers, then folding them – with fresh herbs – into a creamy sauce is a classic way of treating the crisp vegetable. Salting them first draws out their moisture and any trace of bitterness. The sauce will not become watery if the cucumbers stand overnight. This dip and the minted cucumbers are both delicious eaten with a spoon, as a dip with vegetables or even as a salad dressing. They are related to Indian raitas and Greek tzatziki.

- *4 large cucumbers*
- *salt*
- *1 clove garlic, skinned and crushed*
- *30 ml (2 tbsp) white wine vinegar*
- *570 ml (1 pint) very low-fat fromage frais or yogurt*
- *3 spring onions, trimmed and finely chopped*
- *30 ml (2 tbsp) chopped fresh coriander (optional)*
- *60 ml (4 tbsp) finely chopped fresh mint*
- *2.5 ml (½ tsp) ground cumin*
- *2.5 ml (½ tsp) ground coriander*
- *freshly ground pepper to taste*

1 Peel the cucumbers and cut in half lengthways. With a teaspoon, scoop out the seeds from each half and discard them. Slice the cucumber halves about 0.6 cm (¼ inch) thick. Toss the slices with a little salt and leave in a non-reactive colander to drain for ½ hour.

2 While the cucumbers are draining, combine the garlic and wine vinegar in a non-reactive bowl, then leave to marinate.

3 Rinse the cucumbers and dry very well. Add to the garlic and wine vinegar. Fold in the fromage frais, then stir in all remaining ingredients. Taste and adjust seasonings. Serve with crudités, or scoop on to lettuce or chicory leaves.

MARINATED PEPPERS

~

Cut as many red and yellow peppers as you like into their natural sections. Remove the cores, seeds and ribs. Peel the sections with a swivel-bladed vegetable peeler. Cut the peppers into strips. Place them in a shallow non-reactive dish. Season with a little salt and freshly ground pepper. Pour in 30–45 ml (2–3 tbsp) balsamic vinegar and stir until the peppers are well coated with the vinegar. Cover and refrigerate for a few hours or overnight.

MINTED CUCUMBERS

MAKES 1.7 LITRES (3 PINTS)

~

- *4 large cucumbers*
- *salt*
- *570 ml (1 pint) very low-fat yogurt or fromage frais*
- *60 ml (4 tbsp) finely chopped fresh mint*
- *15 ml (1 tbsp) snipped fresh dill*
- *freshly ground pepper to taste*

1 Peel the cucumbers and cut in half lengthways. With a teaspoon, scoop out the seeds from each half and discard them. Slice the cucumber halves about 0.6 cm (¼ inch) thick. Toss the slices with a little salt and leave in a non-reactive colander to drain for ½ hour.

2 Stir together the yogurt, herbs and pepper in a bowl. Rinse the cucumbers and dry well. Fold them into the yogurt mixture. Chill in the refrigerator until needed.

TOMATO HERB SALAD

~

Huge platters of this gorgeously simple salad make Blitz Day a celebration. In the summer, ripe tomatoes are easily acquired and greedily devoured. See page 73 for advice on obtaining good tasting tomatoes out of season.

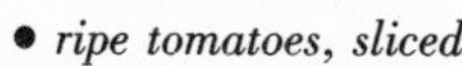

- *ripe tomatoes, sliced*
- *fresh basil or fresh mint, shredded*
- *wine vinegar (preferably balsamic)*

1 Arrange the tomatoes on a platter and scatter the herbs over them.

2 Drizzle with just a little vinegar, then leave to stand for a few minutes. Eat with great pleasure.

NOTE If mint or basil are not available, use snipped fresh chives.

CHERRY TOMATO HERB SALAD

- *ripe cherry tomatoes, halved*
- *a mixture of fresh herbs, such as oregano, thyme, parsley and basil or mint, finely chopped*
- *a spoonful or two of balsamic vinegar*
- *salt and freshly ground pepper to taste*

Toss all the ingredients together. Salt very lightly, grind on some pepper and toss once more. Leave to stand for a few minutes.

FILIPINO TOMATO SALAD

My old friend Consuelo Fernandez Richardson, a brilliant Filipino home cook, taught me to make this in Atlanta in the mid-70's. My son and her two kids were small then, and the three of them used to play elaborate make-believe games that always culminated in a full dress, original production performed for the two mommies. Then it was our turn to provide a quite beautiful meal.

- *cherry tomatoes (a mixture of red and yellow, if you can find them)*
- *watercress*
- *chives or spring onions*
- *salt*

1 Halve the cherry tomatoes and place in a bowl.
2 Steam the watercress over boiling water for 10 seconds. Immediately rinse well under cold running water, then shake dry. Trim off any woody stalks. Cut or tear the watercress into 2.5 cm (1 inch) lengths, using the remaining stalks, leaves and all. Add to the tomatoes.
3 Finely cut the chives. If you are using spring onions, trim them, thinly slice both the white and green parts. Add the chives or spring onions to the tomatoes.
4 Toss the salad together. Allow to stand for an hour or so. Just before serving, salt lightly and toss again.

SPINACH-MUSHROOM SALAD

MAKES ABOUT 570 ML (1 PINT) DRESSING

~

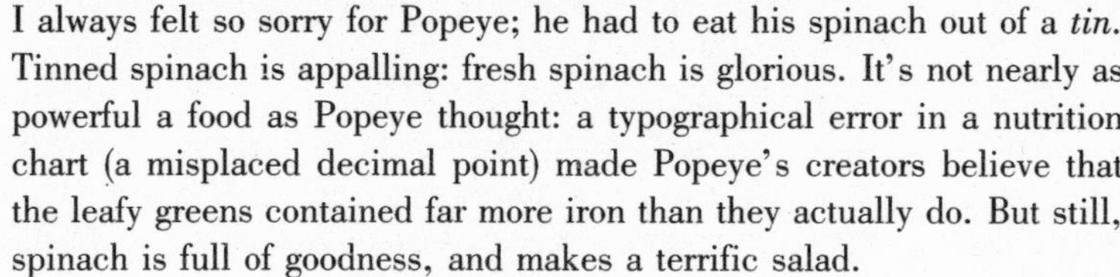

I always felt so sorry for Popeye; he had to eat his spinach out of a *tin*. Tinned spinach is appalling: fresh spinach is glorious. It's not nearly as powerful a food as Popeye thought: a typographical error in a nutrition chart (a misplaced decimal point) made Popeye's creators believe that the leafy greens contained far more iron than they actually do. But still, spinach is full of goodness, and makes a terrific salad.

DRESSING

- *150 ml (¼ pint) buttermilk*
- *300 ml (½ pint) very low-fat fromage frais*
- *7.5 ml (½ tbsp) Dijon mustard*
- *1 clove garlic, skinned and crushed*
- *1 bunch fresh chives, snipped (optional)*
- *salt and freshly ground pepper to taste*

SALAD

- *raw spinach, well cleaned*
- *button mushrooms, well cleaned*

1 Combine the dressing ingredients in a large non-reactive bowl, then whisk well. Refrigerate until needed.

2 Trim the stalks from the spinach leaves. Arrange the leaves on a plate. Chop the stalks into 0.6 cm (¼ inch) pieces and sprinkle over the leaves. Thinly slice the mushrooms, then scatter the slices over the spinach. Put a blob of dressing on each serving and serve at once.

DIPS, SPREADS & DRESSINGS FOR RAW VEGETABLES AND SALADS

~

RED PEPPER – CHIVE SPREAD

Combine chopped, canned red peppers (pimientos), snipped fresh chives and skimmed milk curd cheese or quark in a processor until smooth.

CHIVE SPREAD

Mash or purée quark or curd cheese with snipped fresh chives.

DILL SPREAD

As above, but substitute snipped fresh dill for the chives. Or substitute the feathery fronds of fresh fennel bulbs for a lovely *anise spread*.

RÉMOULADE DIP

Combine skimmed milk fromage frais with some chopped, well drained fresh tomato pulp, a finely chopped spring onion, some chopped fresh parsley, chopped drained capers, a dab of mustard and some crumbled, dried tarragon.

RUSSIAN SALAD

Finely chop radishes, spring onions and peeled, seeded cucumber. Fold into fromage frais. Season with plenty of freshly ground pepper. Sprinkle the top with Hungarian paprika.

MUSTARD DRESSING

Mix 300 ml (½ pint) fromage frais or skimmed milk yogurt with 15 ml (1 tbsp) mustard. Add a dash or two of excellent quality wine vinegar. This is especially delicious with grated carrot, beetroot and mooli (white radish).

'MAYONNAISE'

MAKES 450 ML (¾ PINT)

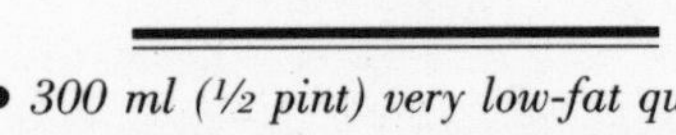

- *300 ml (½ pint) very low-fat quark or curd cheese (or very low-fat yogurt or fromage frais that has been drained overnight in a muslin-lined sieve)*
- *60 ml (4 tbsp) buttermilk or 45 ml (3 tbsp) skimmed milk*
- *15 ml (1 tbsp) mild wine vinegar or balsamic vinegar*
- *5 ml (1 tsp) Dijon mustard*
- *salt and freshly ground pepper to taste*

Place all the ingredients in a bowl and whisk well to combine. Refrigerate until needed.

CREAMY SALAD DRESSING

MAKES 350 ML (12 FL OZ)

~

- *120 ml (4 fl oz) very low-fat quark*
- *120 ml (4 fl oz) very low-fat fromage frais*
- *120 ml (4 fl oz) buttermilk*
- *5 ml (1 tsp) Dijon or German mustard*
- *15 ml (1 tbsp) chopped fresh parsley*
- *dash or two balsamic vinegar or other mild wine vinegar*
- *salt and freshly ground pepper to taste*

Place all the ingredients in a bowl and whisk well to combine. Refrigerate until needed.

CREAMY HERB SAUCE

~

Wonderful as a dip for crudités or – beginning tomorrow – as a filling for jacket potatoes. Alternatively, use as a garnish for vegetable casseroles such as chilli and curry.

- *very low-fat fromage frais or yogurt*
- *shredded or snipped fresh herbs (good combinations are mint and coriander, mint and dill, chives and parsley, thyme and tarragon, oregano and basil, or try one herb at a time)*

Whisk the fromage frais with a generous amount of a single fresh herb or a combination. Refrigerate until needed.

SALSA CRUDA

MAKES ABOUT 475 ML (19 FL OZ)

~

In Mexico, everyone eats beautiful raw chunky sauces based on tomatoes (or tomatillos – husk tomatoes), chillies and herbs, with *everything*. I remember a classic Hungarian meal eaten at a Hungarian restaurant in

Mexico City. Who would eat a Hungarian meal in Mexico City? Everyone – Mexicans in search of the exotic, and foreign visitors looking for a temporary relief from edible fire. But the Mexican diners always call for spicy Salsa Cruda, then smear it all over their Wiener Schnitzel.

Serve this fresh-tasting sauce as a dip for chicory leaves, celery sticks and button mushroom caps, serve as a salad dressing, or eat out of a bowl like Gazpacho. You can also add thinly sliced, seeded cucumbers, more garlic, basil, mint, thinly sliced celery, diced courgette, diced fennel – whatever you like.

- *12–15 ripe fresh tomatoes, skinned, seeded and coarsely chopped (see Note)*
- *canned, drained pimientos (red peppers), or grilled fresh peppers (see page 89), coarsely chopped*
- *fresh chives, snipped, or spring onions, trimmed and finely chopped*
- *finely chopped fresh chilli to taste (optional)*
- *50 ml (2 fl oz) red wine vinegar*
- *1–2 cloves garlic, skinned and crushed*
- *30 ml (2 tbsp) chopped fresh parsley*
- *generous 15 ml (1 tbsp) chopped fresh coriander (optional)*
- *7.5 ml (½ tbsp) fresh oregano leaves*

Combine all the ingredients in a non-reactive bowl. Refrigerate until needed.

NOTE *To ripen tomatoes*: Out of season, put them in a paper bag with a banana and leave in the larder (don't refrigerate them) for a few days to a week. They will emerge lusciously ripened. Alternatively, they may be left in an uncovered bowl in a cool, airy part of the kitchen. In a few days to a week, they will be ripe and tasty.

To skin tomatoes: If you have a gas cooker, hold each tomato on a long fork directly over the gas flame. In seconds, the skin will split. Slip off the skin. Otherwise, immerse tomatoes in boiling water for 10 seconds. Cut out the core, then the skins will slip off easily.

DAYS 2 – 7
TECHNIQUES AND RECIPES

Yesterday's 'Blitz Day' prepared you for action; today is the beginning of the revolution. Today is the day you ditch everything you know about conventional fat and oil based cookery methods. I'm very excited for you: what an adventure of gastronomic discovery you are about to begin! The following section presents an encyclopaedia of fat-free techniques. They are simple, plus they make the difference between boring, insipid 'diet' food, and vibrant, deeply flavoured, 'gourmet' food. Read the techniques section through before you begin to cook. If you are going to embark on an adventure, it pays to be prepared.

Good journey – and good appetite!

A NOTE ON STOCK

Do not use a stock cube for the following techniques; they are woefully salty and 'chemical' tasting, and many of them are extremely high in fat. Use homemade chicken or vegetable stock; Fonds de Cuisine chicken or beef stock (available from the chill cabinets of some supermarkets) or a good Swiss bouillon powder. Marigold vegetable bouillon powder is excellent; Frigg's *Végétal* is even better. If you use such a stock powder, don't even bother to reconstitute it. Simply combine your onions with water, then sprinkle in a little of the powder.

SAUTÉED AND 'FRIED' ONIONS

When I try to explain the precepts of Slim Cuisine to people, the reaction is often one of bewilderment. 'No added fat?!' they exclaim. 'No butter or marge, no olive oil or safflower oil, no suet, dripping, chicken fat or blubber? How is it possible to cook without those things?'

How, indeed? Without that essential step of almost every savoury recipe – 'Sauté the onions in a knob of butter (or a tablespoon of oil)' – how can one achieve even a small measure of deliciousness? Actually, it's easy. I've devised a stock-sauté method that turns out meltingly tender, caramelized and deeply flavoured 'sautéed' onions without a speck of oil or fat. Use this basic technique as the start of any savoury recipe. If you wish, add finely chopped garlic and chopped carrots to the onions as well. I think that you will be astonished at the depth of flavour this method gives to your cookery. And remember – for every 15 ml (1 tbsp) oil, margarine, fat or butter that you leave out, you will be saving over 120 wicked, unhealthy and fattening Calories. The technique works with a heavy, enamelled cast iron frying pan (method 1) or a good quality, non-stick coated pan (method 2).

METHOD 1

Using a heavy, enamelled cast-iron frying pan (this results in the most intense flavour):

- *large Spanish onions, skinned and chopped, sliced or cut into wedges (eighths or sixteenths) with the pieces separated*
- *approximately 450 ml (¾ pint) chicken, beef or vegetable stock*
- *dry white vermouth (optional)*

1 Combine the onion pieces and 300–350 ml (10–12 fl oz) of the stock in the heavy, enamelled cast-iron frying pan. Cover, bring to the boil and boil for 5–10 minutes, uncovering to stir very occasionally.

2 Uncover and reduce the heat a little. Cook and stir until the onions are beginning to stick and brown a little. Pour in a splash of stock or dry white vermouth. Stir and scrape the bottom of the pan to loosen all the browned bits. Continue cooking and stirring for a minute or two, adding a splash of stock or vermouth as necessary, until the onions are amber brown, meltingly tender and syrupy, and the liquid is almost gone.

METHOD 2

Using a frying pan with a non-stick lining:

- *large Spanish onions, skinned and chopped, sliced or cut into wedges (eighths or sixteenths) with the pieces separated*
- *approximately 450 ml (¾ pint) chicken, beef or vegetable stock*
- *dry white vermouth (optional)*

1 Combine the onions and 300 ml (½ pint) of the stock in the non-stick frying pan. Cover, bring to the boil and boil for 5–7 minutes.

2 Uncover and reduce the heat. Cook, stirring, until the onions are very tender, light amber and syrupy, and the liquid is almost gone. Add a little stock or dry white vermouth during cooking, as needed.

> **POT SCRUBBING**
>
> When you let the sautéed onions caramelize and stick in an enamelled pan, the clean up task can seem positively frightening. A blackened, encrusted frying pan is not the prettiest sight in the world. But it is not nearly as daunting as it seems. Soak the blackened pan overnight in a solution of biological detergent and water. In the morning, the encrustation will wash away easily.

SAUTÉED ONIONS FOR CURRIES

To make a curry, the spices and onions must be fried together, so that the spices lose their rawness and harshness. The Slim Cuisine technique eliminates the ghee (clarified butter) or oil, but the finished curries *never* taste 'dietetic'. To this basic onion-curry mixture, add more stock, or chopped tomatoes or tomato purée. Stir in cubed meat, poultry, vegetables, prawns or fish and simmer until cooked. At the very end, yogurt may be added to the sauce. (See index for specific curry recipes.)

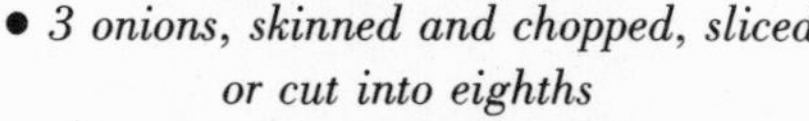

- *3 onions, skinned and chopped, sliced or cut into eighths*
- *300 ml (½ pint) stock*
- *spice mixture (see individual curry recipes)*
- *1–2 cloves garlic, skinned and chopped*

1 Separate the segments of the chopped onion pieces and spread them in a heavy, non-stick frying pan. Add *no* liquid or fat. Heat the frying pan gently. Cook over moderate heat, without stirring, for 7–10 minutes until the onions are sizzling, speckled with dark amber and beginning to stick to the pan.

2 Stir in the stock and let it bubble up, stirring up the browned deposits in the pan with a wooden spoon as it bubbles. Stir in the spices and garlic. Turn the heat down a little and simmer, stirring frequently, until the mixture is very thick (not at all soupy) and the onions and spices are 'frying' in their own juices. Don't rush this step, it is essential that the

spices should not have a raw harsh taste. Taste, then cook very gently for a few more minutes if necessary.

3 If you wish, for a thick sauce, purée half of the mixture in a blender or food processor, then combine the puréed and unpuréed portions.

SAUTÉED MUSHROOMS

~

My no-fat method for sautéing mushrooms never ceases to delight me. Mushrooms pan-fried my way taste so much *better* than those sautéed conventionally with lashings of butter or oil. You will find that the mushroom taste is very intense, and the texture is velvety without being mushy. Eat them plain at breakfast (or any meal), as part of a sauce, or as a garnish to meat, poultry or fish.

- *mushrooms (the more types of mushroom, the more interesting)*
- *50–75 ml (2–3 fl oz) stock*
- *50–75 ml (2–3 fl oz) dry sherry*
- *splash or two of soy sauce (or teriyaki sauce)*
- *freshly ground pepper to taste*

1 Leave button mushrooms whole if desired – larger mushrooms may be sliced or cut into quarters or eighths. If you use fresh shiitakes, trim off the tough stalks.

2 Spread out the mushrooms in a heavy-bottomed pan, then pour in the liquids. Cook over high heat, stirring. The mushrooms will release a great deal of liquid. Reduce the heat a little and keep on cooking, stirring occasionally, until the liquid has been absorbed, and the mushrooms are 'frying' in their own juices. Never let the mushrooms scorch, burn or stick to the pan. Season with pepper.

These mushrooms may be prepared ahead of time and stored in the refrigerator. They also freeze well. They may also be cooked in a non-stick frying pan or a heavy enamelled cast iron one.

STIR 'FRIED' PEPPERS

~

Red and yellow peppers have so much potential to become one of the most luscious of foods. It breaks my heart when people cut them up, throw them into salads, then complain all the rest of the day (between burps) how indigestible they are. Peppers become quite digestible if they are peeled. Peeling them also elevates their taste and texture far above what they were in the unpeeled state. When the peeled peppers are then stir-'fried', Slim Cuisine style in stock, they become one of the most delicious vegetable dishes in all of the vegetable kingdom. Add to all this pepper's nutritional profile: low Calories, no fat and simply bursting with vitamins A and C. This dish may be made in advance and rewarmed later or the next day.

- *3 red peppers*
- *3 yellow peppers*
- *175 ml (6 fl oz) stock*
- *freshly ground pepper to taste*

1 Cut the peppers in half lengthways. Remove the stalks, seeds and ribs. Cut the halves into their natural sections.
2 Peel each pepper piece with a swivel-bladed vegetable peeler. Cut each piece into strips about 1.25 cm (½ inch) wide.
3 Combine the peppers and stock in a heavy frying pan. Grind in some black pepper and bring to the boil. When boiling, use two wooden spoons to toss and turn the peppers in the hot stock until the liquid has cooked down considerably. Turn down the heat a little and 'fry' them for a few minutes in their own juices until very tender, and the pepper juices have formed a thick sauce. Serve with their delicious juices.

STIR 'FRIED' VEGETABLES

~

This technique works with:

- *thin asparagus, trimmed of the tough, woody stalks and cut into 2.5 cm (1 inch) pieces (thick asparagus needs to be peeled first)*
- *courgettes, cut into strips about 5 cm (2 inches) long and 1.25 cm (½ inch) thick*
- *cauliflower florets/mange tout*
- *tiny sweetcorn cobs*
- *carrots, peeled and cut into strips 4–5 cm (1½–2 inches) long and 1.25 cm (½ inch) wide*
- *runner beans*
- *approximately 60–75 ml (4–5 tbsp) stock*
- *15 ml (1 tbsp) lemon or lime juice*
- *salt and freshly ground pepper to taste*

1 Use a heavy bottomed non-reactive frying pan that is wide enough so that the vegetables are not crowded (they should be in one layer) or use a non-stick wok. Put your choice of prepared vegetable, in the pan.
2 Add the stock, lemon or lime juice and seasoning to taste. Bring to the boil. With a wooden spoon, constantly toss and turn the vegetables in the hot stock until they are crisp-tender, and the liquid has almost cooked away. Add a splash of stock and/or lemon or lime juice as needed, during the cooking.

GRILLED VEGETABLES

~

Grilling courgette and aubergine slices is a completely classic and time honoured technique, but traditionally it is done with oceans of olive oil. In an old time Italian deli, one sees trays of grilled aubergine (melanzane) and courgettes (zucchini) absolutely wallowing in turgid pools of the oil. Not only is this woefully calorific, but – to my mind – it ruins the glorious fresh taste of the vegetables, and the exquisitely subtle smokiness of the grilling process. A popular belief is that olive oil is a 'good' fat, i.e. beneficial to the heart. This concept is open to debate and current thinking is that it may *not* be particularly beneficial. However, there is no debate about the fact that it is *fattening*: more than 100 fat Calories per 15 ml (1 tbsp). And it's no secret that fat Calories are metabolized into body fat with heart breaking efficiency and rapidity. So why spoil the taste of your vegetables and the shape of your body? Grill the Slim Cuisine way instead.

GRILLED COURGETTES

~

- *approximately 5 medium courgettes, slant cut crossways, 0.6 cm (¼ inch) thick*

1 Preheat the grill to the highest setting.
2 Spread out the courgette slices in one layer on a non-stick baking sheet. Grill, close to the heat, for 3–5 minutes until speckled with brown. (No need to turn them.)
Serve grilled courgettes or aubergine (see opposite) hot or cold – with a squeeze of lime or lemon juice, a sprinkle of balsamic vinegar, a grinding of fresh pepper – whatever you like. Or use in recipes, such as Vegetable 'Lasagne' (see page 106) and Ratatouille (see page 104).

GRILLED AUBERGINE

- *1 large aubergine, sliced crossways, 0.6 cm (¼ inch) thick*

1 Preheat the grill to the highest setting.
2 Spread out the aubergine slices in one layer on a non-stick baking sheet. Grill, close to the heat, for 5–7 minutes or until lightly browned. (No need to turn them.) Cut each slice in half.

GRILLED PEPPERS

Another classic. Grilled peppers are sweet, smoky and meaty, and splendid on their own or in all sorts of recipes. (Green peppers may be used, but they are not as pretty, or as sweet.)

- *red and yellow peppers*

1 If you have a gas cooker, to grill the peppers place them directly on the flame on the burner plate. As the peppers blacken and char, turn them with tongs. Alternatively, cut them in half, place under the grill, cut side down, and grill until they blacken and char. I do mean *blackened* and *charred*. They will look absolutely awful but that is exactly how they should look. Remember: in this case, Burnt is Beautiful.
2 When blackened and charred, enclose the hot peppers in a plastic food bag and leave for a few minutes. Steam will form between the charred skin and the flesh, making peeling much easier. Strip off the charred skin and discard it. Discard the cores, seeds and stalks.

BAKED VEGETABLES

Baking root vegetables brings out their sweetness and flavour as no other method does. Once baked, they have a gloriously intense and *deep* taste. This technique works for swedes, turnips, carrots and parsnips.
1 Preheat the oven to 220°C, 425°F, Gas Mark 7.
2 Peel the chosen root vegetables. Small roots such as turnips, carrots and parsnips may be left whole. Large ones such as swedes may be cut into halves or quarters. Wrap each single vegetable loosely in foil, shiny side in. Crimp well, so that you have a tightly sealed but roomy pouch.

Bake for 1–1¼ hours until very tender and caramelized.

NOTE: Baked vegetables may be served as they are, or mashed and whipped with buttermilk or fromage frais. They may be mashed with an equal amount of potatoes. If you have garlic, beat in some Baked Garlic purée (see pages 74–75) as well.

BAKED AUBERGINE

~

The pulp of a baked aubergine gives a lovely flavour and texture to sauces, dips and spreads.

- *whole aubergines*

1 Preheat the oven to 200°C, 400°F, Gas Mark 6.

2 Pierce the aubergines in several places with a fork or thin skewer. Bake on the oven rack for 30–40 minutes until soft and collapsed. Cool.

3 Cut away the stalks and strip off and discard the skins. Finely chop or mash the aubergine pulp. (Discard any large, tough clumps of seeds.)

BAKED AUBERGINE – MICROWAVE VERSION

1 Pierce an aubergine in several places with a fork or thin skewer. Place it in a 20 cm (8 inch) square, 2.5–5 cm (1–2 inch) deep glass baking dish. Pour in 1.25 cm (½ inch) water. Cover tightly with microwave cling film. Microwave on HIGH for 6 minutes. Remove (do not uncover) and leave to stand for 5 minutes.

2 Pierce the cling film to allow steam to escape (stand back), then very carefully remove the cling film. Be careful not to get scalded by any residual steam. When cool enough to handle, strip off the skin with a blunt knife. Finely chop the pulp with a chef's knife.

BAKED ONION

~

There is nothing sweeter than a baked onion. Eat it cut into quarters and sprinkled with balsamic vinegar, or purée it in the blender, then stir the purée into mashed potatoes or baked, mashed vegetables.

- *large Spanish onions*

1 Preheat the oven to 220°C, 425°F, Gas Mark 7.
2 Put the onions on a double sheet of foil, shiny side out, but do not wrap them. Bake for 1¼ hours or until very soft and almost collapsed.
3 With a sharp knife, cut off the stem and root ends of the onions. Remove and discard the blackened skin and first layer. Serve as they are with pepper and lemon juice. Alternatively, purée the onions in a blender for use in other recipes.

BAKED POTATOES

The best baked potatoes take time, in a hot oven. Preheat the oven to 220°C, 425°F, Gas Mark 7. Pierce the potatoes in several places with a fork or thin skewer. Bake directly on the oven shelf for 1¼–1½ hours, turning once during the baking. When they are done, the potatoes are creamy – fluffy on the inside and exceptionally crunchy on the outside.

Always open your potatoes like this: with a fork, perforate the potato on top in a dotted cross (X). Then squeeze, so that the fluffy potato flesh surges up through the crunchy skin. If you use a knife to cut them open, instead of perforating with a fork and squeezing, you will not achieve the glorious fluffy, creamy, steamy effect that – against the crunchiness of the skin – makes a baked potato such a pleasure to eat.

Baked potatoes are delicious with a scattering of freshly ground pepper, a squeeze of fresh lemon, a dollop of fromage frais (or any of the creamy Slim Cuisine dips, dressings or spreads) or with lashings of any of the Slim Cuisine sauces.

BAKED POTATOES – QUICKER VERSION

Microwaving baking potatoes before you finish them off in the conventional oven saves at least ½ hour of baking time. They are very good, but not as *spectacular* as the conventional ones.

- *2 baking potatoes*

1 Preheat the oven to 220°C, 425°F, Gas Mark 7.
2 Place a double sheet of absorbent kitchen paper on the microwave turntable. Pierce each potato in several places with a thin skewer. Place the potatoes on the turntable. Microwave on FULL for 5 minutes.
3 Turn them over and cook for another 5 minutes.
4 Switch the potatoes to the conventional oven and bake for 20–30 minutes until cooked through with a very crisp skin.
5 With a fork, perforate the top of the potatoes lengthways and crossways and squeeze, so that the soft potato flesh comes surging up.

BAKED POTATO HALVES

~

This is unconventional, but easily my favourite of all the ways to bake potatoes. It results in a potato that combines the best qualities of baked, mashed and fried potatoes.

The method is very simple:

1 Preheat a conventional oven as hot as possible.

2 Halve two baking potatoes (I've done this – with excellent results – with Cara, Maris Piper and King Edward potatoes). Put a double sheet of absorbent kitchen paper on the microwave turntable. Place the potatoes, skin side down, on the paper. Microwave on FULL for 5 minutes.

3 Turn the potatoes skin side up, then microwave on FULL for another 5 minutes.

4 Place the potatoes directly on the rack of the conventional oven, skin side down. Bake for 10 minutes. Turn skin side up, then bake for another 10 minutes. Serve at once. Eat as is, or serve with a dollop of Slim Cuisine smooth Tomato Sauce (see page 122) and a dollop of fromage frais. Dunk pieces of these exemplary potatoes into the dips, and eat.

'FRIED' POTATOES

~

This technique of 'frying' chip potatoes in the oven is one of the mainstays of my revolution. Renounce the chip pan forever! It's so much easier my way – imagine: never again a chip pan fire, never again the disgusting smell of overheated fat clinging to your clothes and hair, never again the nauseating taste and texture of grease on your lips. And for once, glory in the taste of *potatoes*! When was the last time you ate chips and actually tasted the *potatoes*, and not the abused oil? Use baking potatoes: King Edwards or Maris Pipers are excellent.

1 Preheat the oven to 220°C, 425°F, Gas Mark 7.

2 Don't bother to peel the potatoes. Cut them crossways into 0.6–1.25 cm (¼–½ inch) slices. Cut each slice in half or cut the potatoes lengthways into strips.

3 You will need one or two flat baking sheets with non-stick coating. Spread the potatoes on the sheet(s) in one layer. Cook in the oven for ½ hour.

4 Remove the potatoes and, with a spatula, gently turn them. Return to the oven for about another 10–20 minutes. (The timing depends on the thickness of the slices, and on your oven.) By this time they should be browned, crunchy on the outside and puffed. Serve at once. (They may be sprinkled with salt if desired, but I find they don't really need it.)

NOTE: If you are using more than one baking sheet, you will need to switch their positions during baking, so that they all bake evenly.

'FRIED' POTATOES – MICROWAVE VERSION

- *2 large baking potatoes, approximately 350 g (12 oz) each*
- *salt (optional)*

1 Preheat the oven to 200°C, 400°F, Gas Mark 6.
2 Scrub the potatoes but do not peel them. Pierce them in several places with a fork or thin skewer. Line the microwave turntable with a piece of absorbent kitchen paper.
3 Place the potatoes on the turntable. Microwave on FULL for 6 minutes, turning the potatoes over after 3 minutes.
4 Remove the potatoes and allow to stand for 5 minutes.
5 With a sharp knife, cut each potato lengthways into 0.6–1.25 cm (¼–½ inch) thick strips. Arrange in one layer on one or two non-stick baking sheets. Bake in the conventional oven for approximately 20–30 minutes, turning the potatoes with tongs about half-way through, and shaking the sheet every once in a while so that they do not stick. When they are beautifully browned and a bit puffy, they are done. Salt lightly if desired.

Miss Dell said . . . 'Some heads ask us to limit how often we serve chips. But we feel that if we only serve them one day a week, the children will go mad on that day . . .' One girl waiting to collect her lunch asked the staff: 'Ain't you got no decent food? No chips?'

FROM A REPORT ON SCHOOL MEALS BY ANNABEL FERRIMAN, IN THE *SUNDAY OBSERVER*

POTATO CRISPS

1 LARGE BAKING POTATO MAKES APPROXIMATELY 50 CRISPS

~

It may take you one or two tries to get this technique right for your particular oven, but – believe me – *it's worth it*! If you want these crisps to last for any time at all, you'll have to hide them. Moreish does not begin to describe their allure.

Approximately 275 g (10 oz) potato will probably fill 2 non-stick baking sheets. Prepare as many as are necessary.

- *1 baking potato (King Edward or Maris Piper)*
- *salt (optional)*

1 Preheat the oven to 180°C, 350°F, Gas Mark 4.
2 Slice the potato paper thin, using a mandoline, the slicing disc of a food processor or the slicing side of an old fashioned grater.
3 Place in a single layer on a non-stick baking sheet. It *must* be a trusty, unscratched non-stick sheet. Glass, or anything else, will not work. Salt lightly if desired. Bake for approximately 15 minutes. Reposition the crisps on the sheets, then reposition the sheets if necessary. Bake for another 3–5 minutes or until crisp, browned but not burnt.

♡

ROAST POTATOES

~

Forget drippings – you are going to love fat-free roasted spuds. My Slim Cuisine Diet study subjects dote on these potatoes.

- *stock*

small whole new pototoes, or medium potatoes, halved or quartered

- *salt and freshly ground pepper to taste*

1 Preheat the oven to 200°C, 400°F, Gas Mark 6.
2 Pour stock into a shallow baking dish to a depth of about 0.6 cm (¼ inch). Put the potatoes in the dish in one layer. Season, then stir.
3 Bake, uncovered, for 40–50 minutes, shaking the dish and stirring occasionally. When they are browned and tender, they are done. (Pour a little more stock into the dish as necessary during cooking.)

♡

MASHED POTATOES – BAKED METHOD

In my opinion, to make truly exceptional mashed potatoes, you have to bake them first (see page 91). Scoop the potato flesh out of the baked potatoes into a bowl. Mash well with a potato masher. Using a wooden spoon or an electric mixer, beat in some fromage frais, *or* some buttermilk, *or* some skimmed milk that has been mixed with a little skimmed milk powder for richness. Beat in salt and freshly ground pepper to taste. Eat them out of a large bowl, with a large spoon. If you wish, garnish around the edges with Slim Cuisine 'Fried' Onions (see page 83), Sautéed Mushrooms (see page 86) and warm Peperonata (see page 99). As an evening meal, mashed potoatoes ensure a restful night filled with sweet dreams.

The advantage of the baked potato method is twofold:
1 The quality of the mash is quite marvellous.
2 You have those seductive potato skins left over, just begging to be

eaten. Eat them as is on the spot, or refrigerate and save them for an indulgent snack. At snack time, cut them into strips and grill for a few minutes (not too long) to crisp them. Grind on some pepper and salt lightly, if you wish. Eat plain, or with a Slim Cuisine dip or sauce.

MASHED POTATOES – OTHER METHODS

Of course, you can also prepare mashed potatoes by quartering baking potatoes and boiling them until tender. Then strip off the skins, cut into chunks and toss in the pan to dry; finally mash. Or you can microwave potatoes until tender before peeling and mashing. The choice is yours.

MASHED POTATOES – PACKET METHOD

Many brands of packet potatoes are just not worth eating. Read the labels – if they contain fat or salt, don't buy them. There are a few brands, made in France and available in British supermarkets, that contain neither. They are flakes rather than those awful pellets. Mixed with boiling water or stock, seasoned to your taste, then beaten until creamy with a little buttermilk or a dollop of fromage frais, they can be quite palatable. If you are an extremely busy person, and you crave mashed potatoes (who isn't and who doesn't?), these may be the answer.

. . . 'These mashed potatoes are good' said I one night while I was tucking away a splendid pork roast. 'You must have paralysed your arm mashing them.' 'Instant', she said. 'No', I said. 'Nothing instant

is any good.' 'Are these good?' 'Marvellous.' 'They're instant.' She went into the kitchen and came back with an empty carton. 'Out of here, they came . . .' I have not mashed a potato since that night of revelation. Instant mashed potatoes are as good as instant coffee is unfit to drink.

THE HAPHAZARD GOURMET, RICHARD GEHMAN

BRAISED VEGETABLES

Braised vegetables have a melting tenderness, plus – as they braise in the oven – they fill the kitchen with a mouthwatering fragrance. The braising method works beautifully with the following:

- *fennel, trimmed, halved lengthways and cut into 1.25 cm (½ inch) wedges*
- *cauliflower, trimmed and separated into florets*
- *Brussels sprouts, trimmed*
- *courgettes, trimmed (unpeeled) and cut into 1.25–2.5 cm (½–1 inch) dice*
- *aubergines, trimmed (unpeeled) and cut into 1.25–2.5 cm (½–1 inch) dice*

1 Preheat the oven to 180°C, 350°F, Gas Mark 4.
2 Prepare the chosen vegetable. Spread out the pieces in a shallow baking or gratin dish. Pour in approximately 175 ml (6 fl oz) stock. Sprinkle with a tiny bit of salt and a generous grinding of pepper.
3 Bake, uncovered, shaking the pan and stirring up the vegetable pieces occasionally, for 45 minutes to 1 hour until the vegetables are tender, browned and deeply delicious. Adjust seasonings to taste.

CURRIED GRATIN OF PURÉED BAKED VEGETABLES

This is a beautiful and delicious way of treating baked, mashed vegetables. I'm always amazed at how *fattening* no-fat food can taste. No one would ever guess that this is *diet* food!

- *1 onion, skinned and chopped*
- *300 ml (½ pint) stock*
- *2.5 ml (½ tsp) ground coriander*
- *2.5 ml (½ tsp) ground cumin*
- *2.5 ml (½ tsp) mild chilli powder*
- *2.5 ml (½ tsp) paprika or paprika paste*
- *2.5 ml (½ tsp) ground ginger*
- *salt and freshly ground pepper to taste*
- *1.25 ml (¼ tsp) ground turmeric*
- *1.25 ml (¼ tsp) ground allspice*
- *1.25 ml (¼ tsp) cayenne pepper (optional)*
- *2 baked turnips, puréed or mashed (see technique page 89)*
- *1 head baked garlic, puréed or mashed (see page 74)*
- *2 baked carrots, puréed or mashed (see page 89)*
- *3 baked parsnips, puréed or mashed (see page 89)*
- *1 baked swede, puréed or mashed (see page 89)*
- *30–45 ml (2–3 tbsp) skimmed milk*

1 Preheat the oven to 200°C, 400°F, Gas Mark 6.

2 Separate the segments of the chopped onion pieces and spread them in a heavy frying pan. Add *no* liquid or fat. Heat the frying pan gently. Cook over moderate heat, without stirring, for 7–10 minutes until the onions are sizzling, speckled with dark amber and beginning to stick to the pan.

3 Stir in the stock and let it bubble up, stirring up the browned deposits in the pan with a wooden spoon as it bubbles. Stir in the spices. Turn the heat down a little and simmer, stirring frequently, until the mixture is very thick (not at all soupy) and the onions and spices are 'frying' in their own juices. Don't rush this step, it is essential that the spices should not have a raw harsh taste. Taste, then cook very gently for a few more minutes if necessary.

4 Combine the onion-spice mixture with the puréed vegetables. (To purée the vegetables, cut them into chunks and place in a food processor. Process until very smooth. Or mash with a potato masher.) Spread the mixture into a 20 cm (8 inch) square gratin dish.

5 Pour a thin drizzle of milk evenly over the top of the gratin.

6 Bake for 45–55 minutes until bubbly, puffy and browned on top.

AUBERGINE 'CAVIARE'

MAKES 570 ML (1 PINT)

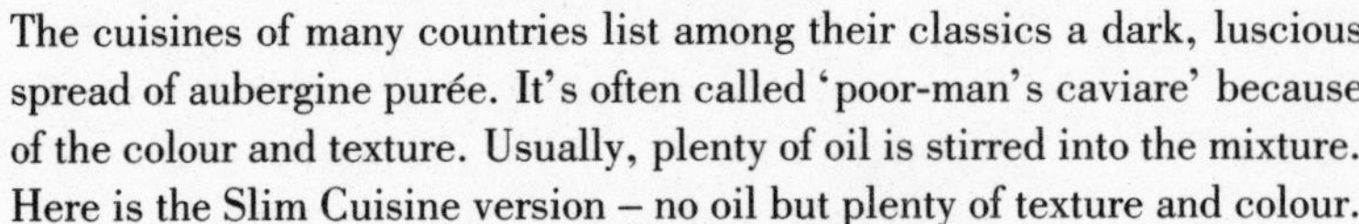

The cuisines of many countries list among their classics a dark, luscious spread of aubergine purée. It's often called 'poor-man's caviare' because of the colour and texture. Usually, plenty of oil is stirred into the mixture. Here is the Slim Cuisine version – no oil but plenty of texture and colour.

- *coarsely chopped flesh from 2 medium roasted aubergines (see page 000)*
- *purée from 1 large head baked garlic (see page 74)*
- *2 red peppers, grilled, peeled and diced (see page 89), or use canned pepper*
- *1 large ripe tomato, skinned, seeded and chopped, or out of season, use 2–3 canned Italian tomatoes, drained and chopped*
- *juice of ½ lemon*
- *2–4 thin spring onions, trimmed, cut in half lengthways and thinly sliced crossways*
- *90 ml (6 tbsp) chopped fresh parsley*
- *45 ml (3 tbsp) chopped fresh mint*
- *salt and freshly ground pepper to taste*

1 Combine all ingredients in a non-reactive bowl. With an electric mixer, beat into a rough purée. Taste and adjust seasoning.
2 Transfer the purée to a glass or ceramic bowl and chill.

BRAISED ONION

MAKES 900 ML (1½ PINTS)

This recipe yields crisp-tender onions, with slightly charred bits here and there, bathed in a sweet and sour sauce.

- *4 large Spanish onions, skinned and cut into eighths*
- *15 ml (1 tbsp) Dijon mustard*
- *30 ml (2 tbsp) balsamic vinegar*
- *300 ml (½ pint) stock*
- *salt and freshly ground pepper to taste*

1 Preheat the oven to 200°C, 400°F, Gas Mark 6.
2 In a bowl, toss all ingredients together until the onions are thoroughly coated. Spread the onions out in a baking dish that can hold them in one layer.
3 Bake, uncovered, for ½–¾ hour, stirring once or twice during this time.

PEPERONATA

MAKES 750 ML (26 FL OZ)

~

This mixture is based on a classic Italian pepper-onion-caper melange.

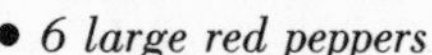

- *6 large red peppers*
- *1 large Spanish onion, skinned, halved and cut into thin half moons*
- *2 cloves garlic, skinned and finely chopped*
- *50 ml (2 fl oz) dry white vermouth*
- *175 ml (6 fl oz) stock*
- *15 ml (1 tbsp) drained capers*
- *salt and freshly ground pepper to taste*
- *30 ml (2 tbsp) chopped fresh parsley*

1 Remove the stalks, cores and seeds from the peppers, then cut them into their natural sections. Peel with a swivel-bladed vegetable peeler. Cut each piece into strips about 1.25 cm (½ inch) wide.
2 Combine the peppers, onion, garlic, vermouth, stock and capers in a heavy bottomed, non-reactive frying pan. Grind in some pepper. Bring to the boil and toss and turn the vegetables in the stock until the liquid has cooked down considerably.
3 Let the vegetables 'fry' in their own juices until beautifully tender. Salt lightly if necessary. Stir in the parsley. Serve hot or cold as a salad, relish, sandwich filling or a vegetable.

VARIATIONS: Squeeze in some fresh lemon juice when you stir in the parsley in step 3. Refrigerate until needed. Alternatively, add some fresh Brussels sprouts, steamed until tender but not mushy, to the vegetables in step 3. Or add thawed baby sprouts. Serve hot or cold.

Simple Vegetable Soup

MAKES 1.4 LITRES (2½ PINTS)

You must try this soup. It is a perfect example of how cooking vegetables in their own juices, with no fat or oil, brings out their depth of flavour.

- *2 medium carrots, peeled and coarsely diced*
- *1 large onion, skinned, halved and sliced into thin half moons*
- *3 cloves garlic, skinned and crushed*
- *1.4 litres (2½ pints) chicken or vegetable stock*
- *3 peppers (1 red, 1 yellow and 1 green), cored, seeded, peeled and coarsely diced*
- *3 small courgettes, coarsely diced*
- *5 ripe tomatoes, skinned, seeded and quartered (see note page 82) (substitute canned tomatoes if necessary)*
- *salt and freshly ground pepper to taste*
- *45 ml (3 tbsp) chopped fresh parsley*
- *1 bunch chives, finely snipped*

1 Combine the carrots, onion, garlic and 300 ml (½ pint) of the stock in a heavy bottomed soup pan. Cover, bring to the boil and boil for 7 minutes. Uncover, reduce the heat a little and simmer briskly until the onions are browning and sticking, and the liquid is almost gone. Add the peppers and a splash of stock. Cook for a few minutes, stirring.

2 Stir in the courgettes, tomatoes and remaining stock. Simmer for 10–15 minutes. Season and stir in the herbs. Cook for 1–2 minutes more.

Soup Of Creamy Greens

MAKES 1.7 LITRES (3 PINTS)

I tried to make an Italian minestrone verde; the kind that involves throwing a bunch of vegetables into a pan of stock or water to simmer for a while. In the classic version, a couple of dollops of fruity olive oil are added at the end; of course I eliminated them. What a disaster! The soup was so bland that it tasted like that horrible four letter word (Diet). How could a potful of beautiful vegetables become so tasteless? On a whim,

I put the disaster into the blender and blended it to green velvet. The difference was astounding; in fact I polished off the potful all by myself.

- *1 large Spanish onion, skinned and coarsely chopped*
- *4 sticks celery, coarsely chopped*
- *2 cloves garlic, skinned and crushed*
- *¼ small green or white cabbage, cored and coarsely chopped*
- *1 small bulb fennel, trimmed and coarsely chopped*
- *3 small courgettes, trimmed and coarsely diced*
- *½ bunch broccoli, trimmed and coarsely chopped*
- *110 g (4 oz) runner beans, trimmed and sliced into 2.5 cm (1 inch) pieces*
- *1 medium all-purpose potato, scrubbed and coarsely diced*
- *1.1 litres (2 pints) stock*
- *salt and freshly ground pepper to taste*
- *90 ml (6 tbsp) chopped fresh parsley*
- *60 ml (4 tbsp) shredded fresh basil*

1 Combine all the ingredients (use only a modest amount of salt), except the herbs, in a large, heavy soup pan. Cover and bring to the boil. Reduce the heat and simmer, partially covered, for 45 minutes, stirring occasionally.

2 Add the herbs and more seasoning if necessary. Simmer for 5–10 minutes more. Cool slightly.

3 Purée in batches in a blender or food processor until *very* smooth and velvety. (This soup should not be chunky.) Reheat, taste and adjust seasoning.

SOUP OF POTATO AND CARAMELIZED ONIONS

MAKES 2 LITRES (3½ PINTS)

There are infinite versions of potato soup; this one, based on the compelling taste of deeply sautéed onions, was inspired by a soup sampled recently in Portugal.

- *3 large Spanish onions, skinned and chopped or sliced*
- *4 cloves garlic, skinned and crushed*
- *1.4 litres (2½ pints) chicken or vegetable stock*
- *4 medium all-purpose potatoes, peeled and coarsely diced*
- *salt and freshly ground pepper to taste*
- *chopped fresh parsley*

1 Combine the onions, garlic and 300 ml (½ pint) of the stock in a heavy bottomed soup pan. Cover, bring to the boil and boil for 5–7 minutes. Uncover, reduce heat a little and simmer until the onions are amber brown and the liquid is almost gone.

2 Stir in the potatoes and a splash or two of additional stock. Stir and cook for a minute or two, scraping up the browned bits as you do so. Add the remaining stock and season to taste. Cook for ½ hour until tender.

3 In batches, purée the soup in a blender or food processor. Be careful not to fill the blender more than halfway or it will overflow. Pulse the machine on and off until the soup is roughly puréed. It shouldn't be perfectly smooth. Return the soup to the pan and reheat. Taste and adjust seasonings. Serve each bowlful of soup garnished with parsley.

HERBED ONION-TOMATO SOUP

MAKES 2 LITRES (3½ PINTS)

~

You either love fresh coriander or you hate it. I, and all members of my household, love it. If you do too, you'll love what it does to this lively tomato soup, but if you find the taste peculiar and musty, leave it out.

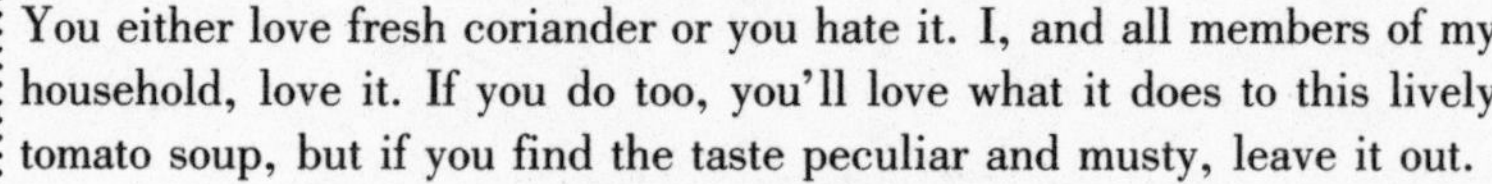

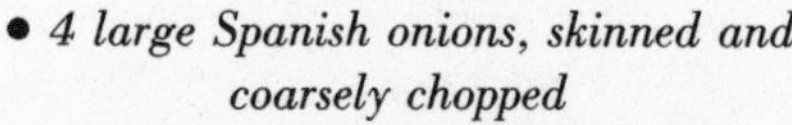

- *4 large Spanish onions, skinned and coarsely chopped*
- *4 large cloves garlic, skinned and crushed*
- *1.4 litres (2½ pints) stock*
- *2 cans (800 g/1 lb 12 oz each) Italian tomatoes, drained*
- *salt and freshly ground pepper to taste*
- *45 ml (3 tbsp) chopped fresh parsley*
- *45 ml (3 tbsp) chopped fresh mint*
- *30 ml (2 tbsp) chopped fresh coriander (optional)*

1 Combine the onions, garlic and 300 ml (½ pint) of the stock in a heavy bottomed soup pan. Cover, bring to the boil and boil for 5–7 minutes. Uncover, lower the heat a little and simmer until the onions are amber brown and beginning to stick, and the liquid is almost gone. Add a splash or two of stock, then cook for a minute or two more, stirring up the browned deposits on the bottom of the pan.

2 Crush the drained tomatoes with your hands. Add them, with the remaining stock, to the pan. Simmer, uncovered, stirring occasionally until thick and savoury. Season to taste and stir in the herbs. Serve at once, or cool and refrigerate until needed.

CREAMY PARSNIP SOUP

MAKES 1.3 LITRES (2¼ PINTS)

The *best* dinner party soup: elegant, very slightly piquant, creamy, and quite outrageously delicious. Make plenty.

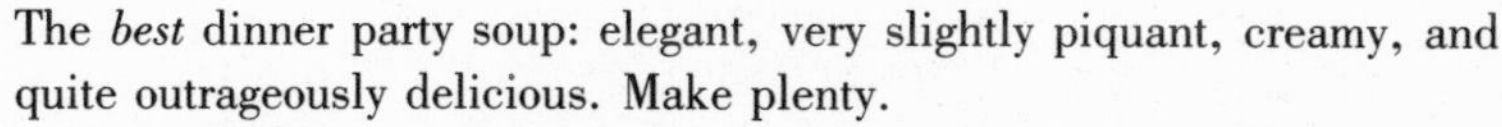

- *1 large Spanish onion, skinned and chopped*
- *5 ml (1 tsp) finely chopped fresh ginger*
- *2 cloves garlic, skinned and crushed*
- *1.7 litres (3 pints) stock*
- *5 ml (1 tsp) garam masala*
- *1.25 ml (¼ tsp) cayenne pepper*
- *450 g (1 lb) parsnips, peeled and diced*
- *1 medium all-purpose potato, scrubbed and coarsely diced*
- *salt and freshly ground pepper to taste*

1 Combine the onion, ginger, garlic and 300 ml (½ pint) of the stock in a heavy bottomed soup pan. Cover, bring to the boil and boil for 5–7 minutes. Uncover, reduce the heat a little and simmer, stirring until the onions are tender and amber brown, and the liquid is almost gone. Add a splash of stock and stir and cook, for another minute or two more, scraping up the browned bits. Add the garam masala and cayenne and stir so that the onions are well coated with the spices.

2 Stir in the parsnips, potato and remaining stock. Simmer for 10–15 minutes until the parsnips and potatoes are very tender. Season to taste. Cool slightly.

3 Purée in batches in a blender until smooth and velvety. (This soup should not be chunky.) Return to the pan and heat gently. Correct seasonings and serve.

RATATOUILLE

MAKES 2.8 LITRES (5 PINTS)

~

This is a very special ratatouille. Between the smokiness of the grilled vegetables and the well rounded taste of the tomato sauce, you'll never miss the olive oil. The recipe makes a large amount of ratatouille, because I can't imagine making a small amount of such a useful recipe. It keeps in the refrigerator for days, freezes beautifully, and can be eaten on its own, with potatoes, or it can be thinned with stock to become soup.

- *2 aubergines, trimmed, sliced and grilled (see page 89)*
- *8 courgettes, trimmed, sliced and grilled (see page 88)*
- *6 grilled peppers (2 red, 2 yellow, 2 green) (see page 89) or use canned peppers*
- *570 ml (1 pint) Tomato Sauce (see page 122)*
- *90 ml (6 tbsp) chopped fresh parsley*
- *90 ml (6 tbsp) shredded fresh basil*

1 Preheat the oven to 180°C, 350°F, Gas Mark 4.
2 Cut the grilled aubergine and courgette slices in half crossways. Cut the peppers into strips.
3 Mix the grilled vegetables with the tomato sauce and herbs. Simmer, uncovered, in a heavy bottomed pan for approximately 15–20 minutes until the ingredients have 'married'.

POTATO-RATATOUILLE PIE

Spread a layer of Mashed Potatoes (see page 94) in a small shallow baking dish. Top with a layer of Ratatouille, then spread another layer of mashed potatoes over the top. Drizzle a little skimmed milk evenly over the top. Bake in the oven at 180°C, 350°F, Gas Mark 4 for 30–40 minutes until browned on top and bubbly.

GRATIN OF MEDITERRANEAN VEGETABLES

MAKES ONE 20 CM (8 INCH) SQUARE GRATIN

~

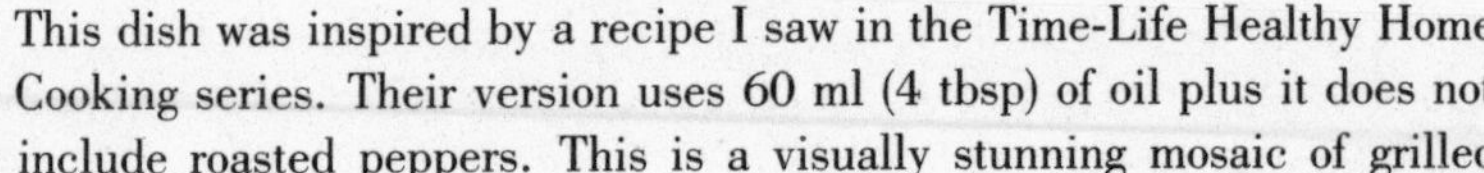

This dish was inspired by a recipe I saw in the Time-Life Healthy Home Cooking series. Their version uses 60 ml (4 tbsp) of oil plus it does not include roasted peppers. This is a visually stunning mosaic of grilled vegetables on a bed of caramelized onions and fennel. It would be a good choice for a dinner party.

- *3 large Spanish onions, skinned, cut in half and sliced into thin half moons*
- *3 cloves garlic, skinned and crushed*
- *2 bulbs fennel, trimmed and sliced thinly crossways*
- *225–300 ml (8–10 fl oz) stock*
- *50–75 ml (2–3 fl oz) dry white vermouth (optional)*
- *1 aubergine, sliced crossways 0.6 cm (¼ inch) thick*
- *3 courgettes, sliced crossways 0.6 cm (¼ inch) thick*
- *2 peppers (1 red, 1 yellow), halved, grilled, each half cut into 4 cm (1½ inch) squares*
- *4 ripe tomatoes, skinned and thinly sliced*

1 Preheat the grill.

2 Combine the onions, garlic, fennel and 225 ml (8 fl oz) stock in a heavy enamelled frying pan. Cover, bring to the boil and boil for 7 minutes. Uncover and cook briskly until the liquid is almost gone, and the vegetables are beginning to stick to the bottom of the pan. Pour in a splash of vermouth or additional stock. Cook and stir, scraping up the browned bits on the bottom of the pan, until the vegetables are meltingly tender and amber brown.

3 Meanwhile, spread out the aubergine in one layer on a non-stick baking sheet. Brush with stock. Grill, close to the heat for 5 minutes or so until browned. (Grill on one side only.) Cut each slice in half.

4 Spread out the courgette slices in one layer on a non-stick baking sheet. Grill, close to the heat, for 3–5 minutes until speckled with brown. (Grill on one side only.)

5 To assemble the gratin, in a 20 cm (8 inch) square gratin dish spread out the onion-fennel mixture. Overlap a row of aubergine slices on the onions. Follow with a row of courgette slices, a row of yellow pepper pieces, a row of aubergine, a row of tomato slices, a row of courgettes, a row of red peppers, and so on, until all the vegetables are used. The finished dish should look like a beautiful jewelled mosaic. The gratin may be refrigerated at this point and kept for a day or two.

6 To cook the gratin, preheat the oven to 190°C, 375°F, Gas Mark 5. Cover the gratin with foil, shiny side down. Bake for ½ hour. Brush the vegetables with a little stock. Bake uncovered for 10 minutes.

VEGETABLE 'LASAGNE'

This is a lasagne that contains no pasta or cheese; simply layers of grilled vegetables, rich tomato sauce and fresh herbs. Oh, the wonderful Therapeutic Binges you can have, when you know how to cook vegetables so they give you the most flavour possible!

- *1 large aubergine, sliced crossways 0.6 cm (¼ inch) thick*
- *5 medium courgettes, sliced crossways 0.6 cm (¼ inch) thick*
- *approximately 570 ml (1 pint) Tomato Sauce (see page 122)*
- *salt and freshly ground pepper to taste*
- *15 ml (1 tbsp) each shredded fresh basil and chopped fresh parsley, mixed*

1 Preheat the grill.

2 Spread out the aubergine slices in one layer on a non-stick baking sheet. Grill, close to the heat, for 5–7 minutes or until lightly browned. (No need to turn them.) Cut each slice in half and set aside.

3 Spread out the courgette slices in one layer on a non-stick baking sheet. Grill, close to the heat, for 3–5 minutes until speckled with brown. Set aside.

4 Preheat the oven to 180°C, 350°F, Gas Mark 4.

5 Spread 300 ml (½ pint) of the tomato sauce on the bottom of a 20 cm (8 inch) square gratin dish. Sprinkle with salt, pepper and 15 ml (1 tbsp) of the mixed herbs. Arrange a single layer of aubergine slices on the herbs. Top with a layer of courgette slices.

6 Spread on the remaining tomato sauce and sprinkle with the remaining herbs. Alternate rows of aubergine and courgettes for the next layer.

7 Bake for 40–50 minutes. Leave to stand for 5–10 minutes before cutting into squares to serve.

POTATO TZATZIKI SALAD

MAKES 1.4 LITRES (2½ PINTS)

I saw a potato tzatziki salad displayed in the refrigerator case in a London deli, and thought it a wonderful idea. I couldn't wait to get home and work on a version. Tzatziki is a creamy Greek mixture of cucumbers, garlic and yogurt: tzatziki and potatoes seem meant for each other. Use fromage frais, rather than yogurt, if you object to the sourness of yogurt.

- *960 ml (1³⁄₅ pints) very low-fat yogurt or fromage frais*
- *2 large cucumbers*
- *salt*
- *2 large cloves garlic, skinned and finely chopped*
- *7.5 ml (1½ tsp) white wine vinegar*
- *freshly ground pepper to taste*
- *steamed new potatoes, halved or quartered, depending on size*
- *90 ml (6 tbsp) chopped fresh parsley*

1 Line a sieve or colander with a long piece of doubled damp muslin. (Rinse it first in cold water, then wring out well.) Place the lined sieve over a large bowl. Add the yogurt, fold the muslin over to cover well and leave for 6–7 hours. Every once in a while, pour off the liquid that accumulates in the bowl.

2 Peel the cucumbers and cut them in half lengthways. Use a teaspoon to scrape out the seeds and discard them. Grate the cucumbers into a non-reactive colander. Salt them and allow to drain for ½ hour. This draws out their bitterness.

3 Place the garlic and vinegar in a small bowl and allow to marinate while the cucumbers are draining.

4 Rinse the drained cucumbers, squeeze them as dry as possible and blot on absorbent kitchen paper. Place in the bowl with the marinated garlic. Add the drained yogurt and a few grindings of fresh pepper, then stir.

5 Fold together the yogurt mixture, potatoes and parsley. Adjust seasoning.

VEGETABLE FILLED CABBAGE ROLLS

MAKES ABOUT 20 CABBAGE ROLLS

~

My vegetarian version of stuffed cabbage has great delicacy. It's best if the sauce is made with ripe summer tomatoes, or with good tomatoes that you've ripened slowly at room temperature (see page 82). If neither are available, try a corresponding amount of ripe cherry tomatoes or canned Italian chopped tomatoes.

Freezing, then thawing the cabbage, softens the leaves and eliminates the need for blanching them. Before you freeze the cabbage, cut out and discard the tough core.

- *1 frozen cabbage, thawed*

STUFFING

- *1 large Spanish onion, skinned and coarsely chopped*
- *2 cloves garlic, skinned*
- *225 ml (8 fl oz) stock*
- *50 ml (2 fl oz) wine*
- *3 small new potatoes, unpeeled and diced*
- *2 carrots, peeled and diced*
- *salt and freshly ground pepper to taste*
- *7.5 ml (½ tbsp) fresh thyme leaves*
- *15 ml (1 tbsp) shredded fresh basil*
- *15 ml (1 tbsp) chopped fresh parsley*
- *2 courgettes, diced*
- *15 ml (1 tbsp) tomato purée*

SAUCE

- *10 large ripe tomatoes, cut into chunks*
- *10 red peppers, cored, seeded and cut into chunks*
- *generous 15 ml (1 tbsp) shredded fresh basil*
- *generous 15 ml (1 tbsp) chopped fresh parsley*
- *7.5 ml (½ tbsp) chopped fresh thyme*
- *salt and freshly ground pepper to taste*

1 For the stuffing, put the onion, garlic and 100 ml (4 fl oz) of the stock in a frying pan. Cover and boil for 5 minutes. Uncover and pour in the wine. Boil, while scraping up the browned bits.

2 When the onion is browned and tender, add the potatoes and carrots. Pour in the remaining stock, cover and simmer until tender but not mushy.

3 Add seasoning and herbs, then stir in the courgettes. Simmer uncovered for approximately 10 minutes until everything is tender, and the liquid is absorbed. Stir in the tomato purée. Taste and adjust seasonings. Set aside.

4 For the sauce, combine the tomatoes and peppers in a frying pan. Simmer uncovered for 20–25 minutes until thickened and the peppers are very tender.

5 Purée in a blender and push through a sieve. Add the herbs and season to taste. Set aside.

6 Separate the cabbage into individual leaves. Place a cabbage leaf on a work surface. With a sharp paring knife, pare down the tough vein. Repeat until all the leaves are trimmed.

7 Preheat the oven to 180°C, 350°F, Gas Mark 4.

8 To assemble the rolls, put a cabbage leaf on a work surface. Place 15–30 ml (1–2 tbsp) stuffing on the leaf (the amount depends on the size of the leaf). Fold the end over the stuffing, fold in the sides and roll to make a neat parcel. Place in a baking dish, seam side down, in a single layer. Repeat until all leaves are filled (about 20 in all).
9 When the rolls are in the dish spread the sauce over them.
10 Cover and bake for 1 hour.

NEW MEXICAN SALAD

MAKES 1.1 LITRES (2 PINTS) SALSA

MAKES APPROXIMATELY 450 ML (¾ PINT) DRESSING

Both the salsa and the creamy dressing may be used on their own. This is a sociable salad, involving plenty of friendly dipping and munching.

CHUNKY SALSA

- *2 cans (800 g/1 lb 12 oz each) Italian tomatoes, drained and coarsely chopped*
- *1 (400 g/14 oz) can red peppers (pimientos), drained and coarsely chopped*
- *finely chopped chilli to taste*
- *2 cloves garlic, skinned and crushed*
- *45 ml (3 tbsp) chopped fresh parsley*
- *15 ml (1 tbsp) chopped fresh coriander*
- *15 ml (1 tbsp) chopped fresh mint*
- *2–4 thin spring onions, trimmed and finely chopped*
- *50 ml (2 fl oz) wine vinegar*

CREAMY DRESSING

- *475 ml (16 fl oz) fromage frais*
- *90 ml (6 tbsp) chopped fresh mint*
- *45 ml (3 tbsp) chopped fresh coriander*

SALAD

- *Cos lettuce leaves, washed and dried*
- *chicory leaves, washed and dried*
- *cherry tomatoes*
- *baby sweetcorn cobs*
- *grilled courgette slices (see page 88)*
- *grilled pepper strips, yellow and red (see page 89)*
- *button mushroom caps*
- *Potato Crisps (see page 93)*
- *jalapeno peppers in vinegar, drained and sliced (optional)*

1 For the salsa, combine all the ingredients together in a large bowl. Refrigerate until needed.
2 For the dressing, combine the fromage frais and herbs together well in a bowl. Refrigerate until needed.
3 For each serving, pour some salsa into a small glass bowl and the creamy dressing into another. Arrange the lettuce leaves, chicory leaves, cherry tomatoes, corn cobs, grilled courgette slices, grilled pepper strips and mushroom caps beautifully on a large plate. Pile a lavish amount of potato crisps in the centre of the arrangement. Provide a bowl of sliced jalapenos for those who can stand the heat.
4 Use the vegetables to dunk into the dips.

BRAISED AUBERGINE, CHINESE STYLE

MAKES 1.1 LITRES (2 PINTS)

Aubergines are like potatoes, they soak up flavourings so well. This version of braised aubergine contains Cantonese seasonings – fresh ginger, soy sauce and sherry.

- *6 medium aubergines, trimmed (unpeeled) and cut into 2.5 cm (1 inch) cubes*
- *3 large cloves garlic, skinned and finely chopped*
- *45 ml (3 tbsp) finely chopped fresh ginger*
- *15 ml (1 tbsp) soy sauce or teriyaki sauce*
- *45 ml (3 tbsp) medium sherry*
- *225 ml (8 fl oz) stock*
- *freshly ground pepper to taste*

1 Preheat the oven to 180°C, 350°F, Gas Mark 4.
2 Spread out the aubergine in a shallow, non-reactive baking or gratin dish. Combine the remaining ingredients and pour over the aubergine. Bake, uncovered, shaking the pan and stirring up the vegetable pieces occasionally, for 45 minutes to 1 hour until the aubergine is tender, browned and deeply delicious. Serve hot.

POTATO-CAULIFLOWER CURRY

MAKES 1.7 LITRES (3 PINTS)

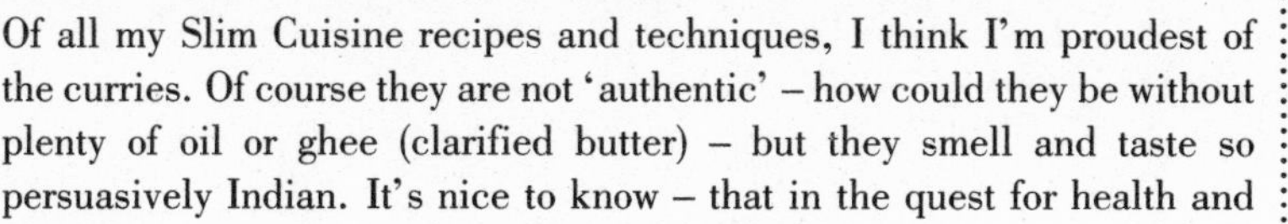

Of all my Slim Cuisine recipes and techniques, I think I'm proudest of the curries. Of course they are not 'authentic' – how could they be without plenty of oil or ghee (clarified butter) – but they smell and taste so persuasively Indian. It's nice to know – that in the quest for health and slimness – you don't have to give up curry meals.

- *3 large onions, skinned and cut into wedges (eighths)*
- *570 ml (1 pint) stock*
- *2 cloves garlic, skinned and crushed*
- *15 ml (1 tbsp) finely chopped fresh ginger*
- *2.5 ml (½ tsp) ground turmeric*
- *1.25 ml (¼ tsp) cayenne pepper*
- *7.5 ml (1½ tsp) ground coriander*
- *2.5 ml (½ tsp) ground cardamom*
- *2.5 ml (½ tsp) ground allspice*
- *15 ml (1 tbsp) tomato purée*
- *1 medium cauliflower, separated into florets*
- *3 medium all-purpose potatoes, cut into 1.25 cm (½ inch) cubes*
- *salt and freshly ground pepper to taste*
- *chopped fresh coriander*

1 Spread out the onions in a heavy bottomed frying pan. Cook over medium heat until they begin to sizzle and stick. Immediately stir in 300 ml (½ pint) of the stock, the garlic, ginger and all the spices. Let it bubble up, stirring up any browned deposits in the pan as it bubbles. Simmer, stirring occasionally, until the onions and spices are 'frying' in their own juices. Stir in the tomato purée.

2 Purée half the mixture in a blender and return it to the pan.

3 Stir in the cauliflower, potato and remaining stock. Cover and simmer until the vegetables are tender and the sauce is thick and savoury. Adjust seasonings. Serve sprinkled with coriander.

VEGETABLE CURRY I

MAKES 1.7 LITRES (3 PINTS)

~

I could write a whole book on vegetable curries alone. This one is particularly easy to do: just sauté the onions and spices Slim Cuisine curry style, throw in a bunch of interesting vegetables and simmer until irresistible.

- *1 large Spanish onion, skinned and coarsely chopped*
- *700 ml (24 fl oz) chicken stock*
- *3 sticks celery, sliced in 1.25 cm (½ inch) pieces*
- *3 carrots, peeled and coarsely chopped*
- *4 cloves garlic, skinned and finely chopped*
- *3 small turnips, peeled and coarsely chopped*
- *3 (1 red, 1 green, 1 yellow) peppers, cored, seeded, peeled and coarsely chopped*
- *1 bulb fennel, trimmed of tough outer layers and sliced into 1.25 cm (½ inch) pieces*
- *7.5 ml (1½ tsp) ground cumin*
- *1.25 ml (¼ tsp) ground allspice*
- *2.5 ml (½ tsp) ground ginger*
- *5 ml (1 tsp) ground turmeric*
- *7.5 ml (1½ tsp) ground coriander*
- *1.25 ml (¼ tsp) cayenne pepper*
- *5 ml (1 tsp) paprika or paprika paste*
- *450 g (1 lb) courgettes, sliced into 1.25 cm (½ inch) pieces*
- *1 small cauliflower, trimmed and separated into florets*
- *90 ml (6 tbsp) fresh lemon juice*
- *60 ml (4 tbsp) chopped fresh parsley*
- *30 ml (2 tbsp) chopped fresh coriander*
- *salt and freshly ground pepper to taste*

1 Spread out the onion pieces in a frying pan. Cook over moderate heat until the onion is sizzling and sticking to the pan. Stir in 300 ml (½ pint) of the stock and let it bubble up, stirring up the browned deposits in the pan as it bubbles. Stir in the celery, carrots, garlic, turnips, peppers, fennel and all the spices. Turn the heat down a little and simmer, stirring frequently, until the mixture is thick (not at all soupy) and the vegetables and spices are 'frying' in their own juices.

2 Stir in the remaining ingredients, including the rest of the stock. Season to taste. Cover and simmer gently for 15 minutes or until tender.

VEGETABLE CURRY II

MAKES 2.3 LITRES (4 PINTS)

~

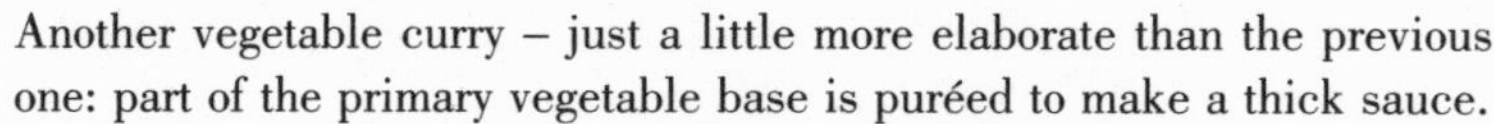

Another vegetable curry – just a little more elaborate than the previous one: part of the primary vegetable base is puréed to make a thick sauce.

- *2 large Spanish onions, skinned and cut into eighths*
- *approximately 570 ml (1 pint) stock*
- *2 cloves garlic, skinned and crushed*
- *15 ml (1 tbsp) ground cumin*
- *15 ml (1 tbsp) ground coriander*
- *15 ml (1 tbsp) Hungarian paprika or paprika paste*
- *2.5 ml (½ tsp) ground allspice*
- *2.5 ml (½ tsp) ground cardamom*
- *5 ml (1 tsp) ground turmeric*
- *2.5 ml (½ tsp) ground ginger*
- *1.25 ml (¼ tsp) cayenne pepper*
- *3 medium peppers, cored, seeded, peeled and coarsely chopped (or use canned peppers)*
- *3 large carrots, peeled and coarsely chopped*
- *350 g (12 oz) button mushrooms, halved or quartered*
- *2 medium white turnips, peeled and chopped in 1.25 cm (½ inch) pieces*
- *1 large cauliflower, trimmed and broken into florets*
- *1 small parsnip, trimmed, peeled and cut into 1.25 cm (½ inch) pieces*
- *1 bulb fennel, trimmed, quartered and sliced 1.25 cm (½ inch) thick*
- *3 sticks celery, sliced 1.25 cm (½ inch) thick*
- *salt to taste*
- *juice of ½ large lemon*
- *3 medium courgettes, chopped into 1.25 cm (½ inch) pieces*
- *225 g (8 oz) runner beans, sliced into 1.25 cm (½ inch) pieces*
- *Mint-Coriander Sauce (see page 173) to garnish*

1 Separate the segments of the onion pieces and spread them in a heavy bottomed pan. Heat gently until the onions are sizzling and sticking to the pan. Stir in 300 ml (½ pint) of the stock and let it bubble up, stirring up the browned deposits in the pan as it bubbles. Stir in the garlic, all the spices, the peppers, carrots and mushrooms. Turn the heat down a little and simmer, stirring frequently, until the mixture is thick (not at all soupy) and the vegetables and spices are 'frying' in their own juices.

2 Purée half the mixture in a blender or food processor. Combine the puréed and unpuréed mixtures in the pan.

3 Add the turnip, cauliflower, parsnip, fennel and celery. Stir together very well. Add enough stock to almost cover the contents of the pan. Season with salt.

4 Bring to the boil. Reduce the heat and simmer, covered, for 15 minutes. Uncover, squeeze in the lemon juice and add the courgettes and beans. Simmer, uncovered, for 10 minutes more or until all the vegetables are tender. Serve in deep soup bowls, with each serving garnished with a dollop of herb sauce.

VEGETABLE BHAJEE WITH CORN COBS

MAKES 2 LITRES (3½ PINTS)

~

My testers and tasters, my family, my friends all agree – this is the vegetable curry of our dreams. And it's a Therapeutic Binge too. I suspect that you will be preparing this one often.

- *2 Spanish onions, skinned and coarsely chopped*
- *300 ml (½ pint) stock*
- *3 sticks celery, sliced 1.25 cm (½ inch) thick*
- *3 carrots, peeled and coarsely chopped*
- *4 cloves garlic, skinned and finely chopped*
- *1 bulb fennel, trimmed, quartered and sliced 1.25 cm (½ inch) thick*
- *225 g (8 oz) button mushrooms, halved or quartered*
- *3 peppers (1 red, 1 yellow, 1 green), cored, seeded, peeled and coarsely chopped (or use canned peppers)*
- *15 ml (1 tbsp) mild chilli powder*
- *15 ml (1 tbsp) Hungarian paprika or paprika paste*
- *5 ml (1 tsp) dried oregano*
- *2.5 ml (½ tsp) ground cinnamon*

- *1.25 ml (¼ tsp) ground allspice*
- *pinch ground cloves*
- *10 ml (2 tsp) ground cumin*
- *15 ml (1 tbsp) ground coriander*
- *2 cans (400 g/14 oz each) chopped tomatoes*
- *2 medium white turnips, peeled and chopped into 1.25 cm (½ inch) cubes*
- *1 small parsnip, peeled and chopped into 1.25 cm (½ inch) cubes*
- *salt and freshly ground pepper to taste*
- *8 baby sweetcorn cobs, sliced into 2.5 cm (1 inch) pieces*
- *225 g (8 oz) runner beans, cut into 2.5 cm (1 inch) pieces*
- *Creamy Herb Sauce with coriander (see page 81) and thinly sliced spring onions to garnish*

1 Spread out the onion pieces in a heavy bottomed pan. Heat, without stirring, until they begin to sizzle and stick a little to the bottom of the pan. Stir in 300 ml (½ pint) of stock and let it bubble up, stirring up the browned deposits on the bottom of the pan with a wooden spoon.

2 Stir in the celery, carrots, garlic, fennel, mushrooms, peppers and all the spices. Turn the heat down a little and simmer, stirring frequently, until the mixture is very thick (not at all soupy) and the vegetables and spices are 'frying' in their own juices. Cook gently for a few more minutes, stirring.

3 Stir in the tomatoes, turnip and parsnip and season to taste. Simmer for 10 minutes.

4 Stir in the corn cobs and runner beans. Simmer for approximately 10 minutes or until all the vegetables are tender. Serve in soup bowls with a dollop of herb sauce and a sprinkling of spring onion on each serving.

VEGETABLE CHILLI WITH POTATOES

MAKES 2 LITRES (3½ PINTS)

A few years ago, I thought that it would be a nifty idea to take the flavour principles of good old fashioned homemade Mexican/American chilli con carne and apply them to vegetable casseroles. It turned out that chilli con legumbres (vegetables) is even better than chilli con carne (meat), because the textures and flavours in the vegetable stew (especially when potatoes are included) marry so well.

- *1 Spanish onion, skinned and coarsely chopped*
- *300 ml (½ pint) stock*
- *3 sticks celery, sliced 1.25 cm (½ inch) thick*
- *3 carrots, peeled and coarsely chopped*
- *4 cloves garlic, skinned and finely chopped*
- *15 ml (1 tbsp) Hungarian paprika or paprika paste*
- *15 ml (1 tbsp) chilli powder*
- *7.5 ml (½ tbsp) ground coriander*
- *5 ml (1 tsp) dried oregano*
- *1.25 ml (¼ tsp) ground cinnamon*
- *15 ml (1 tbsp) ground cumin*
- *3 peppers (1 red, 1 yellow, 1 green), cored, seeded, peeled and coarsely chopped*
- *2 cans (400 g/14 oz each) chopped tomatoes*
- *2 all-purpose potatoes, peeled and cut into 2.5 cm (1 inch) cubes*
- *4 small courgettes, sliced 1.25 cm (½ inch) thick*
- *1 large cauliflower, trimmed and cut into florets*
- *salt and freshly ground pepper to taste*
- *fromage frais and chopped fresh coriander to garnish*

1 Spread out the chopped onion in a heavy frying pan. Cook over moderate heat, without stirring, for 7–10 minutes until the onion is sizzling and beginning to stick to the pan. Stir in 300 ml (½ pint) of the stock and let it bubble up, stirring up the browned deposits in the pan with a wooden spoon as it bubbles. Stir in the celery, carrots, garlic, paprika, chilli powder, coriander, oregano, cinnamon, cumin and peppers. Turn the heat down a little and simmer, stirring frequently, until the mixture is very thick (not at all soupy) and the vegetables and spices are 'frying' in their own juices. Don't rush this step, it is essential that the spices should not have a harsh, raw taste. Taste and cook very gently for a few more minutes if necessary.

2 Stir in the tomatoes and potatoes. Simmer for 10 minutes. Stir in the courgettes and cauliflower and season to taste. Add a little stock if necessary. Simmer for 15–20 minutes until the mixture is thick and the cauliflower is tender. Serve with small bowls of the garnishes.

POTATO-FENNEL GRATIN

~

Fennel has a lovely anise flavour and complements potatoes really well. If you wish, substitute (or augment) the potatoes with swede or turnip.

- *2 large baking potatoes, scrubbed but unpeeled, very thinly sliced*
- *2 bulbs fennel, trimmed and very thinly sliced crossways*
- *approximately 300 ml (½ pint) chicken or vegetable stock*
- *freshly ground pepper to taste*

1 Preheat the oven to 200°C, 400°F, Gas Mark 6.
2 Arrange overlapping rows of potato slices and fennel slices in a single layer in a gratin dish. Evenly pour 225 ml (8 fl oz) of the stock over the vegetables. Season with pepper.
3 Bake for 1–1¼ hours. During the last 15–20 minutes, brush the potatoes with stock occasionally, using a pastry brush.

VARIATION: POTATO-ONION GRATIN Substitute thin slices of Spanish onion for the fennel.

TOMATO RAGOÛT

MAKES 2–2.3 LITRES (3½–4 PINTS)

~

'Thinking person's junk food' is how I like to think of tomato ragoût. The thick, savoury ragoût returns a satisfyingly intense Therapeutic Binge experience for such a small investment of time and effort.

- *2 cans (800 g/1 lb 12 oz each) Italian tomatoes*
- *pinch or two of dried crushed chillies (optional)*
- *1 can (400 g/14 oz) pimientos (red peppers)*
- *handful of coarsely chopped sun-dried tomatoes (optional)*
- *freshly ground pepper to taste*
- *30–45 ml (2–3 tbsp) tomato purée*
- *chopped fresh parsley*

1 Put the tomatoes, juice and all, into a non-reactive saucepan. With a potato masher, roughly crush them. Sprinkle in the chillies.
2 Drain the liquid from the pimientos. With a pair of kitchen scissors, roughly chop the pimientos in the can. Add them to the tomatoes with the sun-dried tomatoes, if using.
3 Bring to the boil, reduce the heat and simmer for about 10 minutes. Season with pepper and simmer for a further 10 minutes. Stir in the tomato purée and simmer for 5–10 minutes more or until thick. Stir in a handful of chopped parsley. Serve with potatoes or in bowls, like soup.
NOTE: You can add all sorts of extra vegetables to make this a tomato-vegetable ragoût.

CURRIED CAULIFLOWER

MAKES 570 ML (1 PINT)

Brightly coloured and fresh tasting, this simple curry is good on its own, or as part of a curry buffet.

- *1 Spanish onion, skinned and chopped*
- *3 cloves garlic, skinned and crushed*
- *300 ml (1/2 pint) stock*
- *2.5 ml (1/2 tsp) ground turmeric*
- *10 ml (2 tsp) ground coriander*
- *5 ml (1 tsp) ground cumin*
- *5 ml (1 tsp) garam masala*
- *1.25 ml (1/4 tsp) cayenne pepper*
- *1 can (400 g/14 oz) chopped tomatoes*
- *1 large cauliflower, trimmed and separated into florets*
- *salt and freshly ground pepper to taste*

1 Spread out the onion pieces in a heavy bottomed frying pan. Cook over moderate heat until the onion is sizzling and sticking to the pan. Add the garlic and stock and let it bubble up, stirring up the browned deposits in the pan as it bubbles. Add the spices, turn the heat down a little and simmer, stirring frequently until the mixture is thick (not at all soupy) and the vegetables and spices are 'frying' in their own juices.
2 Stir in the tomatoes and cauliflower and season to taste. Cover and simmer for 15 minutes. Uncover and simmer, stirring occasionally, for 15–20 minutes until the cauliflower is tender and the sauce thick.

LESCO-POTATO STEW

MAKES 1.7 LITRES (3 PINTS)

The Hungarians seem to eat Lesco (a sort of onion-pepper-paprika stew – almost a thick sauce, in fact) with everything. It's simply marvellous with potatoes (what isn't?).

- *3 large Spanish onions, skinned and coarsely chopped*
- *450 ml (¾ pint) stock*
- *2 cloves garlic, skinned and finely chopped*
- *3 large peppers (1 red, 1 green, 1 yellow), cored, seeded, peeled and coarsely chopped*
- *30 ml (2 tbsp) sweet Hungarian paprika or paprika paste*
- *5 ml (1 tsp) dried marjoram*
- *salt and freshly ground pepper to taste*
- *pinch or two of cayenne pepper (optional)*
- *2 cans (400 g/14 oz each) chopped tomatoes*
- *5–6 medium all-purpose potatoes, scrubbed and cut into 2.5 cm (1 inch) cubes*
- *fromage frais and snipped fresh dill to garnish*

1 Spread out the onion pieces in a heavy bottomed pan. Heat gently until sizzling, speckled with amber and just beginning to stick. Stir in 300 ml (½ pint) of the stock and let it bubble up, stirring up the browned deposits in the pan with a wooden spoon. Stir in the garlic, peppers, paprika and marjoram. Turn the heat down a little and simmer, stirring frequently, until the mixture is very thick (not at all soupy) and the vegetables and paprika are 'frying' in their own juices. Taste – the paprika should not have a harsh raw taste. Cook for a few moments more if necessary.

2 Stir in the remaining ingredients except the garnish. Add enough stock to barely cover the contents of the pan. Bring to the boil, reduce the heat and simmer, covered, for 15–20 minutes or until the potatoes are tender. Serve in soup bowls, garnished with fromage frais and snipped fresh dill.

CURRIED CABBAGE

MAKES 570 ML (1 PINT)

~

Back in the early sixties, my husband and I frequented a tiny Pakistani restaurant tucked away on a side street in New York's theatre district. How well I remember the 'Royal Bengal' dinner for two: soup, samosas, several curries, two kinds of bread, five or six chutneys, salads and relishes, and rose water custard for dessert – all for under four dollars! A meltingly tender melange of cabbage and onions always accompanied the curries. This recipe is very close to my taste-memory of that dish, even though the Slim Cuisine curry technique has been substituted for the traditional one.

- *1 large onion, skinned, halved and sliced into thin half moons*
- *2 cloves garlic, skinned and finely chopped*
- *570 ml (1 pint) stock*
- *1.25 ml (¼ tsp) mild chilli powder*
- *1.25 ml (¼ tsp) ground cinnamon*
- *1.25 ml (¼ tsp) ground turmeric*
- *1.25 ml (¼ tsp) ground ginger*
- *pinch allspice*
- *5 ml (1 tsp) Hungarian paprika or paprika paste*
- *5 ml (1 tsp) ground cumin*
- *2.5 ml (½ tsp) ground coriander*
- *1 small white cabbage, cored, trimmed of tough outer leaves, quartered*
- *¼–½ fresh lime*
- *salt and freshly ground pepper to taste*

1 Spread out the onion pieces in a frying pan. Cook over a moderate heat until the onion is sizzling and sticking to the pan. Add the garlic and 300 ml (½ pint) of the stock and let it bubble up, stirring up the browned deposits in the pan as it bubbles. Add the spices, turn the heat down a little and simmer, stirring frequently, until the mixture is thick (not at all soupy) and the vegetables and spices are 'frying' in their own juices.

2 Meanwhile, shred the cabbage using a sharp knife or the slicing blade of a food processor. Stir the cabbage and remaining stock into the pan. Simmer for 15–20 minutes until the cabbage is tender and the sauce is thick and savoury. Squeeze in a little lime juice. Taste and adjust seasonings.

Colourful Potato and Vegetable Casserole

MAKES 2 LITRES (3½ PINTS)

~

For your potato repertoire: a mixture of baked potato slices, vegetables and chillies. In the baking, the potatoes soak up the vegetable juices, and the chillies give them a slight piquancy.

- *5 medium boiling potatoes, thickly sliced*
- *2 medium onions, skinned, halved and sliced into thick half moons*
- *2 large yellow peppers, peeled, cored, seeded and cut into 2.5 cm (1 inch) chunks*
- *3 sticks celery, cut into 5 cm (2 inch) pieces*
- *2 cans (400 g/14 oz each) Italian tomatoes, crushed*
- *1 can (110 g/4 oz) green chillies, drained of liquid and diced, or 1–2 fresh chillies, seeded and chopped*
- *7.5 ml (½ tbsp) chopped fresh oregano*
- *30 ml (2 tbsp) finely chopped fresh parsley*
- *salt and freshly ground pepper to taste*

1 Preheat the oven to 230°C, 450°F, Gas Mark 8.

2 Put the potatoes and onions in a bowl. Toss with the remaining ingredients. Spread the mixture in the gratin dish and cover tightly.

3 Bake for 45–50 minutes or until the potatoes and celery are very tender.

TOMATO SAUCE

MAKES 900 ML (1½ PINTS)

With a few cans of Italian tomatoes, or with some juicy and ripe fresh tomatoes, you can make splendidly rich tasting, infinitely useful, no-fat sauces. Such sauces are delicious with mashed potatoes, jacket potatoes and steamed vegetables. Later in the plan, you may serve them with pasta or polenta, or as a sauce for steak, fish, chicken breasts or meatballs. This recipe is my basic Slim Cuisine Tomato Sauce; try it as a dip for grilled potato skins (see page 94) as well as all the usual ways.

- *3 shallots, skinned and finely chopped*
- *2 cloves garlic, skinned and crushed*
- *pinch cayenne pepper*
- *175 ml (6 fl oz) stock*
- *175 ml (6 fl oz) dry red wine, white wine or vermouth*
- *15 ml (1 tbsp) chopped fresh parsley*
- *15 ml (1 tbsp) chopped fresh basil or 1.25 ml (¼ tsp) dried*
- *15 ml (1 tbsp) chopped fresh thyme or 1.25 ml (¼ tsp) dried*
- *15 ml (1 tbsp) chopped fresh oregano or 1.25 ml (¼ tsp) dried*
- *3 cans (400 g /14 oz each) chopped tomatoes*
- *salt and freshly ground pepper to taste*
- *30 ml (2 tbsp) tomato purée*

1 Combine the shallots, garlic, cayenne, stock, wine and herbs in a heavy frying pan. Bring to the boil, reduce the heat and simmer briskly until almost all the liquid has been evaporated.

2 Stir in the tomatoes and season to taste. Simmer, partially covered, for 15 minutes. Stir in the tomato purée and simmer for 5 minutes more. Taste and adjust seasonings. For a smooth sauce, purée the tomato mixture in a blender. If you like your tomato sauce chunky, leave it as it is. Freeze tomato sauce in small portions and thaw when needed.

ROASTED TOMATO KETCHUP

MAKES 400 ML (14 FL OZ)

~

Roasting the tomatoes first gives this thick, sweet ketchup a haunting, smoky undertone. Serve it with potatoes or other vegetables until Day 28. After Day 28, lavish it on Slim Cuisine Hamburgers (see page 171).

- *15 very ripe, juicy tomatoes*
- *2 large Spanish onions, skinned and finely chopped*
- *4 cloves garlic, skinned and finely chopped*
- *100 ml (4 fl oz) red wine*
- *75 ml (3 fl oz) stock*
- *45 ml (3 tbsp) chopped fresh parsley*
- *30 ml (2 tbsp) shredded fresh basil*
- *salt and freshly ground pepper to taste*

1 Preheat the oven to 220°C, 425°F, Gas Mark 7.

2 Put the tomatoes in one layer on a baking sheet. Bake, uncovered, for about ½ hour or until blistered and charred. Cool slightly.

3 While the tomatoes are baking, combine the onions, garlic, wine, stock and herbs in a heavy bottomed, non-reactive frying pan. Cover and boil for 5–7 minutes. Uncover and simmer briskly until the onions are tender and beginning to brown, and the liquid is almost gone.

4 When the tomatoes have cooled, squeeze them out of their skins into the frying pan with the onions. Discard the skins. Simmer for about 20 minutes until thick. Season to taste. Cool slightly.

5 Purée the sauce in a blender until smooth. Rub through a sieve to eliminate the seeds.

CHUNKY TOMATO AND PEPPER RELISH

MAKES 570 ML (1 PINT)

~

On Day 28, when you can eat a hamburger, serve this heaped on the burger; in the meantime, it's great in a baked potato or as a side dish.

- *1 onion, skinned and chopped*
- *175 ml (6 fl oz) stock*
- *50 ml (2 fl oz) balsamic vinegar*
- *4 peppers (a mixture of red, yellow and green), cored, seeded and peeled*
- *12–15 ripe tomatoes, skinned, seeded and chopped*
- *generous 15 ml (1 tbsp) chopped fresh basil*
- *generous 15 ml (1 tbsp) chopped fresh oregano*
- *salt and freshly ground pepper to taste*

1 Combine the onion, stock and vinegar in a small non-reactive saucepan. Boil until almost dry.

2 In a non-reactive frying pan, combine the onion mixture with the remaining ingredients. Simmer for 20 minutes.

TOMATO-CARROT SAUCE

MAKES 1.1 LITRES (2 PINTS)

~

This was inspired by a recipe of artist/cook Ed Giobbi, which appeared in the New York Times *years* (almost 30!) ago. The carrots give it a gorgeous colour, creamy texture and a deliciously mysterious taste.

- *2 Spanish onions, skinned and chopped*
- *2 cloves garlic, skinned and chopped*
- *4 large carrots, peeled and diced*
- *225 ml (8 fl oz) stock*
- *225 ml (8 fl oz) dry red wine*
- *4 cans (400 g/14 oz each) chopped tomatoes*
- *30 ml (2 tbsp) shredded fresh basil*
- *45 ml (3 tbsp) chopped fresh parsley*
- *salt and freshly ground pepper to taste*

1 Combine the onions, garlic, carrots, stock and wine in a heavy bottomed frying pan. Cover, bring to the boil and boil for 5–7 minutes. Uncover, reduce heat a little and simmer, stirring, until the vegetables are tender, the onions are amber brown and the liquid is almost gone. Pour in another splash of stock and cook and stir for a minute or two more, scraping up the browned bits as you stir.
2 Stir in tomatoes and herbs and season to taste. Simmer for 20–30 minutes until nicely thickened.
3 Cool the sauce slightly, then purée in batches in a blender or food processor.

GRAVY

MAKES APPROXIMATELY 900 ML (1½ PINTS)

~

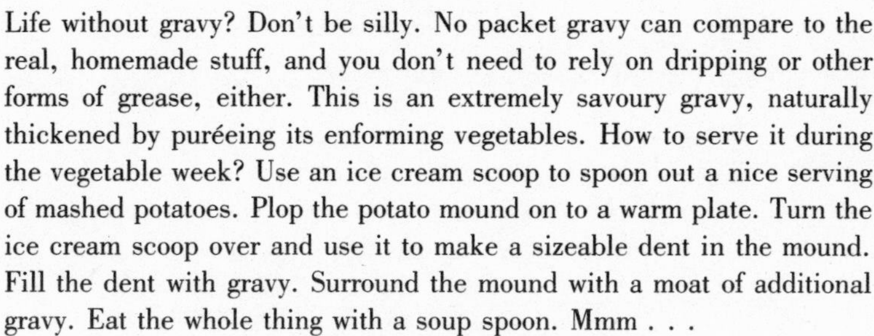

Life without gravy? Don't be silly. No packet gravy can compare to the real, homemade stuff, and you don't need to rely on dripping or other forms of grease, either. This is an extremely savoury gravy, naturally thickened by puréeing its enforming vegetables. How to serve it during the vegetable week? Use an ice cream scoop to spoon out a nice serving of mashed potatoes. Plop the potato mound on to a warm plate. Turn the ice cream scoop over and use it to make a sizeable dent in the mound. Fill the dent with gravy. Surround the mound with a moat of additional gravy. Eat the whole thing with a soup spoon. Mmm . . .

- *4 shallots, skinned and chopped*
- *1 large onion, skinned and chopped*
- *2 sticks celery, chopped*
- *2 cloves garlic, skinned and crushed*
- *2 carrots, peeled and sliced*
- *1.7 litres (3 pints) chicken or beef stock*
- *570 ml (1 pint) dry red wine*
- *1 can (400 g/14 oz) chopped tomatoes*
- *salt and freshly ground pepper to taste*

1 Combine the vegetables and 300 ml (½ pint) of the stock in a heavy bottomed frying pan. Cover, bring to the boil and boil for 5 minutes.
2 Uncover, reduce heat a little and simmer, stirring occasionally until the vegetables are tender and the liquid is almost gone. Cook until the vegetables begin to stick and brown a little. Pour in a splash of stock and stir and scrape up the brown bits.
3 Stir in the wine and tomatoes. Simmer briskly for 10 minutes.

4 Stir in the remaining stock, then simmer for 15 minutes, stirring occasionally. Cool slightly.
5 Purée in a blender until smooth. Sieve into a bowl, rubbing through the solids with a wooden spoon or rubber spatula. Reheat, seasoning to taste.

PEPPER SAUCE

MAKES 1.6 LITRES (2¾ PINTS)

The pepper is one of the most versatile vegetables. It is perfectly suited for eating raw and crunchy, stir-fried and crisp tender, long braised and meltingly tender, or grilled and smoky. But peppers are best of all when simmered, then puréed into a rich, thick sauce. The sauce method works with red or yellow ones.

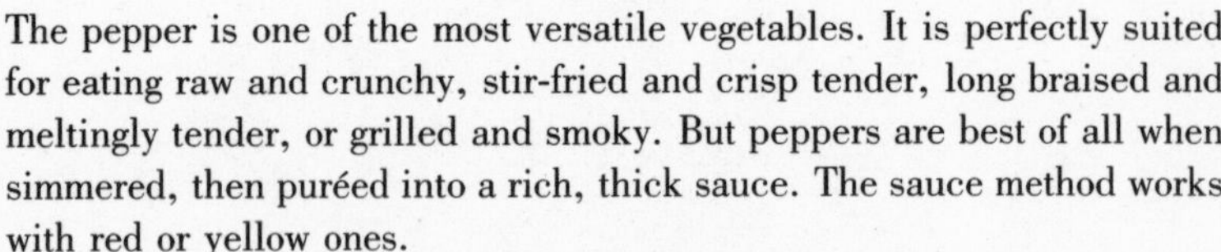

- *570 ml (1 pint) stock*
- *2 large Spanish onions, skinned and chopped*
- *2 cloves garlic, skinned and finely chopped*
- *pinch cayenne pepper*
- *10–12 red peppers, cored, seeded and coarsely chopped*
- *salt and freshly ground pepper to taste*
- *15 ml (1 tbsp) chopped fresh parsley*
- *7.5 ml (½ tbsp) chopped fresh oregano or thyme*
- *30 ml (2 tbsp) tomato purée*

1 Combine 300 ml (½ pint) of the stock, the onions, garlic and cayenne in a heavy bottomed frying pan. Cover, bring to the boil and boil for 5–7 minutes. Uncover, reduce the heat and cook, stirring occasionally, until the onions are tender and amber brown and the liquid is almost gone. Pour in a splash more stock and cook for another minute or so, scraping up the browned bits as it cooks. Add the peppers and stir over a moderate heat for a few minutes.
2 Add the remaining ingredients, except the tomato puree, but including the remaining stock. Simmer, uncovered, for ½ hour or until thick. Stir in the tomato purée and simmer for 5–7 minutes more. Cool slightly.
3 Purée in batches in a blender or food processor, then push the sauce through a sieve. Reheat, taste and adjust seasonings.

DAYS 8–11
TECHNIQUES AND RECIPES

'ICE CREAM' TECHNIQUE

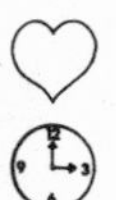

Fresh fruit is going to taste so fabulously OTT to you that you probably won't want to eat it any other way than plain and simple for a while. But when you feel ready to expand your fruit experience, try instant Slim Cuisine Ice Cream. The recipe is quick and easy to make.

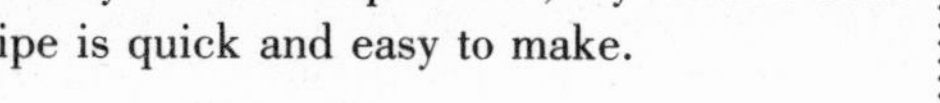

- *frozen fruit or frozen berries*
- *vanilla NutraSweet (see Note overleaf)*
- *buttermilk or skimmed milk mixed with 7.5–15 ml (½–1 tbsp) skimmed milk powder*

1 Put chunks of frozen fruit or frozen berries into a food processor. Add a little vanilla NutraSweet and pour in just a little buttermilk or milk. Process, stopping to scrape the bowl down once or twice if necessary.
2 Taste and add more vanilla NutraSweet to taste, if necessary. Turn on the machine and pour in a little more buttermilk or skimmed milk. Process until the mixture forms a super creamy ice cream. Serve *at once*.

NOTES: The 'ice cream' recipe on the previous page is not suitable for freezing. It freezes into a solid brick and is then impossible to restore to its original creamy perfection. It is so easy and quick to prepare, that it should be no problem – as long as you keep frozen fruit in the freezer to make the 'ice cream' as needed. If necessary, it could be kept in the freezer for up to an hour, but no longer.

Vanilla NutraSweet Buy a vanilla pod and bury it in a jar of NutraSweet. After a few days, the sweetener will be imbued with the vanilla flavour.

GRILLED BANANA

Grilling a banana intensifies its natural sweetness, and turns it into a banana-custard within its skin. This has to be one of the easiest (and sweetest) of puddings! Grilled bananas also feature in several recipes, such as Banana Mousse and Banana Cream Cheesecake (see page 158).

Preheat the grill. Line the grill tray with foil, shiny-side up. Place the rack on the grill tray. Choose a very ripe banana and put it, *unpeeled*, on the grill rack. Grill, about 2.5 cm (1 inch) from the heat, for approximately 3 minutes on each side, until the banana has swelled up, is well speckled with charred bits, and is spitting and spluttering. With tongs, transfer the banana to a plate. Peel a strip off the top. Pour the juices from the grill tray on to the banana. Eat with a spoon.

BANANA MOUSSE

MAKES 900 ML (1½ PINTS)

- *4 grilled bananas, with their juices*
- *4 small cartons (200 g/7 oz each) quark or very low-fat curd cheese*
- *30 ml (2 tbsp) thawed orange juice concentrate*
- *5 ml (1 tsp) natural vanilla essence*
- *2.5 ml (½ tsp) ground cinnamon*
- *NutraSweet to taste*

1 Spoon the bananas out of their skins. Put them, with their juices, into a food processor with the quark, orange juice concentrate, vanilla and cinnamon. Process until very smooth and fluffy. Taste, then process in some sweetener and a little more cinnamon, if needed.

2 Chill for several hours or overnight, so that the flavour develops and the mousse 'sets'.

DAYS 12–14

TECHNIQUES AND RECIPES

SLIM CUISINE 'WHIPPED CREAM' OR VANILLA MILK SHAKE

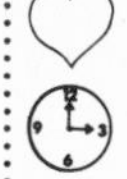

MAKES APPROXIMATELY 1.7 LITRES (3 PINTS)

I hardly know how to tell you about this technique without babbling incoherently. On the one hand, it is unbelievably delicious, creamy and decadent tasting: in fact, it tastes as fattening as hell, yet it's essentially only skimmed milk and air! On the other hand, if you binge on this milk shake, it might cause flatulence, ballooning sensations and general feelings of overindulgence. It's a double problem, really: 1) the incredible ice creamy, milk shaky, whipped creamish delight of the damned thing, and 2) all that *air* that the processor whips into it. The *air* is what makes it so thick and creamy, and it's the *air* that makes you feel – 15 minutes or so after ingesting a *large* amount – that you've swallowed several rapidly expanding balloons. Rude noises quite beyond your control usually follow. So what's the answer to the problem? Well, the milk shake is too delicious (amazing at such low Calories and *no* fat) to ignore, so:

1 Don't eat too much at once (this is a tough direction to obey; it really *is* good). By too much, I mean the whole recipe (yes – it's been done).

2 If you do plan to overeat this recipe, stop processing at 2 minutes, before it gets really stiff and whipped creamish. You will thus lessen the air content – it's the air that causes all the ructions. But if you are a binger, or one who just enjoys over-huge portions of delicious food (I'm not saying this in a pejorative sense, I am your sister-in-appetite), over-consuming the stiffly whipped milk shake may cure you of it. You won't be really ill, but you may be embarrassed. But no matter how much of the recipe you eat, you need not fear the Calories and fat; they are paltry. The recipe makes 1.7 litres (3 pints) because all members of the household will want plenty, and I want to be sure that there is enough for *you*. (Don't tell them that it is a diet recipe: they probably wouldn't believe you anyway.) If you are making it for two, or for one only, cut the recipe by half or by one third.

- *570 ml (1 pint) skimmed milk slush (see Note overleaf)*
- *90 ml (6 tbsp) skimmed milk powder*
- *30 ml (2 tbsp) vanilla NutraSweet (see page 128)*

1 Combine about three-quarters of the milk slush and all the remaining ingredients in a food processor.

2 Process until thick, the consistency of whipped cream, and greatly (unbelievably!) increased in bulk (at *least* 2 minutes of processing). The longer you process the mixture, the stiffer and more like whipped cream it becomes. Add the rest of the slush gradually, as it processes. Spoon into cold glasses and serve at once with spoons, or use as whipped 'cream' for berries, bananas, etc. (Or try a banana split: a halved banana, Slim Cuisine ice cream, raspberry sauce, sprinkled Grape-Nuts cereal and this 'cream'.)

NOTE: To make skimmed milk slush, freeze 570 ml (1 pint) cartons of long life (UHT) skimmed milk. When you want to make a milk shake, remove the carton from the freezer and, with scissors, cut off the top, then cut the carton away from the frozen block of milk. Put the milk into a microwave container and microwave on HIGH for 2–3 minutes until slushy and partially melted. With a spoon or a blunt knife, chop and mush up the milk until the texture is consistently slushy. *To make coffee slush*, store strong filter coffee in the freezer. Defrost in the microwave until slushy.

If you do not have a microwave, freeze the milk, in its carton, until it is partially frozen and slushy. Proceed with the recipe.

VARIATIONS: COFFEE: Use three-quarters the amount of milk slush and add 150 ml (¼ pint) coffee slush (see Note).

MOCHA: When the mixture has become very thick, while the mixture is processing, add 2.5–5ml (½–1 tsp) instant espresso granules. When thoroughly amalgamated, taste and process in a little more sweetener if necessary. Serve at once.

CHOCOLATE MILK SHAKE

MAKES 1.7 LITRES (3 PINTS)

~

- *570 ml (1 pint) skimmed milk slush (see page 130)*
- *90 ml (6 tbsp) skimmed milk powder*
- *45 ml (3 tbsp) vanilla NutraSweet (see page 128)*
- *generous 30–45 ml (2–3 tbsp) low-fat cocoa powder, sifted*

1 Combine three-quarters of the milk slush and all the remaining ingredients in a food processor.
2 Process until thick, the consistency of whipped cream, and greatly (unbelievably!) increased in bulk (at *least* 2 minutes of processing). The longer you process the mixture, the stiffer and more like whipped cream it becomes. Add the rest of the slush gradually, as it processes. Pour into cold glasses and serve at once, with spoons.

MANGO CREAM

MAKES APPROXIMATELY 900 ML (1½ PINTS)

~

The milk shake/whipped cream technique can be used to create outstanding fruit creams and fruit mousses.

- *frozen mango cubes from approximately ½ large mango (see method)*
- *300 ml (½ pint) skimmed milk slush (see page 130)*
- *45 ml (3 tbsp) skimmed milk powder*
- *2.5 ml (½ tsp) natural vanilla essence*
- *approximately 7.5 ml (½ tbsp) vanilla NutraSweet (see page 128)*

1 To cube and freeze mango cubes, slice down on each whole mango with a sharp knife, as if you were slicing it in half, but try to miss the large flat centre stone. Slice down again on the other side of the stone. You will now have two half mangos and the flat centre stone to which quite a bit of mango flesh clings.
2 With a small, sharp paring knife, score each mango half lengthways and crossways, cutting all the way to, but not through, the skin. Push

out the skin as if you were pushing the half mango inside out. The mango flesh will stand out in cubes. Slice these cubes off the skin.

3 With the knife, remove the skin from the mango flesh remaining on the stone. Slice the flesh off the stone. Spread all the mango cubes and pieces on a tray and freeze. When frozen, transfer to plastic bags.

4 Combine the milk slush, milk powder and vanilla in a food processor and process for about 30 seconds.

5 While the machine is running, drop the frozen mango cubes through the feed tube, 1–2 at a time. When all are added, stop and taste. Add sweetener to taste, then continue processing for another minute or so, until the mixture is very thick and the texture of softly whipped cream.

FRESH STRAWBERRY MILK SHAKE

Follow directions for Mango Cream, substituting 1 punnet fresh (unfrozen) hulled, halved, ripe strawberries for the mango cubes.

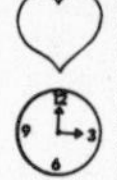

VANILLA-FRUIT PARFAITS

~

Half vanilla 'whipped' cream and half fruit mousse make a festive dessert.

- *570 ml (1 pint) skimmed milk slush (see page 130)*
- *90 ml (6 tbsp) skimmed milk powder*
- *45 ml (3 tbsp) vanilla NutraSweet (see page 128)*
- *110–175 g (4–6 oz) cubes of frozen fruit or berries*

1 Put the milk slush, milk powder and vanilla NutraSweet in a food processor. Process for at *least* 2 minutes until it is the consistency of whipped cream and unbelievably increased in volume. Stop the machine. Divide half of the mixture among large clear glass dessert goblets.

2 Turn the machine back on. As it processes, add the fruit, a few pieces at a time. Stop and push the pieces of fruit down on to the blades. Taste and add a little more sweetener if necessary. Continue processing until the mixture is smooth, thick and all the fruit is amalgamated. Spoon an equal amount of the fruit cream on to the vanilla cream. Serve at once.

CREAMY MOUSSE

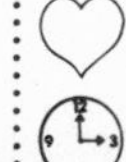

~

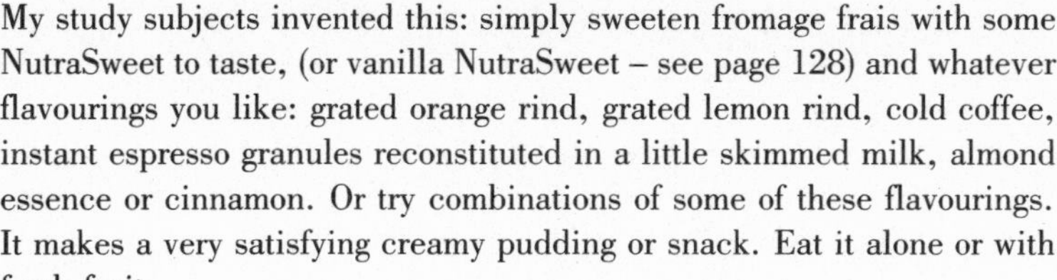

My study subjects invented this: simply sweeten fromage frais with some NutraSweet to taste, (or vanilla NutraSweet – see page 128) and whatever flavourings you like: grated orange rind, grated lemon rind, cold coffee, instant espresso granules reconstituted in a little skimmed milk, almond essence or cinnamon. Or try combinations of some of these flavourings. It makes a very satisfying creamy pudding or snack. Eat it alone or with fresh fruit.

BREAKFAST MUESLI

In the evening, stir Grape-Nuts cereal into the Creamy Mousse. Refrigerate overnight. In the morning, the cereal will have expanded and softened. Eat with fruit.

BLACK-WHITE PARFAITS

MAKES 1.7 LITRES (3 PINTS)

~

- *570 ml (1 pint) skimmed milk slush (see page 130)*
- *90 ml (6 tbsp) skimmed milk powder*
- *45–60 ml (3–4 tbsp) vanilla NutraSweet (see page 128)*
- *22.5 ml (1½ tbsp) low-fat cocoa powder, sifted*

1 Put the milk slush, skimmed milk powder and vanilla sweetener in a food processor. Process for at *least* 2 minutes until it is the consistency of whipped cream and unbelievably increased in volume. Stop the machine. Divide half of the mixture among large clear glass dessert goblets.

2 Turn the machine back on. While it is running, sprinkle the cocoa powder into the mixture through the feed tube. Stop the machine and add more sweetener to taste. Process for another minute or so. Spoon an equal amount of the chocolate mixture on to the vanilla mixture. Eat at once.

DAYS 15 – 20

TECHNIQUES AND RECIPES

FISH SOUP

MAKES APPROXIMATELY 2.8 LITRES (5 PINTS)

~

What a delicious main dish soup this is. It makes a wonderful family meal, or an equally wonderful offering to guests, as does the Italian fish soup that follows.

- *3 medium onions, skinned and cut into wedges (eighths)*
- *3 cloves garlic, skinned and crushed*
- *2 sticks celery, cut into 0.6 cm (¼ inch) slices*
- *1 small bulb fennel, trimmed, quartered and sliced into 1.25 cm (½ inch) pieces (save the feathery fronds)*
- *2 litres (3½ pints) stock, chicken, fish, vegetable or a combination*
- *100 ml (4 fl oz) dry white vermouth*
- *225 g (8 oz) button mushrooms, quartered*
- *350 g (12 oz) new potatoes, scrubbed and quartered*
- *salt and freshly ground pepper to taste*
- *90 ml (6 tbsp) chopped fresh parsley*
- *snipped feathery fronds of the fennel bulb*
- *700 g (1½ lb) cod fillets or other white fish fillets, cut into 5 cm (2 inch) pieces*

1 Combine the onions, garlic, celery, fennel, 300 ml (½ pint) of the stock and the vermouth in a heavy bottomed soup pan. Cover, bring to the boil and boil for 3–4 minutes. Uncover, reduce the heat a little, stir in the mushrooms and simmer until the vegetables are 'frying' in their own juices. Stir and cook until everything is tender.

2 Add the potatoes and remaining stock. Season to taste. Cook, uncovered, until the potatoes are tender.

3 Stir in the herbs and fish. Simmer for 2–4 minutes until the fish is just cooked. Serve at once.

ITALIAN FISH SOUP

MAKES 2 LITRES (3¾ PINTS)

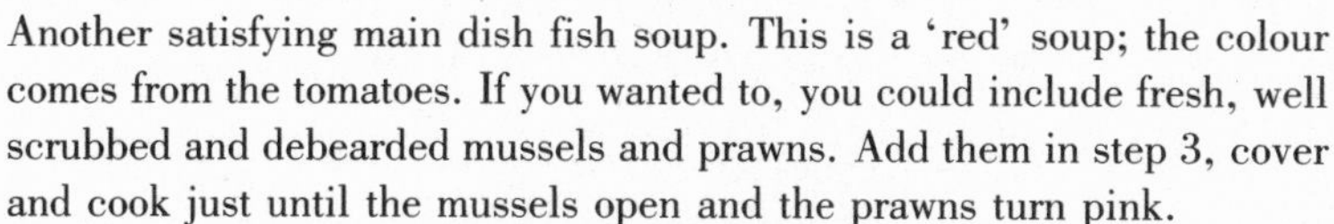

Another satisfying main dish fish soup. This is a 'red' soup; the colour comes from the tomatoes. If you wanted to, you could include fresh, well scrubbed and debearded mussels and prawns. Add them in step 3, cover and cook just until the mussels open and the prawns turn pink.

- *450 ml (¾ pint) stock*
- *2 large cloves garlic, skinned and chopped*
- *1 onion, skinned and chopped*
- *2 bulbs fennel, trimmed and chopped (save the feathery fronds)*
- *1 can (800 g/1 lb 12 oz) Italian tomatoes, drained and cut into strips*
- *450 ml (¾ pint) fish or chicken stock*
- *450 ml (¾ pint) dry white wine*
- *45 ml (3 tbsp) tomato purée*
- *1 bay leaf*
- *2.5 ml (½ tsp) dried marjoram*
- *5 ml (1 tsp) oregano*
- *salt and freshly ground pepper to taste*
- *900 g (2 lb) mixed fish fillets, such as cod, halibut, cut into 7.5 cm (3 inch) chunks*
- *30 ml (2 tbsp) fresh lemon juice*
- *chopped fresh parsley*

1 In a non-reactive soup pan, combine 450 ml (¾ pint) stock, garlic, onion and fennel. Cover, bring to the boil and boil for 5–7 minutes. Uncover, reduce heat a little and simmer until the vegetables are browning and almost all the liquid is gone.

2 Stir in the tomatoes, remaining stock, wine, tomato purée, bay leaf, marjoram and oregano and season to taste. Bring to the boil, reduce the heat, partially cover and simmer gently for ½ hour.

3 Increase the heat to a brisk simmer. Stir in the fish and cook for approximately 3 minutes until just done. Stir in the lemon juice, parsley and reserved fennel fronds.

FISH IN A BAG

SERVES 1

The 'bag' is simply a pouch made from foil. This is my favourite way to steam fish fillets and vegetables. Serve each person an individual bag of fish and vegetables – let each diner slit his or her bag and slide the aromatic contents on to the plate. This preparation is colourful, exquisitely fresh tasting, and fun.

- *1 fillet (110–150 g/4–5 oz) cod or haddock, or other white fish fillet*
- *salt and freshly ground pepper to taste*
- *1 small carrot, peeled and cut into thin sticks*
- *1 small courgette, thinly sliced*
- *4–5 button mushrooms, halved or quartered*
- *½ each small red and small yellow pepper, cored, seeded, peeled and cut into 5 cm (2 inch) squares*
- *6 cherry tomatoes, halved*
- *30 ml (2 tbsp) shredded fresh mint leaves*
- *30 ml (2 tbsp) chopped fresh parsley*
- *15 ml (1 tbsp) chopped spring onion or snipped chives*
- *22.5 ml (1½ tbsp) stock*
- *22.5 ml (1½ tbsp) dry white vermouth*

1 Preheat the oven to 230°F, 450°F, Gas Mark 8.
2 Tear off a sheet of heavy duty foil large enough to generously enclose the fish and all the vegetables. Position the fish, skinside down, in the centre. Season with salt and pepper. Arrange the vegetables, each in a neat, separate heap, around the fish. Place the cherry tomatoes, cut side up, on the fish. Season the vegetables to taste. Sprinkle the herbs and spring onion on the fish and vegetables. Dribble on the stock and vermouth.
3 Fold the foil over and crimp the edges to form a very well sealed, loose tent around the fish and vegetables. Bake on the oven shelf for approximately 15 minutes. When done, slash the foil and slide the fish and vegetables on to a warm plate.

TUNA PÂTÉ

MAKES 350 ML (12 FL OZ)

Tuna pâté makes a delicious sandwich spread or filling for ripe summer tomatoes. To prepare tomatoes, first cut out the core of the tomato. Cut the tomato into quarters or eighths, from the cored end to the bottom, but don't cut all the way – the quarters should remain attached. Spread the tomato open and fill with a mound of tuna pâté. Serve on a bed of beautiful greens and surround with grated carrots, grated beetroot, grated white turnip and sliced fennel. Garnish with leaves of fresh basil and pass the bottle of balsamic vinegar.

- *1 can (185 g/6½ oz) tuna in brine or water, drained*
- *15 ml (1 tbsp) drained capers*
- *60–90 ml (4–6 tbsp) quark*
- *bunch snipped chives*
- *15 ml (1 tbsp) chopped fresh parsley*
- *juice of ¼ lemon*
- *freshly ground pepper to taste*

1 Combine all the ingredients in a food processor. Process to a rough purée.

2 Pour into a muslin lined sieve (or jelly bag) and leave to drain for at least an hour. Serve chilled.

AS THE BIRD FRIES

The following techniques show you how to make 'fried' chicken breasts, or grilled chicken breasts. They are quickly prepared and – especially if you can find breasts from a poulet noir, a corn fed bird or a free range one – make exquisite eating. Serve them simply with lemon wedges, or try one of the following sauces or accompaniments:

Creamy Cucumber Dip (see page 76)/Minted Cucumbers (see page 77)/Salsa Cruda (see page 81)/Stir 'Fried' Peppers (see page 86)/Aubergine 'Caviare' (see page 98)/Peperonata (see page 99)/Chunky Salsa (see page 109)/Tzatziki (see page 106)/Tomato Sauce (see page 122)/Pepper Sauce (see page 126)/Chunky Tomato and Pepper Relish (see page 124)/Tomato-carrot Sauce (see page 124)/Roasted Tomato Ketchup (see page 123)/Gravy (see page 125)

GRILLED CHICKEN BREASTS

- *apple juice or dry white vermouth*
- *pinch ground ginger*
- *pinch ground cumin*
- *pinch ground coriander*
- *boneless, skinless chicken breasts*
- *1 egg white*
- *2.5–5 ml (½–1 tsp) French mustard*
- *2.5 ml (½ tsp) dried tarragon*
- *2.5 ml (½ tsp) dried thyme*
- *plain breadcrumbs seasoned with salt, pepper and a pinch or two of ground cinnamon*

1 Combine the apple juice or vermouth and spices in a bowl. Submerge the chicken breasts in the liquid. Place the egg white in a bowl and lightly beat in the mustard and herbs. Put the seasoned crumbs on a plate.

2 Preheat the grill. Line the grill tray with foil, shiny side up. Place the grill rack on the tray. Remove the chicken breasts from the marinade. Dredge them thoroughly in the egg white, then coat them well with seasoned crumbs. Place on the grill rack.

3 Grill, as far from the heat as possible, for approximately 3 minutes on each side until browned and just cooked through. Try not to let them dry out. Serve with a sprinkling of balsamic vinegar, lemon or lime wedges, or any of the Slim Cuisine sauces (see recipes and lists).

OVEN-FRIED CHICKEN BREASTS WITH MATZO MEAL

- *dry white vermouth or apple juice*
- *dash of soy sauce*
- *generous pinch ground cumin*
- *generous pinch ground coriander*
- *generous pinch ground ginger*
- *boneless, skinless chicken breasts*
- *45 ml (3 tbsp) fromage frais*
- *7.5 ml (½ tbsp) French mustard*
- *matzo meal seasoned with salt, freshly ground pepper and a pinch cayenne pepper*

1 Combine the vermouth or apple juice, soy sauce and spices in a bowl. Dunk the chicken breasts in the mixture, so that they are thoroughly moistened on both sides.
2 Combine the fromage frais and mustard in a shallow bowl. Spread out the seasoned matzo meal on a plate.
3 Preheat the oven to 200°C, 400°F, Gas Mark 6. Line a grill tray with foil, shiny side up. Put a rack on the grill tray.
4 Remove the chicken breasts from the marinade and dredge them thoroughly in the fromage frais and mustard mixture. Dip them in the matzo meal so that they are well coated. Place on the rack.
5 Bake for approximately 10 minutes or until they are *just* done. (They will feel firm, but a little springy when pressed with your finger.) If liked, flash under the grill for 30–40 seconds to brown slightly. Serve as is, with lemon wedges or with any of your Slim Cuisine sauces.

BAKED CRISPY CHICKEN BREASTS

~

- *apple juice or dry white vermouth*
- *pinch ground ginger*
- *pinch ground coriander*
- *pinch ground cumin*
- *1 egg white*
- *2.5–5 ml (½–1 tsp) French mustard*
- *2.5 ml (½ tsp) dried tarragon*
- *2.5 ml (½ tsp) dried thyme*
- *matzo meal seasoned with salt, freshly ground pepper and a pinch ground cinnamon*
- *boneless, skinless chicken breasts*

1 Preheat the oven to 200°F, 400°F, Gas Mark 6.
2 Line the grill tray with foil, shiny side up. Put the grill rack on the tray.
3 Combine the apple juice or vermouth and spices in a bowl. Lightly beat the egg white with the mustard and herbs in a bowl. Spread the seasoned matzo meal on a plate.
4 Dunk the chicken breasts in the apple juice or vermouth, so that they are moistened on both sides. Dredge them in the egg white mixture, then coat well with matzo meal. Put the coated chicken on the grill rack.
5 Bake for approximately 10 minutes, then flash under the grill for 30–60 seconds, to lightly brown. Serve with lemon or lime wedges or with a Slim Cuisine sauce.

GONE FISHING

Any of the 'fried' and grilled chicken breast techniques can be used for fish fillets as well. Time your fish by this rule: *10 minutes* cooking time per 2.5 cm (1 inch) thickness of fish. It is not necessary to skin the fish fillets. Coat them on the non-skin side only. (No need to turn them when grilling.)

GRILLED CHICKEN BREASTS WITH BREADCRUMBS

~

- *dry white vermouth or apple juice*
- *dash of soy sauce*
- *generous pinch ground cumin*
- *generous pinch ground coriander*
- *generous pinch ground ginger*
- *boneless, skinless chicken breasts*
- *salt and freshly ground pepper to taste*
- *45 ml (3 tbsp) fromage frais*
- *7.5 ml (½ tbsp) French mustard*
- *plain breadcrumbs seasoned with salt, freshly ground pepper and a pinch cayenne pepper*

1 Combine the vermouth or apple juice, soy sauce and spices in a bowl. Dunk the chicken breasts in the mixture, so that they are moistened on both sides.

2 Preheat the grill. Line the grill tray with foil, shiny side up. Place the grill rack on the tray.

3 Combine the fromage frais and mustard in a shallow bowl. Spread the seasoned breadcrumbs on a plate.

4 Remove the chicken breasts from the marinade and dredge them thoroughly in the fromage frais mixture, then in the breadcrumbs. They should be well coated on both sides. Place on the grill rack.

5 Grill, approximately 12.5 cm (5 inches) from the heat, for 3–3½ minutes on each side until cooked through but still moist. Serve with lemon or lime wedges, Peperonata (see page 99) or with any of the Slim Cuisine sauces.

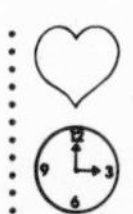

CHICKEN BREASTS PAN SAUTÉ METHOD

You can prepare an elegant and special meal in less than ½ hour, by pan frying chicken breasts and serving them with a quick sauce made in the same pan. The clean up is easy too.

1 Heat a non-stick pan until moderately hot.

2 Season skinless, boneless chicken breasts with salt and freshly ground pepper.

3 Cook, in one layer, for 3–4 minutes on each side until the chicken is just cooked through. (It will feel firm but springy when poked with the finger, and the interior of the chicken breast will be a delicate pearly white.)

Serve with any of the Slim Cuisine sauces. Alternatively, set them aside in one layer on a platter, loosely covered, and make a quick sauce in the same pan in which you've cooked the chicken. (Don't wash the pan, or wipe it out.)

QUICK PAN SAUCES

MUSHROOM TARRAGON

Put some thinly sliced spring onion into the pan with a few spoonfuls stock. Simmer until the onions are tender and the stock is gone. Add some sliced mushrooms, salt and pepper, a pinch or two of dried tarragon, 15 ml (1 tbsp) dry vermouth, 50–75 ml (2–3 fl oz) stock and a dash of soy sauce. Boil, stirring, until the mushrooms are tender and syrupy.

LESCO (HUNGARIAN PEPPER SAUCE)

Put some diced, canned red peppers and some sliced spring onion into the pan with a little stock, a dash of dry vermouth and a pinch or two of paprika or paprika paste. Stir and cook over gentle heat until the onions are tender and the liquid is almost gone. Off the heat, stir in about 15 ml (1 tbsp) room temperature fromage frais.

CURRY

Put a handful of thinly sliced spring onion or finely chopped shallots, 1 crushed clove of garlic, a pinch each of ground ginger, ground turmeric, ground cinnamon, ground cumin and ground coriander into the pan. Add

175–200 ml (6–7 fl oz) stock and a squeeze of lime juice. Boil, stirring, until the onions and spices are 'frying' in their own juices. Stir and cook for a few moments. Stir in 7.5–15 ml (½–1 tbsp) tomato purée. Off the heat, stir in 15–30 ml (1–2 tbsp) room temperature yogurt.

STIR- 'FRIED' CHICKEN

SERVES 4

~

This quite amazingly good stir fry is a basic technique. You may substitute vermouth for sherry, or mix and match vegetables. After you have mastered this version, try it with mushrooms, mange tout, broccoli, spring onions, whatever you like.

- *15 ml (1 tbsp) cornflour*
- *30 ml (2 tbsp) cold stock*
- *2 dashes soy sauce*
- *fresh ginger, peeled and grated*
- *4 chicken breasts, boned, skinned and cut into 2–2.5 cm (¾–1 inch) cubes*
- *approximately 300 ml (½ pint) additional stock*
- *½ large Spanish onion, skinned and quartered*
- *1 small red or yellow pepper, cored, seeded, peeled and coarsely diced*
- *½ ripe tomato, skinned, seeded, juiced and quartered*
- *110 ml (4 fl oz) sherry*
- *freshly ground pepper to taste*
- *30–45 ml (2–3 tbsp) chopped fresh parsley*

1 Combine the cornflour, stock, soy sauce and ginger, stirring to dissolve the cornflour. Marinate the chicken breast cubes in the mixture.

2 In a non-stick wok, heat 100 ml (4 fl oz) of the additional stock. In batches, sauté the vegetables separately over a high heat, turning and tossing constantly. Have a bowl on hand to receive each batch as it is finished; begin with the onion and end with the tomato. Sauté the onion and pepper until they are crisp-tender. The tomato will lose its shape and cook down, with the pan juices, into a sauce. As vegetables are done, transfer to the bowl and keep warm. Add more stock as needed.

3 Heat the remaining stock. Add the chicken and sauté over high heat, tossing and turning constantly with a wooden spatula for 1½–2 minutes or until *just* cooked. Add to the vegetables.
4 Add the sherry to the pan. Over high heat, stir and scrape up any browned particles with a wooden spatula, then let the sherry reduce to about half. Add the chicken-vegetable mixture and all its juices back to the wok. Add pepper to taste and stir to combine and heat through. Sprinkle with parsley and serve immediately.

SALIL'S CHICKEN CURRY

SERVES 6

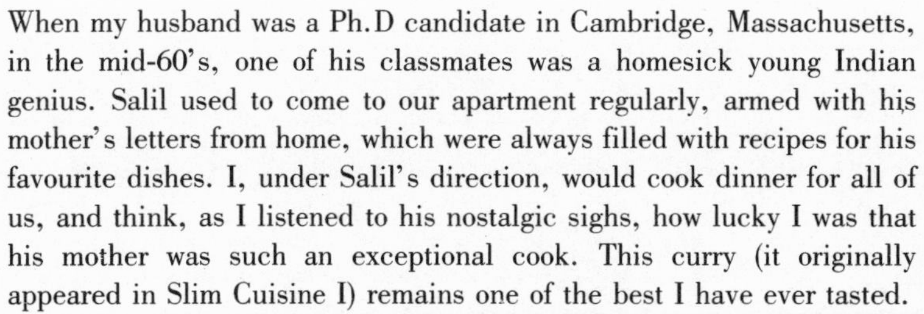

When my husband was a Ph.D candidate in Cambridge, Massachusetts, in the mid-60's, one of his classmates was a homesick young Indian genius. Salil used to come to our apartment regularly, armed with his mother's letters from home, which were always filled with recipes for his favourite dishes. I, under Salil's direction, would cook dinner for all of us, and think, as I listened to his nostalgic sighs, how lucky I was that his mother was such an exceptional cook. This curry (it originally appeared in Slim Cuisine I) remains one of the best I have ever tasted.

- *6 skinless, boneless chicken breasts*
- *juice of 1 large lemon*
- *salt to taste*
- *5 ml ((1 tsp) ground turmeric*
- *5 ml (1 tsp) ground cumin*
- *5 ml (1 tsp) ground coriander*
- *2.5 ml (½ tsp) chilli powder*
- *2.5 ml (½ tsp) ground cinnamon*
- *½ bay leaf, finely crumbled*
- *2 cloves garlic, skinned and finely chopped*
- *2 medium onions, skinned and cut into eighths*
- *400 ml (14 fl oz) stock*
- *30 ml (2 tbsp) tomato purée*
- *25 g (1 oz) raisins*
- *45 ml (3 tbsp) low-fat yogurt, at room temperature*

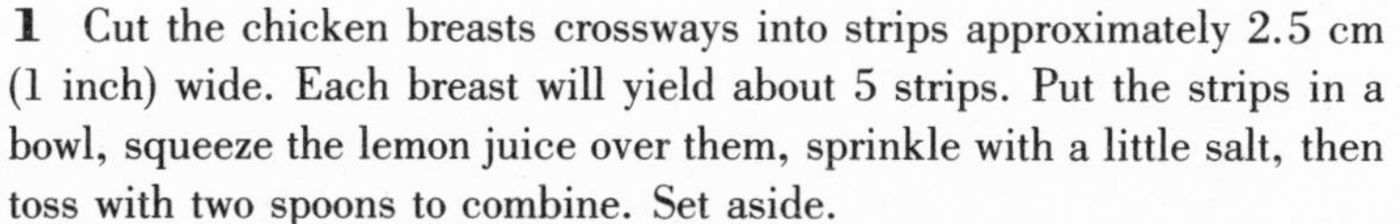

1 Cut the chicken breasts crossways into strips approximately 2.5 cm (1 inch) wide. Each breast will yield about 5 strips. Put the strips in a bowl, squeeze the lemon juice over them, sprinkle with a little salt, then toss with two spoons to combine. Set aside.

2 Measure all the spices and bay leaf into a small bowl. Add the garlic.
3 Separate the segments of onion pieces and spread them in a heavy, non-stick frying pan. Add no liquid or fat. Heat the frying pan gently. Cook over moderate heat, without stirring, for 7–10 minutes until the onions are sizzling and beginning to stick to the pan.
4 Stir in 300 ml (½ pint) of the stock and let it bubble up, stirring up the browned deposits in the pan with a wooden spoon as it bubbles. Stir in the spice and garlic mixture. Turn the heat down a little and simmer stirring frequently, until the mixture is very thick (not at all soupy) and the onions and spices are 'frying' in their own juices. Don't rush this step, as it is essential that the spices should not have a raw harsh taste. Taste. Cook very gently for a few more minutes if necessary.
5 Toss the chicken into the spicy onions in the frying pan. Stir and turn the chicken over low heat for 1 minute until everything is well combined. Stir in the remaining stock, the tomato purée and raisins. Spread out the mixture evenly in the pan. Cover and cook over lowest heat for 4 minutes.
6 Uncover and add 30 ml (2 tbsp) of the yogurt. Stir over low heat for a few moments until everything is amalgamated. Stir in the remaining yogurt and cook, stirring, for a moment or two more. Check the chicken for doneness, it should feel firm and springy, not soft and mushy. If you wish, cut into several pieces, you may even cut each strip in half. Each piece should be pearly white in the centre. Try to catch them when they are just done, at the moment they are turning from blush pink to creamy white. A minute or two of overcooking turns them tough and stringy. If the chicken is not quite cooked, cover, turn off the heat and leave to stand for a minute or two more. Stir everything up once more and serve warm or at room temperature.

LEMON ROASTED CHICKEN

SERVES 4–6

This recipe originally appeared in Slim Cuisine I, but my study subjects love it so much, I've decided to reprint it here. *You* eat the breast, serve the remainder to the rest of the family.

- *juice of 1½ lemons*
- *5 ml (1 tsp) black pepper*
- *10 ml (2 tsp) ground cumin*
- *5 ml (1 tsp) paprika or paprika paste*
- *1 medium (1.1–1.4 kg/2½–3 lb) roasting chicken, trimmed of fat*
- *120–175 ml (4–6 fl oz) dry white wine*

1 Mix the lemon juice with the pepper, cumin and paprika. Make small incisions all over the chicken (except in the breast) and rub in the lemon mixture. Loosen the breast skin and rub the lemon mixture under the skin. Place the squeezed lemon halves in the chicken cavity. Marinate overnight.

2 Next day, preheat the oven to 230°C, 450°F, Gas Mark 8. Place a rack across a flameproof shallow roasting tin. Place the chicken on the rack and roast, breast side down, for 15 minutes, then breast up for approximately 45 minutes until just done.

3 Allow the chicken to rest on a plate, loosely covered with foil. Tilt the roasting tin and prop it in the tilted position. With a large spoon, spoon out all the fat (there will be plenty) and discard. Put the roasting tin on the cooker and turn the heat on full. Stir and scrape up the dripping and browned bits. Pour in the dry white wine. Boil, stirring and scraping, until you have a dark, thick, rich sauce, and the alcohol has cooked away. Serve this powerful juice with the carved chicken.

EDDIE MUI'S STEAMED CHICKEN

SERVES 2–3

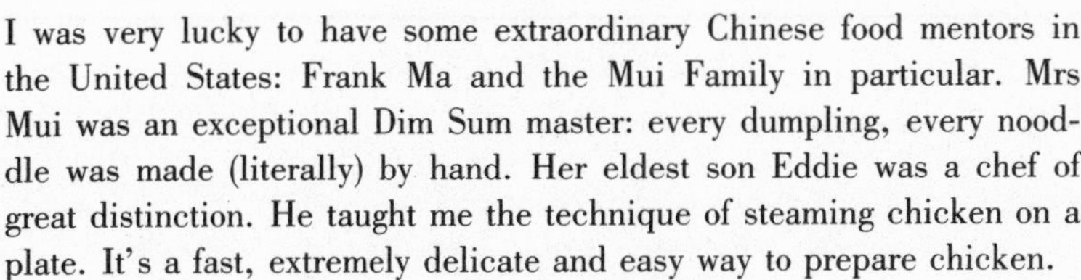

I was very lucky to have some extraordinary Chinese food mentors in the United States: Frank Ma and the Mui Family in particular. Mrs Mui was an exceptional Dim Sum master: every dumpling, every noodle was made (literally) by hand. Her eldest son Eddie was a chef of great distinction. He taught me the technique of steaming chicken on a plate. It's a fast, extremely delicate and easy way to prepare chicken.

- *275 g (10 oz) boneless, skinless chicken breast*
- *110 g (4 oz) fresh shiitake mushrooms, stalks removed, cut into quarters or eighths*
- *8 spring onions, trimmed and cut into 5 cm (2 inch) pieces*
- *1 piece fresh ginger, 6.25 cm (2½ inches) thick, peeled and very thinly sliced*
- *15 ml (1 tbsp) soy sauce*
- *22.5 ml (1½ tbsp) oyster sauce (see Note overleaf)*
- *15 ml (1 tbsp) dry sherry*
- *freshly ground pepper to taste (preferably white)*

1 Remove every bit of fat and gristle from the chicken. Slant cut into 2.5 cm (1 inch) pieces and set aside. Combine the mushrooms, spring onions and ginger. Set aside.

2 Combine all the remaining ingredients. Toss the liquid mixture, the chicken and the vegetable mixture together.

3 Spread the mixture in an even layer on a china plate that fits into a wok or steamer. Put some water in the wok or steamer, put in the steamer rack and bring to the boil. Place the plate on the rack, cover and steam for 12 minutes or until the chicken is opaque and just cooked through. Serve at once.

NOTE: Oyster sauce is available in Chinese food markets and many supermarkets and specialist food stores. Read the labels and buy a brand with no added fat. It keeps well in the refrigerator, so buy a bottle and keep it to use for this dish.

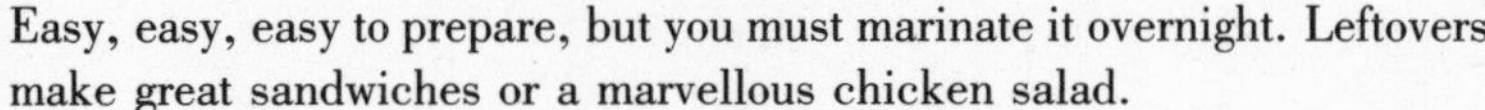

TANDOORI CHICKEN

SERVES 4

~

Easy, easy, easy to prepare, but you must marinate it overnight. Leftovers make great sandwiches or a marvellous chicken salad.

- *4 chicken breasts, boned and skinned*
- *salt and freshly ground pepper to taste*
- *15 ml (1 tbsp) ground coriander*
- *5 ml (1 tsp) ground cumin*
- *5 ml (1 tsp) ground turmeric*
- *5 ml (1 tsp) garam masala*
- *1.25 ml (¼ tsp) grated nutmeg*
- *pinch ground cloves*
- *1.25 ml (¼ tsp) ground cinnamon*
- *1.25–2.5 ml (¼–½ tsp) cayenne pepper*
- *350 ml (12 fl oz) yogurt*
- *6 cloves garlic, skinned and crushed*
- *1 onion, skinned and chopped*
- *1 piece fresh ginger, 2.5 cm (1 inch) long, peeled and finely chopped*

1 Season the chicken with salt and pepper. Set aside.

2 Combine the remaining ingredients. Mix the chicken with this mixture in a shallow non-reactive baking dish that holds them in one layer. Cover and allow to marinate in the refrigerator overnight.

3 Preheat the oven to 180°C, 350°F, Gas Mark 4. Take the baking dish directly from the refrigerator and bake in the oven for 30 minutes or until the chicken is just done, but still creamy textured.

4 Preheat the grill to its highest setting. Using tongs, remove the chicken from the marinade and shake off the excess liquid and onion pieces. Do *not* shake off the spice paste. Place the chicken breasts on to the grill rack in one layer and grill for approximately 1–2 minutes. Serve at once.

ROSIE'S FAMILY HEIRLOOM CURRY

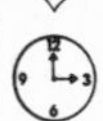

MAKES 900 ML (1½ PINTS)

~

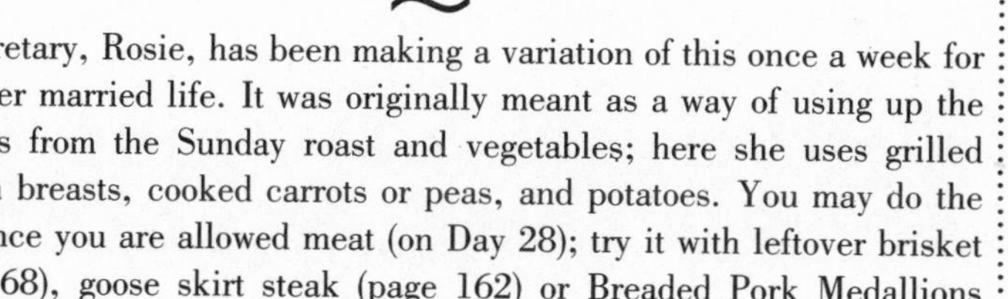

My secretary, Rosie, has been making a variation of this once a week for all of her married life. It was originally meant as a way of using up the leftovers from the Sunday roast and vegetables; here she uses grilled chicken breasts, cooked carrots or peas, and potatoes. You may do the same once you are allowed meat (on Day 28); try it with leftover brisket (page 168), goose skirt steak (page 162) or Breaded Pork Medallions (page 170). It's also great with all vegetables – as many as you like.

- *1 large onion, skinned and diced*
- *375 ml (13 fl oz) stock*
- *crushed chillies, to taste (Rosie uses 5 ml (1 tsp) but you may want quite a bit less)*
- *10 ml (2 tsp) paprika*
- *cayenne pepper to taste*
- *5 ml (1 tsp) ground turmeric*
- *7.5 ml (1½ tsp) ground coriander*
- *12.5 ml (2½ tsp) ground cumin*
- *5 ml (1 tsp) ground ginger*
- *2.5 ml (½ tsp) ground cinnamon*
- *2 cloves garlic, skinned and crushed*
- *225 g (8 oz) potatoes, cooked and cut into 1 cm (½ inch) cubes*
- *110 g (4 oz) cooked sliced carrots (or garden peas after Day 28)*
- *2 grilled chicken breasts (see page 138), cut into 2.5 cm (1 inch) cubes*
- *1 can (213 g/7½ oz) Italian tomatoes, drained and chopped*
- *30 ml (2 tbsp) tomato purée*

1 Spread out the onion in a heavy, non-stick frying pan. Add no liquid or fat. Heat the frying pan gently. Cook over moderate heat, without stirring, for 7–10 minutes until the onion is sizzling, speckled with dark amber and beginning to stick to the pan.
2 Stir in 225 ml (8 fl oz) of the stock and let it bubble up, stirring up the browned deposits in the pan with a wooden spoon as it bubbles. Stir in the spices and garlic. Turn the heat down a little and simmer, stirring frequently, until the mixture is very thick (not at all soupy) and the onions and spices are 'frying' in their own juices. Don't rush this step, it is essential that the spices should not have a raw harsh taste. Taste. Cook very gently for a few more minutes if necessary.
3 Add the remaining ingredients, including the remaining stock. Turn up the heat slightly and simmer for approximately 15 minutes. Serve hot.

LUXURIOUS POTATO-TURKEY SALAD

MAKES 1.1 LITRES (2 PINTS)

~

Mayonnaise – who needs it? Diet or no diet, this is the finest potato salad in the galaxy. The warm potatoes become imbued with the compelling taste of balsamic vinegar; the turkey adds a subtle smokiness and the sun dried tomatoes add flavour intensity. The mere thought of adding mayonnaise to this perfection is ludicrous!

- *700 g (1½ lb) small new potatoes (unpeeled)*
- *1 large clove garlic, halved*
- *75 g (3 oz) smoked turkey breast, diced*
- *15 ml (1 tbsp) drained capers*
- *1 grilled pepper (see page 89), diced (roasted pepper from a can may be used)*
- *30 ml (2 tbsp) balsamic vinegar*
- *300 ml (½ pint) chicken stock*
- *3–4 dry-pack sun dried tomatoes, finely diced (use scissors)*
- *pinch or two dried chilli flakes to taste*
- *freshly ground pepper to taste*
- *30 ml (2 tbsp) chopped fresh parsley*
- *3 spring onions, trimmed, cut in half lengthways, then thinly sliced crossways*

1 Steam the potatoes until tender but not falling apart. Halve or quarter them.
2 Rub a glass bowl thoroughly with the cut sides of the garlic. Set the garlic aside.
3 While the potatoes are still warm, toss them with the smoked turkey, capers and diced pepper in the bowl. Add the balsamic vinegar.
4 Combine the stock, tomatoes and chilli flakes in a small frying pan. Finely chop the garlic and add it to the pan. Boil rapidly until the liquid is reduced by half. Immediately pour the stock mixture over the potatoes. With a wooden spoon, turn the potatoes so that they are coated with the stock mixture. Season with pepper. Mix in the parsley and spring onions just before serving.

FRUIT FONDUE

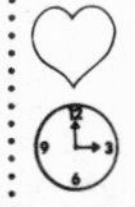

This is the simplest of fruit puddings, yet it is also one of the most festive and convivial. It's a wonderful way for a family to end a celebration meal, and dinner party guests love it too. Fruit Fondue is at its best during the summer, but a pleasing version can be assembled with winter fruits as well. Choose plates and bowls that show off the brilliant colours of the fruit and the fruit sauces.

Choose the best and most interesting fruits the market can offer: strawberries, melons, oranges, mangos, papayas, lychees . . . leave the strawberries whole and unhulled, slice the melons, mangos and papayas; peel the oranges, remove every bit of pith and then slice; peel and stone the lychees. Prepare several different fruit coulis (see below). Provide each diner with a plate of beautifully arranged prepared fruit and several bowls, each containing a different coulis. Decorate the fruit plates with sprigs of mint, and provide forks for spearing the fruit and dipping.

FRUIT COULIS

This method works beautifully with fresh, or frozen, thawed fruits and berries. Try mango, raspberries, blueberries, strawberries, tayberries, blackcurrants, blackberries . . .

Purée the fruit or berries in a food processor or blender. If the fruit or berries contain pips, sieve the purée to eliminate them. Sweeten to taste with just a little NutraSweet. If the taste needs sharpening, squeeze in a little lemon juice. Refrigerate until needed.

DAY 21
TECHNIQUES AND RECIPES

GRAIN TECHNIQUES

Grains are a wonderful source of essential fatty acids, fat soluble vitamins and complex carbohydrate. They are also, as are potatoes, a natural tranquillizer, and can be used in so many different ways, in so many delicious recipes. If you learn to cook with some of the more unusual grains you will add much pleasure to your daily fare.

POLENTA

Polenta is coarse corn (maize) meal. It is a beloved staple in Italian cuisine, although – like many other foodstuffs – it was a gift of the New World and didn't reach Italy until the middle of the 17th century. The Rumanians love it too; they call it '*mamaliga*'. The Americans call it cornmeal mush – it sounds awful, but it is just as delicious as when it's called polenta. Quick cooking polenta is easy and fast to prepare. You can eat it fresh and hot, as it comes out of the pot, or cooked, cut into squares, then baked, grilled or microwaved.

BASIC POLENTA

MAKES APPROXIMATELY 1.4 LITRES (2½ PINTS) COOKED POLENTA

- *750 ml (1¼ pints) very well seasoned stock*
- *175 g (6 oz) quick cooking polenta*

1 In a heavy pan, heat the stock until very hot, but not quite boiling. With a whisk, stir in the polenta.
2 Switch to a wooden spoon, then stir over low heat for 3–5 minutes until very thick and smooth. At this point, the polenta should be thick, cooked and pull away from the sides of the pan in a mass as it is stirred. Be careful not to scorch it. Serve at once, or cool for later eating.

Freshly cooked polenta is delicious eaten with Tomato Sauce, Sautéed Mushrooms, 'Fried' Onions (see pages 122, 86 and 83) or with any of the Slim Cuisine sauces. To eat later, spread the hot, freshly cooked polenta evenly on to a baking sheet or into a baking dish. Cool, cover and refrigerate until needed.

TO HEAT LEFTOVER POLENTA

cooked, chilled polenta (see previous recipe)

1 Cut a square of polenta. Put it in a small baking dish and cover with foil for conventional oven or microwave cling film for the microwave.

2 Heat in the conventional oven at 180°C, 350°F, Gas Mark 4 for 30–40 minutes, or in the microwave on FULL for 6 minutes. If you have used the microwave, pierce the cling film with a sharp knife to release the steam, then carefully uncover. Serve with Tomato Ragoût (see page 117), Vegetable Chilli (see page 115) or any Slim Cuisine sauce.

TO GRILL LEFTOVER POLENTA

cooked, chilled polenta (see previous recipe)

1 Preheat the grill to its highest setting. Cover the grill tray with foil, shiny side up. Cut squares of polenta and place on the tray.

2 Grill, close to the heat, for approximately 2 minutes until speckled with brown. Turn and grill for a minute or two on the second side.

BULGHUR

Bulghur is cracked wheat, available in packets from most supermarkets and wholefood shops. Prepare bulghur by soaking it in cold water to cover for 30–40 minutes (it will greatly expand as it soaks), then squeezing dry with clean hands. It has a wonderfully nutty taste and texture.

Bulghur may be also cooked by the pilaf method:

WHEAT PILAF

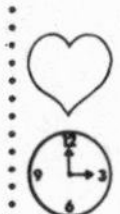

MAKES APPROXIMATELY 900 ML (1½ PINTS)

- *1 large onion, skinned and coarsely chopped*
- *2–3 cloves garlic, skinned and crushed*
- *1 carrot, peeled and coarsely chopped*
- *570 ml (1 pint) stock*
- *1 red pepper, cored, seeded, peeled and chopped*
- *1 small courgette, coarsely chopped*
- *1 bunch chives, snipped*
- *45 ml (3 tbsp) chopped fresh parsley*
- *30 ml (2 tbsp) shredded fresh mint*
- *salt and freshly ground pepper to taste*
- *225 g (8 oz) bulghur*

1 Combine the onion, garlic, carrot and 300 ml (½ pint) of the stock in a heavy, lidded frying pan. Cover, bring to the boil and boil for 5–7 minutes. Uncover, reduce the heat a little and simmer briskly until the onions are browning and sticking and the liquid is almost gone. Add the pepper, courgette and a splash of stock and cook for a few more minutes, stirring and scraping up the browned bits.
2 Bring the remaining stock to the boil in a separate saucepan.
3 Stir the herbs and seasoning into the vegetables. Add the bulghur and stir so everything is well combined. Pour in the boiling stock and stir well.
4 Cover the pan and simmer over lowest heat for about 20 minutes until the bulghur is tender but not mushy, and all the liquid is absorbed. Fluff with a fork. Taste and adjust seasonings. Remove from the heat. Place a tea towel over the pan, then put the cover on the pan over the tea towel. Leave to stand until you are ready to serve.

Cous Cous

Cous cous is made up of tiny bits of semolina: in fact, you might say that cous cous is a collection of tiny grains of pasta. Because most cous cous that you will find in supermarkets and whole food shops is precooked, it needs only a brief soaking in hot liquid. It goes beautifully with sauces, curries and chilli preparations. Leftover cous cous reheats very well in the microwave.

Basic Cous Cous

MAKES APPROXIMATELY 1.1 LITRES (2 PINTS) COOKED COUS COUS

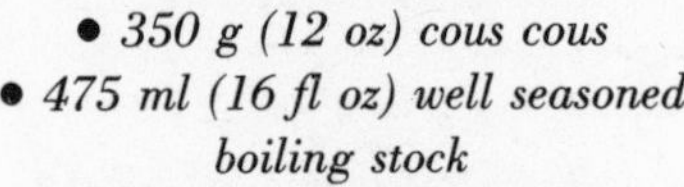

- *350 g (12 oz) cous cous*
- *475 ml (16 fl oz) well seasoned boiling stock*

1 Combine the cous cous and boiling stock in a large bowl. Soak for 10–15 minutes until the liquid is absorbed and the grains are tender. Fluff with a fork.

Buckwheat Groats

Buckwheat is a staple food in much of Eastern Europe, where it is known as kasha. Many wholefood shops here stock it. Kasha is one of the most delicious foods in the world; easy to cook, satisfying to eat. I must say, though, that some people find the smell of cooking kasha strong and vulgar, and the taste unrefined. But if you have Russian or Polish ancestry, or if you love earthy, deep flavours, you'll love kasha too. Cooked kasha goes especially well with Slim Cuisine 'Fried' Onions and Sautéed Mushrooms (see pages 83 and 86).

BASIC KASHA

MAKES APPROXIMATELY 900 ML (1½ PINTS) COOKED KASHA

- *2 egg whites, very lightly beaten*
- *225 ml (8 fl oz) kasha (roasted buckwheat groats)*
- *475 ml (16 fl oz) boiling stock*
- *salt and freshly ground pepper to taste*

1 Heat a large, heavy frying pan.
2 Stir the egg white into the kasha. Mix until the grains are well coated.
3 With a wooden spoon or spatula, stir the kasha in the hot pan over moderate heat until each grain is dry and separate. It will take about 5 minutes and will smell deliciously toasty. Scrape the kasha into a lidded pan. (When choosing your pan, remember that the kasha will expand and so needs room.)
4 Stir the boiling stock into the kasha, then season to taste with salt and pepper. Cover and simmer over lowest heat for 30 minutes. Remove from the heat, uncover and drape a clean tea towel over the pan. Re-cover, over the tea towel, and leave to stand for 5–10 minutes until the liquid is absorbed and the kasha is fluffy and tender, each grain separate. Season.

POLENTA PIZZA

SERVES 6–8

Spread just cooked polenta on to a baking sheet, bake briefly and you have a delightful pizza base. The yellow of the polenta 'crust' and the deep red of the tomato sauce make a lovely contrast. Top the pizza with your favourite Slim Cuisine vegetables.

- *750 ml (1¼ pints) very well seasoned stock*
- *175 g (6 oz) quick cooking polenta*
- *570 ml (1 pint) Tomato Sauce (see page 122)*
- *toppings of your choice, such as 'Fried' Onions (see page 83), Sautéed Mushrooms (see page 86), Grilled Peppers (see page 89)*

1 Preheat the oven to 180°C, 350°F, Gas Mark 4.

2 Heat the stock in a pan until very hot but not quite boiling. With a whisk, stir in the polenta. Switch to a wooden spoon, then stir over low heat for 5 minutes until thick and smooth. At this point, the polenta should be thick, cooked and pull away from the sides of the pan in a mass as it is stirred. Be careful not to scorch it. As it cooks, taste for seasoning, you do not want the polenta to taste bland.

3 Immediately pour and scrape the polenta on to a 38 cm × 25 cm (15 × 10 inch) non-stick baking sheet. Smooth it with a spatula and build up the sides a bit. Bake for 15 minutes.

4 Spread the baked polenta base with tomato sauce. Arrange the chosen topping ingredients over the sauce. Bake for 10–15 minutes until heated through.

♡

BULGHUR-TUNA SALAD

MAKES 1.1 LITRES (2 PINTS)

~

A delicious change from plain old tuna salad. It is, essentially, tabouli with tuna added.

- *225 g (8 oz) bulghur*
- *100 ml (4 fl oz) lemon juice*
- *45 ml (3 tbsp) shredded fresh basil*
- *15 ml (1 tbsp) shredded fresh mint*
- *90 ml (6 tbsp) chopped fresh parsley*
- *4–5 ripe tomatoes, skinned, seeded and chopped (or use canned tomatoes)*
- *4 spring onions, trimmed and finely chopped*
- *1 can (185 g/6½ oz) tuna in brine, drained and flaked or chunked*
- *salt and freshly ground pepper to taste*

1 Soak the bulghur in cold water to cover, using a large bowl as it expands quite a bit. After 30–40 minutes, squeeze the grains with your (clean!) hands to drain them. Place the squeezed grains in a clean bowl.
2 Stir in the lemon juice, then toss in the herbs. Fold in the tomatoes, spring onions and tuna pieces. Season to taste.
NOTE: Substitute shredded cooked turkey or chicken breast, or cooked prawns for the tuna, if desired.

TOMATO-TUNA SAUCE

MAKES APPROXIMATELY 1.4 LITRES (2½ PINTS)

This can easily be halved if you wish, but it makes a great family supper, and freezes so well, why not make a big batch?

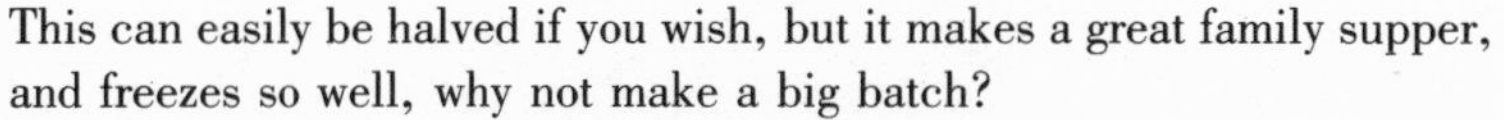

- *2 large onions, skinned and coarsely chopped*
- *2 cloves garlic, skinned and crushed*
- *pinch or two of flaked, dried chillies*
- *175 ml (6 fl oz) stock*
- *175 ml (6 fl oz) dry white vermouth*
- *15 ml (1 tbsp) chopped fresh basil*
- *15 ml (1 tbsp) chopped fresh parsley*
- *15 ml (1 tbsp) chopped fresh oregano*
- *15 ml (1 tbsp) drained capers*
- *3 cans (400 g/14 oz each) chopped tomatoes*
- *salt and freshly ground pepper to taste*
- *30 ml (2 tbsp) tomato purée*
- *90 ml (6 tbsp) chopped fresh parsley*
- *Baked Garlic purée (see page 74) – optional*
- *1–2 cans (185 g/6½ oz each) tuna in water or brine, drained and flaked*

1 Combine the onions, garlic, chillies, stock, vermouth, herbs and capers in a pan. Cover and bring to the boil. Uncover and simmer briskly until the onions are tender and the liquid has almost cooked away.
2 Stir in the chopped tomatoes. Simmer, partially covered, for 15 minutes. Stir in seasoning and tomato purée. Simmer, uncovered, for 5 minutes.
3 Stir in the parsley, optional garlic purée and tuna. Serve with cous cous or over pasta.

DAYS 22–25
TECHNIQUES AND RECIPES

PEARS FILLED WITH ORANGE CREAM

MAKES 8 PIECES

~

I contrived the idea for this recipe on a train somewhere between Bath and London. When I finally got home, and my assistant and I tested it, I was tempted to fling myself to my knees to give heartfelt thanks for my whole Slim Cuisine regime. This is *good*!! And this recipe set me off on a frenzy of new technique development ending with cheesecake – in fact, a positive flurry of cheesecakes. Did you hear me? I said, CHEESE-CAKE!! Can you believe it? Is it really possible?

- *400 g (14 oz) quark or very low-fat curd cheese*
- *45 ml (3 tbsp) NutraSweet*
- *45 ml (3 tbsp) thawed orange juice concentrate*
- *5 ml (1 tsp) natural vanilla essence*
- *pinch grated nutmeg*
- *4 large pears*
- *juice of 1 lemon*
- *Grape-Nuts cereal*
- *Raspberry Coulis (see page 149) optional*

1 In an electric mixer, beat together the quark, sweetener, orange concentrate, vanilla and nutmeg. Set aside.
2 Peel the pears, halve and remove the cores, with a small spoon, forming a cavity. Roll the pears thoroughly in lemon juice.
3 Stuff the cavities with the quark mixture and spread the cut sides of the pears with the mixture. Place the cereal on a plate. Press the pears, cut side down, in the cereal, so they are evenly coated. Sprinkle some cereal on top. Cover with cling film and refrigerate until needed.
4 Place each pear half on a plate. Pour on the raspberry Coulis.

CHEESECAKE TECHNIQUE

~

You are going to have lots of fun making cheesecakes, both for yourself, and for your friends and relations. When I researched cheesecake for a book I wrote in the United States about New York-Jewish cuisine, I learned two important facts from the man in charge of cheesecakes at the Carnegie Delicatessen on New York's 7th Avenue: a perfect cheesecake should have a crumb crust and *no* fruit topping. Jane and Michael Stern, writing about New York cheesecake in *Good Food*, called it 'The richest dessert in history; pure edible ivory, like some new element on the atomic chart – perhaps a fusion of lead and satin!' What I have done here is *emphasized* the satin, and *eliminated* the lead. Enjoy!

CHEESECAKE CRUSTS

Unbaked: To make the very simplest of cheesecake crusts, pour approximately 110 g (4 oz) Grape-Nuts cereal into the bottom of a 25 cm (10 inch) diameter, non-stick round flan tin. With the back of a dessertspoon, or a serving spoon, spread the cereal evenly over the bottom of the tin, and as far up the sides as you can manage. Then, gently swirl and spread the filling over the crust. Chill the cheesecake for a few hours, or overnight; the 'crust' will soften to just the right consistency.

Baked: This method makes a more traditional crust. Preheat the oven to 180°C, 350°F, Gas Mark 4. Put 150 g (5 oz) Grape-Nuts cereal into a bowl. Lightly beat 2 egg whites. With two spoons, toss together the cereal and egg white until the cereal is thoroughly coated with the egg white. Pour the mixture into a 25 cm (10 inch) non-stick, round flan tin. With the back of a dessert spoon or a serving spoon, spread the cereal evenly over the bottom and up the sides to form a thin layer. Bake for 5–7 minutes. Cool. When cool, spread and swirl the cheesecake mixture over the crust. Chill for several hours or overnight. During chilling, the crust will soften to just the right consistency.

CHEESECAKE

These cheesecakes are substantial. They are not really meant to be a dessert following a main meal; they are to be eaten as a snack, as breakfast or even as a meal in themselves. How much is a serving? Well, your Grape-Nuts cereal allowance is 30 g (1¼ oz). Therefore approximately a quarter of a cheesecake made with the unbaked crust, and a fifth of a cheesecake made with the baked crust would provide you with the requisite allowance. That doesn't mean that you *have* to eat a quarter or a fifth of a cheesecake; it is just a guide to help you from going over your cereal limit.

BANANA CREAM CHEESECAKE

MAKES ONE 25 CM (10 INCH) CHEESECAKE

~

Rich tasting banana mousse swirled into a crumb crust. *This* is dieting??

- *4 grilled bananas and their juices (see page 128)*
- *4 small cartons (200 g/7 oz each) quark or very low-fat curd cheese*
- *30 ml (2 tbsp) thawed orange juice concentrate*
- *5 ml (1 tsp) natural vanilla essence*
- *2.5 ml (½ tsp) ground cinnamon*
- *NutraSweet to taste*
- *Cheesecake crust (see page 157)*
- *freshly grated nutmeg*

1 Spoon the bananas out of their skins. Put them, with their juices, into a food processor with the quark, orange juice concentrate, vanilla and cinnamon. Process until very smooth and fluffy. Taste, then process in some sweetener and a little more cinnamon if needed.

2 Spread and swirl the banana cream mixture over the crust. Sprinkle with a little nutmeg. Chill for several hours or overnight, so the flavours can blend and the filling can 'set'.

STRAWBERRY CHEESECAKE

MAKES ONE 25 CM (10 INCH) CHEESECAKE

~

A beautiful pink cheesecake to make when strawberries are at their sweetest and juiciest.

- *1 punnet very ripe strawberries, hulled and halved*
- *4 small cartons (200 g/7 oz each) quark*
- *15 ml (1 tbsp) thawed orange juice concentrate*
- *5 ml (1 tsp) natural vanilla essence*
- *NutraSweet to taste*
- *Cheesecake crust (see page 157)*
- *fresh strawberry halves and mint leaves to decorate*

1 Put the strawberries in a shallow bowl. Mash them with a potato masher until they form a lumpy, juicy purée.
2 Put the quark, strawberries and their juices, the orange concentrate and vanilla in a food processor and process for a moment or so. Taste and add sweetener as needed, then process until fluffy.
3 Spread and swirl the mixture over the crust. Chill for several hours or overnight. Just before serving, decorate the cake with fresh strawberry halves and mint leaves.

ORANGE CHEESECAKE

MAKES ONE 25 CM (10 INCH) CHEESECAKE

~

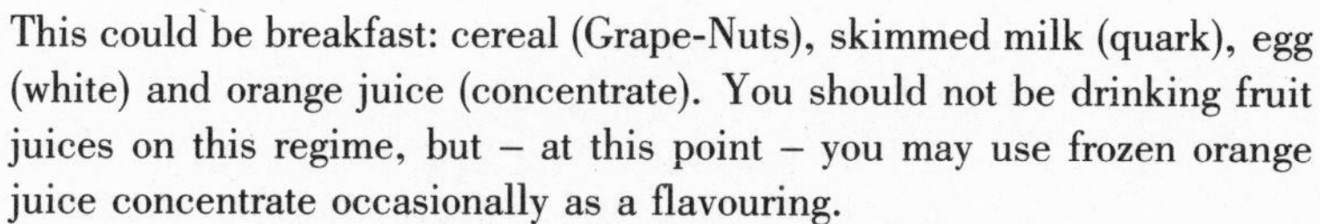

This could be breakfast: cereal (Grape-Nuts), skimmed milk (quark), egg (white) and orange juice (concentrate). You should not be drinking fruit juices on this regime, but – at this point – you may use frozen orange juice concentrate occasionally as a flavouring.

- *4 small cartons (200 g/7 oz each) quark or very low-fat curd cheese*
- *75–90 ml (5–6 tbsp) granulated NutraSweet*
- *60 ml (4 tbsp) thawed orange juice concentrate*
- *7.5 ml (1½ tsp) natural vanilla essence*
- *Cheesecake crust (see page 157)*

1 In a food processor, whip the quark, sweetener, orange juice concentrate and vanilla until they are fluffy and well blended.
2 With a rubber spatula, gently and evenly spread and swirl the quark mixture over the crust. Chill for a few hours or overnight, so the flavours can blend and the filling can 'set'.

QUARK FOR CHEESECAKES

There is a brand of quark available in some supermarkets that contains modified food starch. This particular quark is not suitable for cheesecake making; it is too runny and the cheesecake will not set properly. Read the labels and buy the quark that lists 'plain quark, made with skimmed milk'.

DAYS 26–27

TECHNIQUES AND RECIPES

POLENTA WITH TOMATO-SWEETCORN SAUCE

It is a good idea to cook more polenta than you need, so you can keep some in the refrigerator for fast meals, like this one. Of course, it helps to keep a supply of tomato sauce in the freezer as well.

- *cooked, chilled polenta (see page 150)*
- *Tomato Sauce (see page 122)*
- *frozen sweetcorn kernels, defrosted and cooked until just done (they should not be mushy)*

1 Cut a square of polenta. Put it into a small baking dish and cover with foil (for the conventional oven) or cling film (for the microwave). Heat in the conventional oven at 180°C, 350°F, Gas Mark 4 for 30 minutes or microwave on FULL for 6 minutes.
2 Combine the tomato sauce and sweetcorn in a pan, then bring to simmering point. Preheat the grill.
3 Carefully uncover the polenta. Pour the sauce over and around it. Grill, not too close to the heat, for a few minutes until the sauce is beginning to bubble. Serve at once.

VARIATIONS Add sweetcorn to Pepper Sauce (see page 126) or Tomato-Carrot Sauce (see page 124). The sauces are delicious with pasta as well as polenta.

CORN SALAD

MAKES 1.4 LITRES (2½ PINTS)

Corn salad will keep in the refrigerator for several days, and improve in flavour day by day. I make this with thawed frozen sweetcorn. The recipe is at its best prepared with grilled fresh peppers, but canned red peppers will do when time is short. In fact, you could use canned tomatoes too, but the salad is so much more scintillating with fresh, ripe beauties.

- *450 g (1 lb) sweetcorn kernels, steamed until barely tender (the microwave is perfect for this)*
- *6 fresh ripe tomatoes, skinned, seeded, juiced and coarsely chopped*
- *6 grilled red peppers, peeled and coarsely chopped (see page 89), or use canned red peppers*
- *½ can (50 g/2 oz) green chillies, drained and coarsely chopped, or 1–2 fresh chillies, chopped*
- *salt and freshly ground pepper to taste*
- *30 ml (2 tbsp) balsamic vinegar or wine vinegar*
- *30 ml (2 tbsp) chopped fresh coriander*
- *30 ml (2 tbsp) chopped fresh parsley*

1 Combine all the ingredients together in a shallow dish. Toss together.
2 Chill, stirring occasionally. Serve cold.

HERBED PEA PURÉE

MAKES 570 ML (1 PINT)

~

Thawed frozen peas, puréed with herbs and a little lime juice, taste so vibrant and fresh-from-the-garden. Scoop it on to Slim Cuisine Potato Crisps (see page 93), spread it on bread, stuff it into pita pockets, eat it with a spoon or serve it with raw vegetable dippers.

- *60 ml (4 tbsp) shredded fresh mint*
- *30 ml (2 tbsp) chopped fresh parsley*
- *30 ml (2 tbsp) lime juice*
- *1 fresh chilli, seeded and coarsely diced (optional)*
- *450 g (1 lb) defrosted frozen peas*
- *salt to taste*
- *2 spring onions, trimmed and chopped*

1 Place the herbs, lime juice and chilli in a blender or food processor. Add the peas and salt, then blend to a rough purée.
2 Scrape the purée into a bowl and stir in the spring onion.

DAY 28

TECHNIQUES AND RECIPES

GOOSE SKIRT STEAK

~

Don't ask me why it's called goose skirt – I have no idea. It is not an article of apparel for a gander; it's a flat, paddle shaped, extremely lean, deeply flavoured cut of beef – about 450–700 g (1–1½ lb) in weight. Ask your butcher. You might request that he make a habit of putting one aside for you each week. As beef cuts go, goose skirt is just about perfect. It is as lean as can be, can be cooked *very* quickly (grilled, pan fried or stir fried) or braised for a longer (unattended) time in the oven, and lends itself to all sorts of interesting recipes.

BASIC GOOSE SKIRT TECHNIQUES

GRILLING METHOD

1 Preheat the grill to its highest setting. Line the grill tray with foil, shiny side up. Place the rack on the grill tray.

2 Season the goose skirt steak on both sides with salt and freshly ground pepper. Grill, 7.5 cm (3 inches) from the heat, for 4–5 minutes (depending on thickness and your preference) on each side. (It tastes best and most tender when it is *not* well done.) Leave to rest for 7–10 minutes for the juices to redistribute. With a sharp carving knife, slice thinly, on the diagonal, across the grain.

PAN FRYING METHOD

1 Heat a heavy bottomed non-stick frying pan until hot. Season the goose skirt steak. Sear it on both sides in the hot pan, turning it with tongs. Once seared, reduce the heat a little and cook for 3–4 minutes on each side. Remove to a platter, cover loosely with foil and leave to rest for 5 minutes.

NOTE You can pan *grill* your goose skirt, if you purchase a non-stick ridged grill pan. Simply heat the ridged pan on the hob, then cook your steak in the pan, turning it with tongs. Goose skirt cooked in such a pan has a delicious, smoky, barbecued taste. You'll need a good extractor fan over your cooker, or the kitchen may get a bit smoke-filled.

PAN SAUCES FOR PAN FRIED GOOSE SKIRT

(PREPARED IN A FRYING PAN)

~

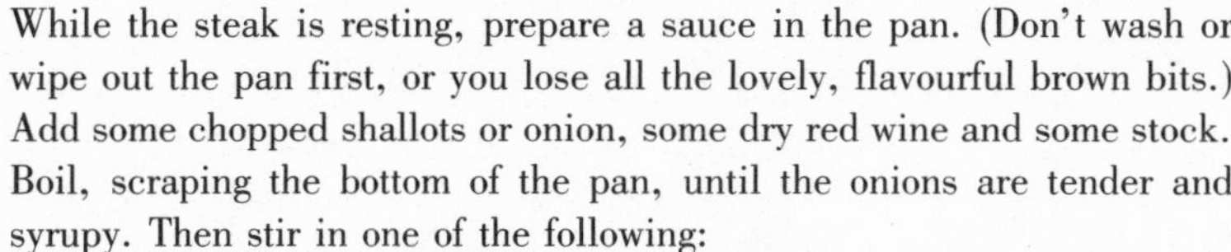

While the steak is resting, prepare a sauce in the pan. (Don't wash or wipe out the pan first, or you lose all the lovely, flavourful brown bits.) Add some chopped shallots or onion, some dry red wine and some stock. Boil, scraping the bottom of the pan, until the onions are tender and syrupy. Then stir in one of the following:

- *a dab of Dijon mustard*
- *a good dollop of Baked Garlic purée (see page 74)*
- *Sautéed Mushrooms (see page 86)*
- *Peperonata (see page 99)*
- *Stir-'Fried' Red Peppers (see page 86)*

Pour the meat juices that have collected under the resting goose skirt into the pan sauce. Thinly slice the steak on the diagonal, crossways (against the grain), and arrange the slices on the platter. Pour the sauce over the steak.

CHINESE STIR-FRY METHOD

This is the basic technique; see page 165 for a specific recipe. Add any vegetables you like in the last step, such as mushrooms, cauliflower, broccoli.

1 Cut the goose skirt steak down the centre, lengthways, into 2 equal sized pieces. With a very sharp carving knife, carve each piece of steak on the diagonal, crossways (across the grain), into slices as thin as you can manage.

2 Whisk together 30 ml (2 tbsp) soy sauce or teriyaki sauce, 15 ml (1 tbsp) dry sherry and 15 ml (1 tbsp) cornflour. Toss this mixture into the beef slices.

3 Heat a non-stick wok or large frying pan. Pour in 50 ml (2 fl oz) stock. When it boils furiously, add the meat. Stir and cook with 2 wooden spoons, using the spoons to pull apart the meat strips as they cook. When the meat strips have lost their red, raw look, scoop them on to a plate.

4 Add 100 ml (4 fl oz) stock to the wok with some finely chopped fresh ginger and garlic. Add whatever vegetables you like, such as cauliflower, broccoli, mange tout, sliced mushrooms. Cook and stir until tender and surrounded by a thick but scant sauce. Return the beef and its juices. Cook and stir for another minute or so. This is lovely with rice.

BRAISING METHOD

Braising the meat takes much longer, but it is an ideal method for those who don't find meat appetizing if it is at all pink. When the steak is casseroled for approximately 1½ hours, it becomes meltingly tender.

1 Preheat the oven to 200°C, 400°F, Gas Mark 6.

2 Heat a heavy bottomed non-reactive frying pan. When moderately hot, sear the goose skirt steak on both sides, then set aside on a platter.

3 Put some chopped vegetables into the pan (onions, celery, carrots – whatever you like) and some stock or some wine or a mixture. Cover and boil for 5–7 minutes. Uncover and cook until the vegetables are tender. Stir and scrape up the browned bits with a wooden spoon.

4 Season the beef. Transfer the vegetables to a shallow baking dish. Put the meat on the vegetables. Pour some stock over and around the meat. (Don't swamp it – just a little will do.) Add some herbs or spices of your choice, and some sliced potatoes, if you like. Cover tightly with foil. Bake for ½ hour. Reduce the oven temperature to 130°C, 250°F, Gas Mark ½ and bake for 1–1½ hours more until beautifully tender.

OPEN FACE STEAK SANDWICHES WITH MUSHROOMS

SERVES 4

Imagine this – crusty slices of toast slathered with a creamy garlic spread with juicy pink slices of steak oozing meat juices, laid across the top, then sautéed mushrooms, heady with the taste of sherry, generously ladled on to the meat . . . isn't dieting wonderful?

- *1 goose skirt steak, very well trimmed*
- *coarsely ground pepper*
- *purée from 1 freshly baked head of garlic (see page 74)*
- *275 g (10 oz) quark*
- *350 g (12 oz) button mushrooms, halved or quartered*
- *100 ml (4 fl oz) stock*
- *a dash or two of soy or teriyaki sauce*
- *50–75 ml (2–3 fl oz) sherry*
- *4 slices crusty bread*

1 Preheat the grill. Coat the goose skirt steak on both sides with the pepper. Cook until medium rare under the grill or in a ridged grill pan. When it is done, remove to a board and leave to rest for 5 minutes.

2 While the steak is grilling, cream together the garlic and quark (or process together in a food processor). Set aside.
3 Cook the mushrooms in the stock, soy sauce and sherry in a frying pan. When the mushrooms are tender, and the liquid is greatly reduced and syrupy, set aside.
4 Toast the bread and spread it with the garlic mixture.
5 Slice the steak on the diagonal, against the grain. Overlap the slices on the bread. Pour the meat juices, that have accumulated on the board, evenly over the meat. Divide the mushrooms and their juices evenly over the sandwiches. Eat at once with a knife and fork.

> *I began to entertain lustful thoughts. I desired a roast beef sandwich with horse-radish and pickled onions with a wanton savagery that I had never felt for any man.*
>
> *THE THIN WOMAN*, A NOVEL BY DOROTHY CANNELL

CHINESE BEEF WITH SPRING ONIONS ♡

~

My friend Frank Ma taught me to stir fry slices of goose skirt steak by mixing them with egg white, then stir frying them in a wok full of very hot oil. The first time I tried a beef stir-fry without oil, I was haunted by visions of Frank rolling his eyes and shrugging his shoulders at my utter madness. But dear Frank (and dear reader) it works just fine! As with all Slim Cuisine, it turns up its nose at *tradition* but it sure tastes good.

Before you begin to stir fry, have all ingredients chopped, sliced, diced, measured and ready on your work surface. The actual cooking is very fast.

- *1 very well trimmed goose skirt steak (about 550 g/1¼ lb)*
- *15 ml (1 tbsp) chopped fresh ginger*
- *4 cloves garlic, skinned and crushed*
- *45 ml (3 tbsp) soy sauce*
- *15 ml (1 tbsp) cornflour*
- *300 ml (½ pint) chicken stock*
- *1 clove garlic, skinned and chopped*
- *2 bunches spring onions, trimmed and cut into 6.25 cm (2½ inch) pieces*
- *freshly ground pepper*

1 Cut the goose skirt steak down the centre, lengthways, into 2 pieces. With a very sharp carving knife, slice each piece of steak on the diagonal, against the grain, into slices that are as thin as you can manage. Toss them in a bowl with the ginger, crushed garlic, soy sauce and cornflour. With 2 wooden spoons, toss very well so that everything is well combined. Set aside to marinate for at least 1 hour. It may marinate for as long as 12 hours, if you wish.

2 Heat 75–100 ml (3–4 fl oz) of the stock in a wok with the chopped garlic. Stir in the spring onions and toss in the hot stock until they are becoming tender. With tongs, remove the onions to a plate.

3 Pour in another 100 ml (4 fl oz) or so of stock. When very hot, add the beef. With 2 wooden spoons, toss and turn, pulling the meat strips apart as you do so, until the meat has lost its raw look. Add a little more stock as the meat begins to stick.

4 When the beef has lost its red, raw look, remove it with tongs, and put it on another waiting plate. Return the spring onions to the wok and stir fry for a few seconds. Pour in the meat juices that are accumulating under the beef, then stir fry for a few moments more. Return the beef to the wok, season with pepper and toss. Heat through and serve.

Goose Skirt Steak Braised With Wine and Onions

~

What a wonderful Sunday lunch this dish makes; it braises slowly and fills the kitchen with delicious Sunday smells. Serve it with Roast Potatoes (see page 94) and an array of Slim Cuisine vegetables. Or slice some unpeeled new potatoes and let them braise with the meat.

- *1 goose skirt steak*
- *1 large Spanish onion, skinned, halved and sliced into thin half moons*
- *2 sticks celery, sliced 0.6 cm (¼ inch) thick*
- *3 cloves garlic, skinned and finely chopped*
- *150 ml (¼ pint) dry red wine*
- *100 ml (4 fl oz) stock*
- *2.5 ml (½ tsp) dried tarragon*
- *15 ml (1 tbsp) tomato purée*
- *5 ml (1 tsp) Dijon mustard*
- *salt and freshly ground pepper*

1 Preheat the oven to 200°C, 400°F, Gas Mark 6.

2 Heat a heavy bottomed non-reactive frying pan. When it is moderately hot, sear the goose skirt steak well on both sides, turning it with tongs. Remove and set aside on a plate.

3 Put the onion, celery and garlic into the frying pan and pour in the wine. Cover, bring to the boil and boil for 5–7 minutes. Uncover, reduce the heat and simmer, stirring with a wooden spoon, until the onion is very tender and beginning to stick and burn, and the liquid is gone. Add a splash of stock and stir with a wooden spoon to loosen the browned bits. Stir in the tarragon, tomato purée and mustard.

4 Season the goose skirt. Put the onion wine mixture into a shallow baking dish. Place the meat on top. Pour a little stock over and around the meat. Cover tightly with foil.

5 Cook in the oven for ½ hour. Reduce the oven temperature to 130°C, 250°F, Gas Mark 1 and cook for 1–1¼ hours longer or until beautifully tender. I find that the meat slices best if made in advance, then cooled and refrigerated for several hours, or – even better and certainly more convenient – overnight. Slice the cold meat against the grain, return to the sauce and heat, covered, in a moderate oven.

OLD FASHIONED POT ROAST

~

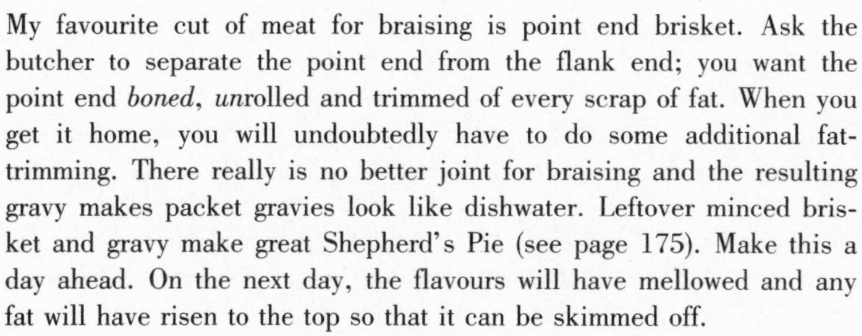

My favourite cut of meat for braising is point end brisket. Ask the butcher to separate the point end from the flank end; you want the point end *boned*, *un*rolled and trimmed of every scrap of fat. When you get it home, you will undoubtedly have to do some additional fat-trimming. There really is no better joint for braising and the resulting gravy makes packet gravies look like dishwater. Leftover minced brisket and gravy make great Shepherd's Pie (see page 175). Make this a day ahead. On the next day, the flavours will have mellowed and any fat will have risen to the top so that it can be skimmed off.

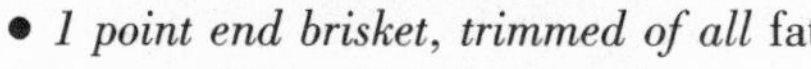

- *1 point end brisket, trimmed of all* fat
- *175 ml (6 fl oz) stock*
- *3 Spanish onions, skinned and sliced*
- *3 red peppers, cored, seeded, peeled and cut into strips*
- *225 ml (8 fl oz) red wine*
- *175 ml (6 fl oz) passata (sieved plum tomatoes)*
- *1 large carrot, peeled and sliced*
- *8 cloves garlic, skinned*
- *1 chilli, coarsely chopped, seeds, stalk and all*
- *salt and freshly ground pepper to taste*

1 Preheat the oven to 180°C, 350°F, Gas Mark 4.
2 In a large non-stick frying pan, sear the brisket on both sides. When browned on both sides, put it on a plate and loosely cover with foil.
3 Pour any fat drippings out of the pan and blot the pan with absorbent kitchen paper, but do not wipe off the browned bits. Pour the stock into the pan and add the onions. Cover and boil for 4–5 minutes. Uncover, turn down the heat and cook gently. When the onions are browning and almost tender, add the peppers. Stir and cook until the liquid is gone and the vegetables are tender. Scrape up the browned bits in the pan.
4 While the onions are cooking, pour the wine and tomato passata into a saucepan. Boil until reduced and thickened.
5 When the vegetables are tender, spread them out in a 23 × 33 × 5 cm (9 × 13 × 2 inch) non-reactive baking dish. Add the carrot, garlic and chilli. Pour in any meat juices that have accumulated under the meat. Put the meat on the vegetables and season to taste. Pour the tomato-wine mixture over and around the meat.
6 Cover with foil, shiny side in, so that no steam can escape. Cook in the oven for 1 hour. Reduce the oven temperature to 130°C, 250°F, Gas Mark 1 and cook for an additional 2–2½ hours or until very tender.
7 When tender, remove the meat to a plate and cover to prevent it drying out. Cool. Pour the pan juices and vegetables into a jug, add any juices that have accumulated under the meat, cool and refrigerate. When the meat has cooled, wrap well in cling film and refrigerate.
8 The next day, skim any fat from the juices in the jug. Purée the vegetables and juices in a blender, then rub the purée through a sieve.
9 With a sharp knife, slice the meat thinly against the grain and arrange in a baking dish. Pour and spread some of the puréed sauce over the slices. Cover and refrigerate until serving time. To serve, reheat, covered, in the oven at 170°C, 325°F, Gas Mark 3 for 35–40 minutes. Reheat the remaining sauce in a saucepan and serve in a gravy boat.

BRISKET AND ONIONS

The easiest of all the brisket recipes I have ever developed, this dish is simply onions and meat, slowly braised together.

- *3 large Spanish onions, skinned, halved and sliced into thin half moons*
- *1 point end brisket, trimmed of all fat*
- *salt and freshly ground pepper to taste*
- *generous 15 ml (1 tbsp) tomato purée*
- *15 ml (1 tbsp) Dijon mustard*
- *100 ml (4 fl oz) dry white vermouth*

1 Preheat the oven to 170°C, 325°F, Gas Mark 3.
2 Arrange the onions in the bottom of a shallow baking dish that can be tightly covered. Choose a dish in which the brisket will fit *snugly*.
3 Season the brisket on both sides. Place it on the bed of onions. Cover *tightly*. Bake for 1 hour.
4 Uncover and, with tongs, turn the meat over. Re-cover the meat tightly. Return to the oven for another 2 hours.
5 Uncover. Tilt the dish and, with a large cooking spoon, remove all the juices (there will be plenty!) to a jug. Refrigerate the juices. Re-cover the meat tightly and continue to roast until very tender, about another ½–1 hour.
6 Remove the meat to a chopping board. Leave to rest for 10–15 minutes. While it is resting, degrease the refrigerated pan juices. (The fat will have risen to the top and congealed. Simply remove it with a spoon.) Pour the defatted juices into a non-reactive saucepan. Stir in the remaining ingredients. Boil, stirring occasionally, for 3–4 minutes.
7 Slice the meat across the grain. Overlap the slices in a shallow baking dish or gratin dish. Spread the onions evenly over the slices, then pour the pan juices over them. Serve or, if necessary, cover and refrigerate or freeze until needed.

ROAST PORK

~

Pork tenderloin is sometimes labelled pork fillet or 'tenderlean' fillet. It is one of the leanest cuts there is. Sometimes the tenderloin is sold in two pieces, in which case simply marinate and roast the two pieces. This recipe makes an extremely juicy, flavourful roast pork. A little honey is used in the marinade, but it is so small that it makes no difference to your weight loss plan. Its purpose is to contribute to the beautiful glaze of the finished roast.

- *3 cloves garlic, skinned and crushed*
- *7.5 ml (½ tbsp) chopped fresh ginger*
- *4 spring onions, trimmed and chopped*
- *salt and freshly ground pepper to taste*
- *generous pinch ground cumin*
- *generous pinch cayenne pepper*
- *pinch ground coriander*
- *7.5 ml (½ tbsp) soy sauce*
- *juice of ½ lemon*
- *5 ml (1 tsp) honey*
- *1 pork tenderloin (275–350 g/ 10–12 oz), trimmed of fat*

1 Purée all the ingredients (except the pork) in a blender. Rub the mixture all over the pork. Put the pork with the mixture in a plastic bag and seal. Marinate for at least 4 hours, turning occasionally. (It may be marinated overnight.)
2 Preheat the oven to 240°C, 475°F, Gas Mark 9.
3 Put the pork on a rack in a shallow roasting tin. Put the marinade in the tin with 175 ml (6 fl oz) water. Roast for 25–35 minutes, turning once half way through, until cooked (the internal temperature will be 155–160°F). Slice thinly on the diagonal to serve.

BREADED MEDALLIONS OF PORK WITH ONION SAUCE

MAKES 45–50 PIECES

~

Breading and grilling slices of pork tenderloin is a basic Slim Cuisine technique. Here the grilled slices are tossed with an intense caramelized onion-wine sauce. If you wish, as a change, you may toss the slices with *any* of the Slim Cuisine sauces instead, or you can toss them with Stir-'Fried' (in stock) vegetables. Or you may serve them crispy (without a sauce) in which case, pass the lemon wedges. This can easily and generously feed at least 4 people. Cold leftovers make a delicious snack or meal the next day.

- *1 pork tenderloin (225–275 g/ 8–10 oz), trimmed of all fat*
- *plain flour seasoned with salt, a pinch of cayenne and freshly ground pepper*
- *2 egg whites, lightly beaten with 15 ml (1 tbsp) water*
- *plain breadcrumbs, seasoned with freshly ground pepper*
- *2 large Spanish onions, skinned and chopped*
- *570 ml (1 pint) stock*
- *225 ml (8 fl oz) dry sherry, dry white wine or dry white vermouth*
- *salt and freshly ground pepper to taste*
- *watercress (optional)*

1 Cut the pork tenderloin into slices, approximately 0.6 cm (¼ inch) thick. Pat them dry with absorbent kitchen paper. Spread the seasoned flour on a plate, then dip pork slices on both sides, shaking off the excess.

2 Dip each floured pork medallion into egg white, then let the excess egg white drip off. Spread the seasoned breadcrumbs on a plate, then dredge the pork slices in them. They should be well coated with crumbs on both sides. Place the coated pork on a platter and refrigerate for at least 15 minutes.

3 Preheat the grill. Line the grill tray with foil, shiny side up. Place the rack on the tray.

4 Combine the onion and 350 ml (12 fl oz) of the stock in a large frying pan. Cover, bring to the boil and boil for 5–7 minutes. Uncover and simmer until the onions are browning and sticking, and the liquid is almost gone. Pour in the sherry, wine or vermouth and cook, stirring and scraping up the browned bits, until the onions are amber brown and syrupy. Stir in the remaining stock. Season and simmer for 2–3 minutes.

5 Remove the medallions from the refrigerator and place on the rack. Grill, 7.5 cm (3 inches) from the heat, for 1½–2 minutes on each side.

6 Put the browned pork in the frying pan with the onion mixture. Stir and cook over medium heat for 1–2 minutes until well combined. Serve hot on a platter, surrounded by watercress.

I've always loved meatballs. The tender meaty little morsels, nestling in an interesting sauce, are comforting and homely, yet elegant too. Meatballs are the sort of food children eat with pleasure, yet meatballs could be served at a dinner party without embarrassment. I consider myself a Matisse of meatballs; an artist whose medium is mince; a Paginnini of polpetti as it were. My meatball recipes would fill a sizeable cookery book all by themselves. Always use *very* lean mince – whether pork, veal, lamb or beef – for meatball making. To rescue them from the dry dustiness that is the fate of most meatballs (or hamburgers) made from very lean meat, I often mix the meat and spices with . . . roasted aubergine pulp. Don't run away screaming. The technique is quite amazing; the resulting meatballs have an ineffably tender and juicy texture; you need use *less* meat (and subsequently ingest less fat and Calories) because the aubergine bulks it out nicely, and the taste is exquisite. It's interesting that the aubergine taste does not really come through; but the lovely meat and spice flavour does.

HAMBURGERS

MAKES 4 GENEROUS BURGERS

~

These are big, fat juicy burgers, although each burger contains only 75 g (3 oz) lean meat. Serve them on hamburger buns with Sautéed Onions or

Braised Onions, Chunky Tomato and Pepper Relish, and Roasted Tomato Ketchup (see pages 83, 124 and 123). For convenience, make a big batch and store them in the freezer. These burgers are very quick and very easy (and very delicious) prepared from the frozen state. Keep the buns, as well as the onions, ketchup and relish in the freezer as well.

- *350 g (12 oz) very lean minced beef*
- *scant 15 ml (1 tbsp) tomato purée*
- *10 ml (2 tsp) low-fat fromage frais or yogurt*
- *1 small onion, skinned and very finely chopped*
- *1 (450 g/12 oz–1 lb) aubergine, baked, peeled and coarsely chopped (see page 90)*
- *1–2 cloves garlic, skinned and finely chopped*
- *salt and freshly ground pepper to taste*

1 Preheat the grill to its highest temperature. Place the grill shelf on the middle position. Line the grill tray with foil, shiny side up. Place the grill rack on the tray.

2 Thoroughly mix together all ingredients. Shape the mixture into 4 fat, oval cakes. (If you plan to freeze them, wrap each burger in cling film, put them in one layer on a baking sheet, then freeze. When thoroughly frozen, put them, still wrapped, into a plastic bag. Close the bag and store in the freezer until needed.)

3 Place the burgers on the rack and grill for 3–4 minutes on each side, until crusty on the outside and done to your liking within. Turn the burgers with a fish slice and tongs. (Cook to your taste, but please don't incinerate them!)

4 Serve as they are, or in wholewheat buns with onions and Chunky Tomato and Pepper Relish.

NOTE: To serve from frozen, cook under a hot grill with the grill tray in the middle position for 5–7 minutes on each side. (To test if they are done: poke a thin metal skewer into the centre of one of the burgers and leave for 2 seconds. Pull it out and hold the skewer against your lower lip. If cold, or barely warm, the burger is not done. If quite warm, or hot, it is done.)

SHAMI KEBAB

MAKES 24 PATTIES

~

More wonderful Indian food: plump grilled lamb balls, laced with ginger, spring onions, herbs and spices. Serve with a creamy herb sauce (recipe follows). Shami Kebab would be wonderful as part of a gala Indian dinner party (see menu suggestions – page 66).

- *350 g (12 oz) very lean minced lamb*
- *8 spring onions, trimmed and finely chopped*
- *4 cloves garlic, skinned and crushed*
- *15 ml (1 tbsp) finely chopped fresh ginger*
- *5 ml (1 tsp) ground cumin*
- *2.5 ml (½ tsp) ground cardamom*
- *1.25–2.5 ml (¼–½ tsp) cayenne pepper*
- *90 ml (6 tbsp) shredded fresh mint*
- *90 ml (6 tbsp) chopped fresh coriander*
- *chopped flesh from 1 small baked aubergine (see page 90)*
- *salt and freshly ground pepper to taste*
- *lemon or lime wedges*
- *Mint-Coriander sauce (see below)*

1 Combine all the ingredients, except the lemon wedges and mint-coriander sauce, in a bowl. Mix well with your hands or a fork. Fry a tiny piece in a small frying pan (use no oil!) and taste. Adjust seasonings.
2 Preheat the grill. Line the grill tray with foil, shiny side up.
3 Form the lamb mixture into small patties and place on the grill rack. Grill for 3–5 minutes on each side until just cooked through but not dried out. Serve with lemon or lime wedges and Mint-Coriander Sauce.

MINT-CORIANDER SAUCE

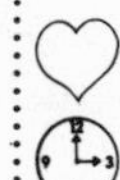

- *150 ml (¼ pint) fromage frais*
- *15 ml (1 tbsp) finely chopped spring onion*
- *2.5 ml (½ tsp) finely chopped fresh ginger*
- *1 green chilli, seeded and finely chopped*
- *60 ml (4 tbsp) shredded fresh mint*
- *150 ml (10 tbsp) chopped fresh coriander*
- *salt to taste*

Combine all the ingredients in a blender. Process until it forms a green flecked sauce. Refrigerate until needed.

VEAL-MUSHROOM PATTIES

MAKES 35 PATTIES

Here, duxelles (an intensely flavoured mushroom hash) are mixed with minced veal (you may also use lean minced pork) and quick grilled. This is a very special recipe. If you want to freeze the patties, freeze them in Tomato-Carrot, Tomato or Red Pepper Sauce. See pages 122–126.

- *2 bunches spring onions, trimmed and sliced*
- *3 cloves garlic, skinned and crushed*
- *stock*
- *450 g (1 lb) very lean minced veal*
- *Duxelles made from 450 g (1 lb) mushrooms (see recipe below)*

1 Preheat the grill to its highest setting. Line the grill pan with foil, shiny side up. Put a rack on the grill pan.
2 Sauté the spring onions and garlic in stock in a pan until tender, but not browned and the stock is almost gone.
3 Mix the veal, duxelles and spring onion mixture together. Form into 35 patties. Grill for 2 minutes on each side.
4 Serve on a bed of Tomato-Carrot Sauce (see page 124).

DUXELLES

Duxelles are also fine on their own; try them spread on toast, or mixed into one of the Slim Cuisine sauces.

- *450 g (1 lb) mixed mushrooms, cleaned well*
- *175 ml (6 fl oz) stock*
- *75 ml (3 fl oz) sherry*
- *several dashes soy sauce*
- *5 ml (1 tsp) dried tarragon, crumbled*
- *salt and freshly ground pepper to taste*

1 Chop the mushrooms very, very finely. This is best done in a food processor if you have one. Quarter the mushrooms and put them into the food processor, then pulse on and off until very finely chopped. You will need to do this in two or more batches.
2 Empty the chopped mushrooms into a deep, non-reactive frying pan. Add the stock, sherry, soy sauce and tarragon, stirring well. The mushrooms will be barely moistened but it doesn't matter.
3 Cook over moderate heat, stirring occasionally, until the mushrooms have rendered quite a bit of liquid. Turn the heat up a little and simmer briskly, stirring occasionally, until the mushrooms are very dark, very thick and quite dry. Season to taste. Refrigerate until needed.

SHEPHERD'S PIE

SERVES 4

I had never tasted a Shepherd's Pie until I moved to England. I have since used the basic Shepherd's Pie formula as a springboard to some wild flights of culinary fantasy but this one is no wild flight; it is a basic, very satisfying rendition of the classic.

- *450 g (1 lb) very lean minced pork, lamb or beef*
- *3 onions, skinned and finely chopped*
- *3 cloves garlic, skinned and finely chopped*
- *300 ml (½ pint) stock*
- *dash of soy sauce or teriyaki sauce*
- *300 ml (½ pint) dry red wine*
- *15 ml (1 tbsp) reduced-salt Worcestershire sauce*
- *30 ml (2 tbsp) tomato purée*
- *salt, freshly ground pepper and cayenne pepper to taste*
- *several pinches grated nutmeg*
- *chopped pulp of 3 baked aubergines (see page 90)*
- *well-seasoned mashed potatoes made from 900 g (2 lb) potatoes and 100 ml (4 fl oz) buttermilk (about 1.1 litres/2 pints mashed potatoes)*
- *purée from one head roasted garlic (see page 74) – optional*
- *skimmed milk*

1 Cook the pork in a large non-stick frying pan, breaking up the lumps as it cooks. When the pork is cooked through, drain it well in a colander set over a bowl. Spread it out on absorbent kitchen paper and blot with more paper. Wash and dry the pan. Return the pork to the pan.

2 Meanwhile, combine the onion, garlic, 150 ml (¼ pint) of the stock, the soy or teriyaki sauce and 150 ml (¼ pint) of the wine in a non-reactive frying pan. Simmer briskly, stirring occasionally, until the onions are tender and the liquid is almost gone. Add this mixture to the pork.

3 Stir in the Worcestershire sauce, tomato purée, salt, peppers and nutmeg. Stir in the aubergine, remaining stock and wine. Simmer, uncovered, for 20–30 minutes, stirring occasionally. Taste and season.

4 Spread the meat mixture in a gratin dish or 4 individual casseroles. Season the potatoes with a little nutmeg, mix in the garlic purée, if using. Spread the mashed potatoes over the meat.
5 Preheat the oven to 190°C, 375°F, Gas Mark 5. Dribble the top of the pie with a little skimmed milk. Bake, uncovered, for 30–40 minutes (40–60 minutes if frozen) until browned and bubbly. Serve at once.

BOLOGNESE SAUCE

MAKES 1.4 LITRES (2½ PINTS)

~

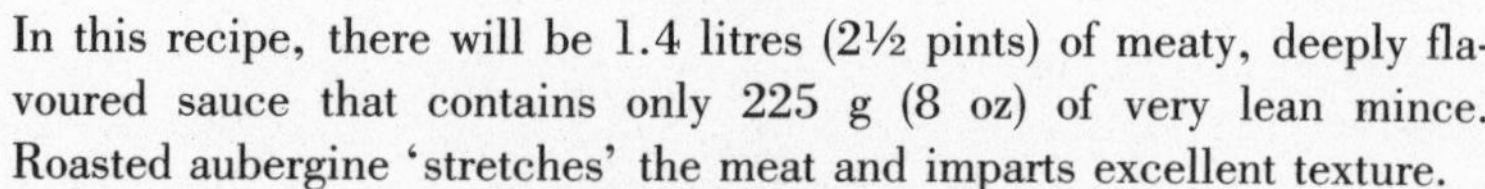

In this recipe, there will be 1.4 litres (2½ pints) of meaty, deeply flavoured sauce that contains only 225 g (8 oz) of very lean mince. Roasted aubergine 'stretches' the meat and imparts excellent texture.

- *225 g (8 oz) very lean minced beef*
- *1 medium onion, skinned and chopped*
- *2 large cloves garlic, skinned and crushed*
- *1 small carrot, peeled and chopped*
- *1 small red pepper, cored, seeded, peeled and chopped*
- *1 small yellow pepper, cored, seeded, peeled and chopped*
- *2 cans (450 g/1 lb each) chopped tomatoes*
- *chopped pulp of 1 (350–450 g/¾–1 lb) baked aubergine (see page 90)*
- *generous 60 ml (4 tbsp) tomato purée*
- *salt and freshly ground pepper to taste*
- *15 ml (1 tbsp) chopped fresh oregano or 1.25 ml (¼ tsp) dried*
- *15 ml (1 tbsp) chopped fresh basil or 1.25 ml (¼ tsp) dried*

1 Cook the beef and onion over medium heat in a non-stick, heavy frying pan. As it browns, break up any lumps with a wooden spoon. When the meat is almost browned, stir in the garlic, carrot and peppers. Continue to stir and cook until the meat is completely cooked through and the onions are soft. Transfer the mixture to a colander over a bowl to drain away any fat. Spread it out on absorbent kitchen paper and blot with more paper. Return to the frying pan. Add the remaining ingredients. Partially cover the pan and simmer for 15 minutes.
2 Season the sauce to taste and simmer, partially covered, for approximately 10 minutes more until thick. Serve with pasta or as a filling for baked potatoes.

MAINTENANCE
RECIPES

ADAPTING TO MAINTENANCE

The next few recipes are meant to show you how to adapt the Slim Cuisine recipes and techniques you have learned so far, to Maintenance. The Vegetable-Cheese Gratin is simply the Vegetable 'Lasagne' (see page 106) from the vegetable week, enriched with a layer of Mozzarella and Parmesan cheese. The Potato Pizza shows you how to combine basic mashed potatoes, tomato sauce and sautéed vegetables into a family-pleasing pizza. You will be able to ring many changes yourself: add a modest shower of grated Mozzarella to the Polenta Pizza (see page 153); enrich Mashed Potatoes (see page 94) with a spoonful or two of grated Parmesan; braise vegetables (see page 96) with a sprinkling of Parmesan, so that the cheese melts down during the baking; add rinsed, drained canned kidney beans to Slim Cuisine Tomato Sauce (see page 122), then toss with pasta; or add drained beans (borlotti, kidney beans, chick peas) to Vegetable Soup (see page 100) or Herbed-Onion Tomato Soup (see pages 102–103). Eat pulses as often as you want, but save Mozzarella and Parmesan for an occasional treat. If you find it hard to eat a small amount, if you find yourself wolfing down all you have in the refrigerator, if you find your weight soaring, *forget* it: you will live (and eat) very happily without it.

POTATO PIZZA

SERVES 6–8

~

Mashed potatoes work very well as a pizza base.

- *1.1 kg (2½ lb) baking potatoes*
- *60 ml (4 tbsp) grated Parmesan cheese*
- *freshly ground pepper to taste*
- *450 ml (¾ pint) Chunky Tomato Sauce (see page 122)*
- *toppings of your choice, such as Sautéed Onions, Sautéed Mushrooms, Roasted or Stir-'Fried' Peppers (see pages 83 and 86)*
- *175 g (6 oz) part-skim Mozzarella cheese, grated*

1 Preheat the oven to 220°C, 425°F, Gas Mark 7.
2 Scrub the potatoes and pierce them in several places with a thin skewer or the prongs of a fork.
3 Bake directly on the oven shelf for about 1¼ hours or until soft.
4 Reduce the oven temperature to 180°C, 350°F, Gas Mark 4.
5 Scoop out the potato flesh into a bowl, add 30 ml (2 tbsp) of the Parmesan cheese and some pepper. Mash well with a potato masher.
6 Spread out the mashed potato on a 34 × 25 cm (15 × 10 inch) baking sheet. Bake in the oven for 15 minutes.
7 Spread the baked mashed potato with the tomato sauce. Arrange the topping ingredients over the sauce. Sprinkle the Mozzarella and the remaining Parmesan over the top. Bake for 15–20 minutes.

VARIATION: Omit cheese.

QUICK CHILAQUILES

~

Mix some frozen sweetcorn kernels with Slim Cuisine Tomato Sauce (see page 122) in a saucepan. Simmer until the corn is thawed and the sauce is hot. Spread some Tortilla Chips (see page 186) on the bottom of individual shallow ovenproof ramekins. Cover with the sauce and top with some grated Mozzarella cheese. Grill until the cheese is melted.

VEGETABLE-CHEESE GRATIN

SERVES 4

~

This gratin is very similar to the Therapeutic Binge on page 106, but here, Mozzarella and Parmesan cheeses are layered in between the grilled aubergines, courgettes and Chunky Tomato Sauce (see page 122).

- *1 large aubergine, sliced crossways 0.6 cm (¼ inch) thick*
- *5 medium courgettes, sliced crossways 0.6 cm (¼ inch) thick*
- *approximately 570 ml (1 pint) Chunky Tomato Sauce (see page 122)*
- *salt and freshly ground pepper to taste*
- *15 ml (1 tbsp) each chopped fresh basil and parsley, mixed together*
- *225 g (8 oz) Mozzarella cheese, grated*
- *30 ml (2 tbsp) grated Parmesan cheese*

1 Preheat the grill.

2 Spread out the aubergine slices in one layer on a non-stick baking sheet. Grill, close to the heat, for 5–7 minutes or until lightly browned. (No need to turn them.) Cut each slice in half. Set aside.

3 Spread out the courgette slices in one layer on a non-stick baking sheet. Grill, close to the heat, for 3–5 minutes until speckled with brown. Set aside.

4 Preheat the oven to 180°C, 350°F, Gas Mark 4.

5 Spread 300 ml (½ pint) of the tomato sauce on the bottom of a 20 cm (8 inch) square gratin dish and sprinkle lightly with seasoning. Sprinkle on 15 ml (1 tbsp) of the mixed herbs. Arrange a single layer of aubergine slices on the herbs. Top with a layer of courgette slices, then layer on half the Mozzarella cheese.

6 Spread the remaining tomato sauce over the Mozzarella cheese, followed by a light sprinkling of pepper, and the remaining mixed herbs. Alternate rows of aubergine and courgettes for the next layer. Sprinkle the remaining Mozzarella cheese and the Parmesan cheese on top.

7 Bake for 40–50 minutes until bubbling. Leave to stand for 5–10 minutes, then cut into squares and serve.

VEGETABLE-CHEESE LASAGNE

SERVES 4

~

A more elaborate version of the Vegetable-Cheese Gratin, this variation includes a pasta (lasagne) layer and a creamy quark-based cheese sauce.

- *1 aubergine, sliced crossways 0.6 cm (¼ inch) thick*
- *4–5 courgettes, sliced crossways 0.6 cm (¼ inch) thick*
- *225 g (8 oz) quark*
- *175 g (6 oz) Mozzarella cheese*
- *90 ml (6 tbsp) grated Parmesan cheese*
- *30 ml (2 tbsp) skimmed milk*
- *570 ml (1 pint) Chunky Tomato Sauce (see page 122)*
- *salt and freshly ground pepper to taste*
- *30 ml (2 tbsp) mixed fresh herbs, such as basil and parsley*
- *6 sheets lasagne (the kind that needs no pre-cooking)*

1 Preheat the grill.
2 Spread out the aubergine slices in one layer on a non-stick baking sheet. Grill, close to the heat, for 5–7 minutes or until lightly browned. (No need to turn them.) Cut each slice in half. Set aside.
3 Spread out the courgette slices in one layer on a non-stick baking sheet. Grill, close to the heat, for 3–5 minutes until speckled with brown. Set aside.
4 Preheat the oven to 180°C, 350°F, Gas Mark 4.
5 Mix the quark with 75 g (3 oz) of the Mozzarella cheese, 45 ml (3 tbsp) of the Parmesan cheese and the skimmed milk.
6 Spread 300 ml (½ pint) of the tomato sauce on the bottom of a 20 cm (8 inch) square gratin dish. Add a sprinkling of salt and pepper. Sprinkle over 15 ml (1 tbsp) of the mixed herbs. Arrange 3 sheets of lasagne over the sauce. Top with half of the grilled aubergine slices. Follow this with a layer of half of the grilled courgette slices, then all of the quark-cheese mixture.
7 Spread the remaining tomato sauce over the cheese mixture, then a sprinkling of pepper, followed by the remaining mixed herbs. Arrange the remaining sheets of lasagne on top, followed by a layer of alternate rows of aubergine and courgette. Sprinkle the remaining Mozzarella and Parmesan cheese over the top.
8 Bake for 40–50 minutes until bubbling. Leave to stand for 5–10 minutes, then cut into squares and serve.

TUNA-TOMATO-BEAN SALAD

MAKES 1.1 LITRES (2 PINTS)

~

- *10–12 beautiful summer tomatoes, skinned and seeded*
- *1 clove garlic, skinned and crushed*
- *generous 90 ml (6 tbsp) chopped fresh parsley*
- *generous 90 ml (6 tbsp) shredded fresh basil or mint*
- *30–45 ml (2–3 tbsp) balsamic vinegar or other mild wine vinegar*
- *salt and freshly ground pepper to taste*
- *1 can (185 g/6½ oz) tuna in water or brine, drained and flaked*
- *1 can (425 g/15 oz) beans drained, (chick peas, borlotti beans, kidney beans or a combination)*

Coarsely chop the tomatoes and place in a non-reactive bowl. Stir in the garlic, herbs, vinegar and seasoning. Toss in the tuna and beans.

RE-FRIED BEANS

Re-fried beans are a delicious Mexican staple, made by mashing cooked beans, then cooking them again in oil or lard in a frying pan. Here they are cooked without the oil or lard. The beans form a savoury, thick, rough mass. To make *Black bean nachos*, mound the re-fried beans on Tortilla Chips (see page 186), sprinkle with a little medium fat Mozzarella cheese, then grill until the cheese melts – great party food. When cooking dried beans, ensure tenderness by a) salting *after* the beans have simmered for 1 hour. b) Use bottled water if your tap water is very hard.

- *450 g (1 lb) dried black beans (or use borlotti beans or kidney beans, if black beans are unavailable), washed and picked over*
- *1 large Spanish onion, skinned and chopped*
- *300 ml (½ pint) stock*
- *4 cloves garlic, skinned*
- *2.5 ml (½ tsp) ground cumin*
- *pinch ground cloves*
- *1.25 ml (¼ tsp) ground allspice*
- *2.5 ml (½ tsp) ground coriander*
- *pinch or two of cayenne pepper*
- *1.8 litres (3¼ pints) stock*
- *salt and freshly ground pepper to taste*

1 In a cool part of the kitchen, soak the beans overnight in 1.8 litres (3¼ pints) water. The next day, drain them.
2 Spread the onion pieces on the bottom of a heavy saucepan. Heat until they sizzle and begin to stick to the pan. Pour in the 300 ml (½ pint) stock and stir in the garlic and all the spices and seasoning. Simmer, stirring occasionally, until the mixture is thick and the onion and spices are 'frying' in their own juices. When the onion is tender, add the drained beans.
3 Stir in the 1.8 litres (3¼ pints) stock. Cover and simmer for 1 hour.
4 Season to taste. Simmer for an additional hour or more until very tender. Taste and adjust seasonings. If necessary, refrigerate or freeze until needed.

5 Put any amount of drained, cooked beans into a non-stick frying pan. Mash them roughly with a potato masher. Stir, mash and cook over low heat until they are quite dry. Spoon in some bean liquid and stir it in. Continue cooking, stirring, and adding spoonfuls of bean liquid until a thick, savoury mass is formed. Serve with Tortilla Chips (see page 186), Minted Pea Purée (see page 161), Salsa Cruda (see page 81), grated Parmesan cheese and fromage frais mixed with chopped fresh coriander.

BREAD PUDDING WITH RASPBERRIES

SERVES 4–6

~

Now that you are on Maintenance, you may use sugar occasionally. Slim Cuisine Bread Puddings are made with egg whites only and a small amount of sugar. These bread puddings are exceedingly light, delicate and fluffy, imbued with the taste of their particular fruit. They puff up like soufflés – on cooling, they subside. Eat bread puddings hot, warm or at room temperature – they make wonderful breakfasts.

- *175 g (6 oz) 1–2 day old unsliced bakery white or brown bread*
- *5 egg whites*
- *60 ml (4 tbsp) caster sugar*
- *425 ml (16 fl oz) skimmed milk*
- *5 ml (1 tsp) natural vanilla essence*
- *pinch or two of ground cinnamon (optional)*
- *450 g (1 lb) frozen raspberries, thawed*

1 Cut the bread into 2–2.5 cm (¾–1 inch) chunks. Put them in a 30.5 × 18 × 5 cm (12 × 7 × 2 inch) baking dish.
2 Beat the egg whites with the sugar. Gently beat in the milk and flavourings. Pour the mixture over the bread. Use a broad spatula to push the bread into the liquid. Add the raspberries and their juices. Stir well, but be careful not to break up the bread. Cover the dish and refrigerate for several hours or overnight.
3 Remove the dish from the refrigerator and leave to stand at room temperature while you preheat the oven to 180°C, 350°F, Gas Mark 4.
4 Choose a baking dish larger than the one with the bread. Put it in the preheated oven. Put the bread pudding dish in the larger dish. Pour boiling water in the larger dish to come about halfway up the sides of the smaller dish. Bake for 30–40 minutes until puffed and firm. (A knife inserted near the centre will emerge clean.)

5 Cool the bread pudding on a wire rack. Serve warm or at room temperature.

VARIATION: Use mixed summer fruits in place of raspberries. Before baking, sprinkle 7.5 ml (½ tbsp) caster sugar evenly over the surface of the pudding.

ORANGE BREAD PUDDING

SERVES 4–6

~

Beautiful to look at – it looks jewelled – and utterly delicious.

- *175 g (6 oz) 1–2 day old unsliced bakery white or brown bread*
- *2 (295 g/10½ oz) cans mandarins in natural juice, drained*
- *150 ml (¼ pint) juice from mandarins*
- *5 egg whites*
- *75 ml (5 tbsp) brown sugar*
- *475 ml (16 fl oz) skimmed milk*
- *45 ml (3 tbsp) skimmed milk powder*
- *15 ml (1 tbsp) orange brandy (Cointreau or Grand Marnier)*
- *5 ml (1 tsp) natural vanilla essence*
- *grated rind of ½ orange*

1 Cut the bread into 2–2.5 cm (¾–1 inch) chunks. Put them in a 30.5 × 18 × 5 cm (12 × 7 × 2 inch) baking dish, together with the mandarins and the juice.
2 Beat the egg whites with the brown sugar. Gently beat in the milk and remaining ingredients. Pour the mixture over the bread. Use a broad spatula to push the bread into the liquid. Stir well, but be careful not to break up the bread. Cover the dish and refrigerate for several hours.
3 Remove the dish from the refrigerator and leave to stand at room temperature while you preheat the oven to 180°C, 350°F, Gas Mark 4.
4 Choose a baking dish larger than the one with the bread. Put it in the preheated oven. Put the bread pudding dish in the larger dish. Pour boiling water in the larger dish to come about halfway up the sides of the smaller dish. Bake for 30–40 minutes until puffed and firm. (A knife inserted near the centre will emerge clean.)
5 Cool the bread pudding on a wire rack. Serve warm or at room temperature.

CARROT CHEESECAKE

MAKES ONE 25 CM (10 INCH) CHEESECAKE

~

I love this cheesecake, and it is very popular with my tasters, too. It combines the best characteristics of three old fashioned desserts: cheesecake, carrot cake and pumpkin pie.

- *generous 90 ml (6 tbsp) raisins*
- *grated rind of 1 lemon*
- *30 ml (2 tbsp) dark rum*
- *5 ml (1 tsp) natural vanilla essence*
- *approximately 900 g (2 lb) carrots, baked in foil in a 220°C, 425°F, Gas Mark 7 oven for 1½ hours, cooled and puréed in a food processor*
- *4 small cartons (200 g/7 oz each) quark*
- *pinch ground allspice*
- *pinch ground ginger*
- *pinch grated nutmeg*
- *2.5 ml (½ tsp) ground cinnamon*
- *NutraSweet to taste*
- *Cheesecake crust (see page 157)*
- *7.5 ml (½ tbsp) brown sugar*
- *15 ml (1 tbsp) Grape-Nuts cereal*

1 Combine the raisins, lemon rind, dark rum, 90 ml (6 tbsp) water and vanilla in a small frying pan or saucepan. Simmer until the raisins are plump and the liquid has reduced to 7.5–15 ml (½–1 tbsp). Cool.

2 In a food processor, combine the cooled raisins with all the remaining ingredients except the sweetener, cheesecake crust, brown sugar and cereal. Process until almost smooth. Taste and add sweetener to taste. Process again until very smooth and fluffy (the raisins should be almost totally puréed). Line a sieve with muslin or a jelly bag and place over a bowl. Scrape the carrot-cheese mixture into the sieve. Refrigerate for approximately 2 hours to drain.

3 Swirl and spread the drained carrot-cheese filling over the crust. Combine the brown sugar and cereal. Sprinkle evenly over the top of the cheesecake. Chill for several hours or overnight.

CHOCOLATE CHEWIES

MAKES APPROXIMATELY 18

~

Sweet biscuits are a notorious diet underminer. I always say: 'Don't keep them in the house! Throw them away! Why have such temptation right under your nose at all times?' But all sorts of answers come back: 'My husband can't live without biscuits. My kids love them. I need them for when guests show up.' And so on. Nonsense, I say. Kids shouldn't eat junk, spouses don't need it. Why not bring the whole family into the healthy eating game? Here are some *very* low-fat chocolate-almond biscuits to keep in the pantry for those times (during Maintenance) when biscuit-mania strikes. Amaretti biscuits, although almond flavoured, contain no nuts; their almond flavour comes from apricot kernels.

- *75 g (3 oz) amaretti biscuits*
- *50 g (2 oz) Grape-Nuts cereal*
- *2 egg whites, lightly beaten*
- *10 ml (2 tsp) unsweetened, low-fat cocoa powder, sieved (see mail order page 189)*

1 Preheat the oven to 180°C, 350°F, Gas Mark 4.

2 Crush the amaretti biscuits and the cereal. Combine with the lightly beaten egg whites.

3 Add the cocoa and mix. Drop the mixture on to a non-stick baking tray in 5 ml (1 tsp) dollops.

4 Bake for approximately 20–25 minutes. Remove from the tray and allow to cool.

FRUIT BRÛLÉE

~

A fruit brûlée is lovely made with any berries, such as raspberries, strawberries, blueberries, tayberries, or with sliced peaches, sliced plums, sliced apricots, or sectioned oranges that have been trimmed of every scrap of peel and pith. To prepare the brûlée, spread out the fruit or berries in a gratin dish. Cover them with a thick layer of cold fromage frais. Sprinkle evenly with 15–30 ml (1–2 tbsp) brown sugar. Preheat the grill. Grill, close to the heat, for approximately 1 minute until the sugar is melted and bubbly. Serve at once.

SNACKS

BE GOOD to yourself, and keep your store cupboard and refrigerator well stocked with things you can nibble freely at a moment's notice. In addition to homemade tortilla chips and popcorn, always have plenty of Slim Cuisine Potato Crisps (see page 93), raw vegetable crudités, fruit and cereal, (Grape-Nuts, puffed grain, puffed rice and so on). There is absolutely no reason *not* to snack: just stay out of the way of Demon Fat.

POPCORN

Once you've scoffed down a bowl of home-popped popcorn, you'll wonder why you ever choked down the greasy, salty stuff ladled out at most cinemas. A *huge* bowlful of dry-popped popcorn (1.1 litres/2 pints) contains only 125 fat-free Calories. Compare that to an equal amount of almonds: 8205 Calories and 810 grams of fat!

To pop popcorn without oil or butter, you'll have to choose your pan carefully. I use a long handled wok with a non-stick interior and a high domed lid. Heat the pan until it is moderately hot. Pour the popcorn in a single, even layer on the bottom, cover the pan and leave on the burner until you hear the first pop, then shake the pan. When you begin to hear rapid popping, shake again, and hold the pan a few cm (inches) above the burner, shaking occasionally. It should pop furiously. If the fusillade of popping seems to be slowing down, put the pot back on the burner for a few seconds, but not too long, or the kernels will scorch. When all the corn is popped, transfer it to a bowl and leave to stand for 3–4 minutes. This method produces fluffy, yet crunchy, popcorn.

TORTILLA CHIPS

Not only are these excellent with Re-Fried Beans (see page 181), they make a wonderful, no-fat crunchy snack. Make them in bulk and store in a biscuit tin. Eat them plain or with any of the Slim Cuisine dips, spreads and sauces.

Corn tortillas (see box)

1 Preheat the oven to 150°C, 300°F, Gas Mark 2.
2 Bake the tortillas directly on the oven shelf for 15–20 minutes, turning once until crisp right through (they will break with a clean 'snap'). Break into quarters or eighths, then store in an airtight tin.

MICROWAVE VERSION

1 Put a double layer of absorbent kitchen paper on the microwave turntable.

2 Arrange 5 tortillas around the outer edge of the paper. They should not quite touch each other. Microwave on FULL for 2–2½ minutes.

3 If the paper is wet, replace it. Turn the tortillas over. Microwave on FULL for another 2–2½ minutes.

4 Remove to a wire rack and allow to rest for 5 minutes. Break into quarters or eighths, then store in an airtight tin.

TORTILLAS

Tortillas are like chapattis made from maize meal. They contain *no* fat whatsoever. Many specialist food shops sell canned tortillas, or they are available through mail order (see page 189).

APPENDIX

After the 'Fast' (refeeding after losing weight on a VLCD regime)

If you have lost weight on a VLCD (very low-Calorie formula diet), what you do *after* the 'fast' is as important as the VLCD regime itself. If you immediately leap off the liquid, low-Calorie regime, into quantities of high carbohydrate, high fat, high Calorie food, you might as well kiss your newly discovered cheekbones, willowy waist and firm chinline goodbye. Say hello again to your billowing backside, bulging tummy, double chins; you'll hardly know they were – briefly – gone. You must engineer your first few weeks off the VLCD properly, and then you must engineer the rest of your gastronomic life properly (as must any one who has lost weight by any means) or the whole weight loss process will have been futile.

After a VLCD regime, a high carbohydrate meal will cause your glycogen and water stores to fill up again quickly causing an *immediate* weight gain of 3–4.5 kg (7–10 lb). This is not a *fat* gain – it is a fluid (water) gain – but it is demoralizing, none-the-less, to see such a jump on the scales. The following plan will help you ease into conventional food in a manner that will not cause such weight elevation. The plan will help you establish a pattern that you can live on happily for the rest of your life, *without* the awful yo-yo that plagues so many people with weight problems.

REFEEDING AFTER SOLE SOURCE

FIRST DAY

BREAKFAST VLCD Formula

LUNCH OR DINNER Boneless, skinless chicken breast or fish fillet (any size) or tuna in water or brine (drained), cooked according to any recipe in the diet plan.

With the chicken or fish, you may have a moderate serving of Slim Cuisine Tomato Sauce or Gravy and a moderate serving of non-starchy vegetables, cooked the Slim Cuisine way (see recipes). No potatoes or other root vegetables, no bread or grains, no fruit – not yet! But very soon. Snack on raw vegetables and skimmed milk dairy products; such as quark and fromage frais. Eat them as is, or make into dips and dressings (see page 79). And you may have a Milk Shake (see page 129).

THIRD MEAL VLCD Formula

SECOND DAY

BREAKFAST VLCD Formula

LUNCH Some non-starchy raw vegetables with one of the Slim Cuisine dressings or dips, or a leafy green salad with one of the Slim Cuisine dressings. Some tuna in brine or water (drained) or prawns or fish fillet. One of the fish soup/stews would be fine too, but leave out the potatoes (see pages 134 and 135). If you would like a dessert, have a Vanilla milk shake (see page 129).

DINNER Chicken breast or fish fillet or fish soup and a medium serving of non-starchy vegetables – cooked according to any recipe in the The Plan. Slim Cuisine Tomato Sauce or other vegetable based sauce or Gravy, if you wish.

THIRD DAY

BREAKFAST VLCD Formula

LUNCH Hooray! You may eat one 225 g (8 oz) potato now – cooked any way you like from the Diet Plan: chips, crisps, mashed, baked. You may have a medium serving of non-starchy vegetables too, plus chicken breast, tuna, fish fillet or shellfish. And Slim Cuisine Tomato Sauce or Gravy or any of the vegetable based sauces are still just fine. Plus you can still have a milk shake for dessert.

DINNER Same as lunch (above) except no potato. Don't get bored though, use different recipes for your vegetables, chicken, fish and sauces.

FOURTH DAY

Keep having your VLCD Formula for breakfast for the remainder of this week. But for the rest of each day, you may go directly to the plan for Day 15. Stay at this level (*without* the breakfast) until your weight stabilizes. When stabilization occurs, follow the plan from Day 15 right through. (Stabilization means that your weight has been stable for at least 4 days.)

MAIL ORDER GUIDE

~

ANTON'S DELICATESSEN

101 Hare Lane, Claygate, Esher, Surrey KT10 0QX
Tel: 0372 62306

Tinned tortillas; Mexican specialities; Balsamic vinegar
Dry pack sun-dried tomatoes

~

CULPEPER LIMITED

Hadstock Road, Linton, Cambridgeshire CB1 6NJ Tel: 0223 894054

Californian dry pack sun-dried tomatoes, no added salt
Natural vanilla essence

~

HEALTH CRAZE

Cromwell Court, 115 Earls Court Road, London SW5
Tel: 071 244 7784

Vegetable stock powders and pastes including Frigg's Végétale
Balsamic vinegar; Tinned tortillas
Dry pack sun-dried tomatoes; Quick cooking polenta
Pulses and dried beans including black beans

~

PARSONS TRADING LIMITED

P.O. Box 995, Purton, Swindon, Wiltshire SN5 9WB
Tel: 0793 772200

Excellent quality fat-reduced cocoa powder

~

CAMBRIDGE SLIM CUISINE PRODUCTS

202A Brakey Road, Corby, Northants NN17 1LU

For Cambridge Slim Cuisine Products and
assistance with locating hard-to-find ingredients

~

INDEX

The author and publishers would like to thank the publishers mentioned below for permission to print extracts from the following publications:

UPS AND DOWNS: *Memoirs of Another Time* by Nika Hazelton. Copyright 1989 by Nika Hazelton. Reprinted by permission of HarperCollins Publishers Inc.

THE DIETER by Susan Sussman. Copyright 1989 Susan Sussman. Reprinted by permission of Pocket Books, a division of Simon and Schuster, Inc.

LADY ORACLE by Margaret Atwood. Copyright 1982 Margaret Atwood. Reprinted by permission of André Deutsch Ltd.

WITH BOLD KNIFE AND FORK by M.F.K. Fisher. Copyright 1968, 1969 M.F.K. Fisher. Reprinted by permission of The Putnam Publishing Group.

EAT WHAT YOU ARE by Russell Baker. Copyright 1982 by The New York Times Company. Reprinted by permission.